PRAISE FOR *TO BE A MAN*

"Any book that unveils the male mystique with empathy and compassion, helping men understand themselves and helping women understand men, and that helps the culture understand the masculine dilemma, should be hailed as a miracle. This is what Robert Augustus Masters does in *To Be a Man*. Every man should read it as autobiography, every woman should read it as revelation, and our culture should embrace it as a healing balm."

> HARVILLE HENDRIX, PhD, author of *Getting the Love You Want*

"A masterpiece of transformational wisdom."

> ALAN CLEMENTS, author of *Instinct for Freedom* and *A Future to Believe In*

"Robert Augustus Masters has written a powerful guide for men that integrates rigor and receptivity, aggression and authority, vulnerability and potency. With highly developed emotional intelligence, and a nuanced understanding of adult development including the importance of shadow work, Masters delivers a vision of mature, embodied male empowerment."

> DIANE MUSHO HAMILTON, author of *Everything Is Workable*

"Masters' insights populate every page of this compelling book, and offer creative ways of thinking about many of our era's most complex issues, among them: pornography; sexual violence; militarism and war; the effects of trauma on men's psyches and identities; and much more." JACKSON KATZ, PhD, author of *The Macho Paradox*

"In this essential book, Robert Augustus Masters challenges current ideas about what it means to be a man, and explores crucial gender issues that affect every man, boy, woman, and girl on our planet. By uncoupling anger from aggression, sexuality from rape and porn, and masculinity from brutality, Robert supports men and boys in reclaiming the sacredness, magnificence, and true power of healthy masculinity."

> KARLA MCLAREN, author of *The Language of Emotions*

"*The* classic handbook for men. *To Be a Man* calls out the 'warrior' to do battle inside, to find authentic masculine power, allowing truly intimate relationships with women, other men, and self."

> BILL KAUTH, cofounder of The ManKind Project® and author of *A Circle of Men*

"*To Be a Man* is a book every man should read, especially if they long for their deepest sense of inner peace and wholeness. It's honest. Raw. Thorough. Deep. Such an important book!" MARY ALLEN, author of *The Power of Inner Choice*

"I have rarely heard such textured thinking from anyone: subtle energetic distinctions on the continuum of destructive and wholesome anger; the willingness to de-normalize pornography and a range of sexual and nonsexual immaturities that many would defend as 'being myself'; and the willingness to boldly put happiness as the basis of grown-up sex. *To Be a Man* is a brilliant, compassionate, paradigm-exploding instruction manual for any man—or woman—on the planet. A beautiful, brilliant, fearless, and amazing book!"

> NANCY DREYFUS, PsyD, author of *Talk To Me Like I'm Someone You Love*

"*To Be a Man* dissects the three words that echo in every man's psyche: 'Be a man!' As a seasoned therapist, Masters identifies the accompanying shame men manifest and gives us a guide toward healthy, sustainable masculinity."

JOE EHRMANN, former NFL player and author of
InSideOut Coaching: How Sports Can Transform Lives

"This book honors, challenges, teaches, and nurtures me all at once. It shows me where I have the greatest opportunity to grow. Best of all, it celebrates what's truly sacred about being a man." RAPHAEL CUSHNIR, author of *The One Thing Holding You Back*

"Every once in a while someone comes along and writes a masterpiece, and Robert Augustus Masters' *To Be a Man* falls into this category. His book is a true hero's journey of healing and awakening."

HANK WESSELMAN, PhD, author of *The Bowl of Light* and the *Spiritwalker* Trilogy

"The old question, 'What does it mean to be a man?' has been answered wisely and completely by Robert Masters in the pages of this amazing book. I want every male on the planet to read it, and soon! It could help to heal our deeply wounded masculinity." ROBERT K. HALL, MD, cofounder of the Lomi School

"Compassionately written and wise, this book invites men to make a conscious distinction between their benevolent and malevolent identifications, and paves the way for a way of being that is both sturdy and heartfelt. Highly recommended for anyone who has grown tired of limiting gender identifications!"

JEFF BROWN, author of *Soulshaping*

"*To Be a Man* is a very useful guide through the thicket of confusing options in exactly what 'being a man' means, or can mean, in today's postmodern world."

KEN WILBER, author of *The Integral Vision*

"A brave and full-blooded dive into the challenges and opportunities facing men in the 21st century." VANESSA D. FISHER, co-editor and author of
Integral Voices on Sex, Gender & Sexuality: Critical Inquiries

"This important book covers the whole spectrum of men's experience and challenges today. Masters explains the development of men's many strengths as well as their compensations, the downsides that so many adopt to 'be a man,' including burying some parts of themselves so deeply that they forget that such parts are even there. A book for men who want to embrace their inner life as well as for women who want to understand them."

IAN MACNAUGHTON, PhD, author of *Body, Breath, and Consciousness*

"Robert Augustus Masters is one of the essential wisdom teachers of our time. *To Be a Man* reflects his deep learning, humility, and decades of experience as a therapist, clinician, and healer. In the section of my library where I have a small collection of books about being a man, this book has moved to the top of my list."

JOHN DUPUY, author of *Integral Recovery*

TO BE A MAN

TO BE A

A Guide
to True
Masculine
Power

MAN

ROBERT AUGUSTUS MASTERS, PHD

souɴds true
BOULDER, COLORADO

Sounds True
Boulder, CO 80306

Published 2015
Cover design by Rachael Murray
Book design by Beth Skelley

Printed in the United States of America

Library of Congress Cataloging-in-Publication Data
Masters, Robert Augustus.
  To be a man: a guide to true masculine power / Robert Augustus Masters, PhD
    pages cm
  ISBN 978-1-62203-229-7
  1. Men—Psychology. 2. Masculinity. 3. Intimacy (Psychology) 4. Sex. I. Title.
  HQ1090.M3826 2015
  155.3'32—dc23
                          2014029390

Ebook ISBN 978-1-62203-388-1

10 9 8 7 6 5 4 3 2 1

For Diane

Through being with you, beloved,
I have found my deepest healing and growth,
and the fullest embodiment of my manhood.
Every day I'm grateful I get to be with you.
Bound together are we yet free,
twin flames of intimacy.

Contents

True Masculine Power

"BE A MAN!"

This demand does a lot more harm than good. It's a powerful shame amplifier, packed with "shoulds"—and the last thing males need is more shaming, more degradation for not making the grade.

Men—and boys—who are on the receiving end of "be a man!" get the message that they are lacking in certain factors that supposedly constitute manliness.

And what are some of these factors? Showing no weakness; emotional stoicism; aggressiveness; holding it together and not losing face, no matter what's going on; sucking it up. (Think of what pride boys may feel when they're successful at this, especially when they're "strong" enough to not cry or show any signs of vulnerability.)

A manly handshake is a firm one, even a steely one; a manly approach means, among other things, keeping it together emotionally, not losing one's cool. To be unmanned is to "lose it" emotionally (except when it comes to anger), such a loss of face often being taken to mean a loss of strength. (When Abraham Lincoln couldn't help crying publicly over the killing of a friend, he described his very visible upset as having "unmanned" him.) To be *unmanned* means being visibly vulnerable, being ball-less ("chickening out"), being brought low by shame, being subservient to dominant others.

To *man up* is an expression originally used in football and military contexts, and means not much more than toughen up, move into battle, grow a pair, with the apparent failure to do so often resulting in a male getting referred to as a girl or lady (who in this context epitomize softness, equated in many a male mind with weakness). Imagine a masculine icon, a famous leader or athlete, not just misting up, not just shedding a few silent tears or fighting back his tears, but crying hard and with abandon. This would be very, very uncomfortable for all too many men to watch, no matter how understandable the sadness or grief was.

Men may respond to the exhortation "be a man!" by getting harder or tougher, more ruthlessly driven, more competitive, more uncaring about their unresolved wounds, making "getting over it" more important than "feeling it" or "going through it." Conversely, men might also respond to the exhortation "be a man!" by rebelling against its certainties of what constitutes a man, driving their hardness and competitiveness into the shadows, and making too much of a virtue out of their softness and more "feminine" qualities. But in either case, they are reacting to whatever notion of manhood has been or is being authoritatively held aloft before them, defining themselves through—and impaling themselves upon—such reactivity.

So let's consider other factors or qualities that ought to—but generally don't—count for much in making a male a "real" man, factors that many men keep in the shadows: vulnerability, empathy, emotional transparency and literacy, the capacity for relational intimacy—all qualities more commonly associated with being female than male.

The visible presence of these "soft" qualities induces far more discomfort in most men than the "hard" ones do. But once they are brought out into the open, respected, and honored—which takes courage—they can coexist with the capacity to express anger skillfully and take strongly directed action, empowering men in ways that serve everyone's highest good. True masculine power is rooted in this dynamic blend of "soft" and "hard" attributes—showing up as a potent alignment of head, heart, and guts. When head (thinking, rationality, analysis), heart (caring, compassion, love), and guts (resolve, resilience, bravery) all inform each other and work together, a truly healthy manhood cannot help but arise.

Getting to such power requires facing and outgrowing less-than-healthy forms of power. There is great beauty and much to celebrate when men step more fully into their authentic manhood, a beauty at once rough and tender, caring and fierce, raw and subtle, anchored in standing one's true ground, whatever the weather.

SOFTENING DOES NOT NECESSARILY MEAN EMASCULATION

Many boys are subjected to the demand "be a man!"—or "man up"—from an early age. Such pressure, however well-meaning, can shame and harden a boy well before he reaches adolescence, shrinking him emotionally, making him shun softness and overvalue performance and the appearance of "having it together." Showing vulnerability may invite gibes about being less than masculine. Many a boy has had to force himself to learn not to cry or show tenderness in order to become "one of the boys" rather than a reject or someone to shun.

Softness is rarely associated with manliness, except perhaps in superficial, tightly controlled ways. What it *is* commonly associated with is weakness and being feminine, and not just in conventionally masculine contexts: the kick-ass, militaristic warrior heroines of contemporary cinema usually are just as hard and removed from softness (read: weakness) as their male counterparts.

Telling a man that he's soft is usually far from a compliment. Softness—or perceived softness—is ordinarily taken to be a failing for men (and boys and youths), a sign of being gutless or spineless, a damning proof of emasculation. No wonder so many men take pains not to appear soft, except perhaps for noiselessly shedding a few tears at certain events, such as funerals or the retirement press conference of an admired athlete. Softness in a man is also very commonly equated with sexual failure, an inability to get it up or keep it up—a hard-not-to-notice failure to stay *hard*. More than a few men refer to their genitals as their manhood; not being able to sustain an erection—that is, being soft—easily gets associated with a loss of manhood.

Men nonetheless *need* to soften, and also to strip "softening" of its negative connotations. Yes, a man can be overly soft, marooned from power and the capacity for rock-solid firmness, but softness itself makes possible vulnerability, empathy, compassion, emotional literacy, and genuinely deep connections with others. Softness does not necessarily mean an absence of courage! To be unapologetically vulnerable is not to be unmanned, but to be deepened in your manhood.

Softening can be a profoundly healing undertaking, helping to make more room for pain and difficulty, enriching a man's capacity for deep relationship, rendering him more flexible and permeable, more *heartful*—especially when that softening coexists with steadfastness and firmness. An example of such coexistence can be seen in *fierce compassion,* wherein we're both forceful and soft, both angered and caring.

SHAME LEFT UNATTENDED IS SHAME THAT RUNS US

"Be a man!" may seem a straightforward statement, but it is packed to varying degrees with pressures and expectations—and often an in-your-face shaming—the delivery of which can alienate men from much of their basic humanity. Such alienation has enormous consequences. When we are thus cut off—emotionally and relationally disconnected or numbed—we are far more capable of dehumanizing activity, far more able to rationalize harmful behavior, far more likely to be caught up in abuses of power and sex. But nothing can truly compensate for what's been lost through such disconnection and numbing. Dissociation from one's soul—one's individuated essence or core of being—is hell, regardless of one's comforts and distractions, and all too many men are suffering this, doing little more than just getting by or dutifully manning up.

There is such pain in the drivenness to be a man, such deep and often debilitating hurt, however much it might be camouflaged by stoicism, excessive pride, apparent sexual prowess, aggression, and conventional success. Men in general are hurting far more than they are showing, and *everyone* is paying the price for this, regardless of gender, age, nationality, or occupation. Attempts to address this have barely made a dent in the conventional armoring of manhood, one key reason is that such efforts can, however unintentionally, shame men for not meeting yet further standards of what a man ought to be.

Until such shame (and shame in general) is recognized and understood, it will dominate men's emotional and relational lives, obstructing their capacity to face and work through their unresolved wounding. Shame left unattended, shame left in the shadows, is shame that will run us from behind the scenes, disempowering us and determining far more of our behavior than we might imagine.

To tell a man (or boy) to "be a man" carries the implication that he is not enough of a man (or enough of a person), that he is not measuring up. Not only is he being told that he's failing to meet a certain standard, a preset expectation or "should," but he is also being shamed for this, however subtly or indirectly.

This shaming effect is rarely seen for what it is, being commonly viewed as just a kind of tough love (psychologically akin to "spare the rod and spoil the child"), especially in authoritarian or militaristic contexts. And such shaming usually becomes internalized in the form of the inner critic (a heartlessly negative self-appraisal that originates in childhood), who waggles its finger in our face so often that its shaming of us becomes normalized. This internal drill sergeant, this love-barren, relentless inner overseer, wears us down through self-castigation, even as it pushes us to be better, to be more successful, to be more of a man. And if the delivery of such internalized self-shaming is sufficiently harsh, we may lose much or all of our drive to better ourselves, sinking into depression, apathy, and self-loathing—so long as we leave our inner critic unquestioned and in charge.

The pressure to "be a man" is generally little more than oppression in good intentions' clothing. Such pressure, such insensitive or out-of-tune motivational intensity, is but unhealthy or toxic challenge. From an early age, boys thrive in the presence of healthy challenge—non-shaming, age-appropriate, loving encouragement infused with a significant but safe degree of risk—learning firsthand how to both extend their edge and respect their limits. But boys who are steered by overly zealous (though commonly well-meaning) parents and teachers into overachieving and being "little men" (often taking on a premature responsibility) quickly learn to make a problem out of whatever in them counters such parental ambitions and pressures—like their tenderness and empathy and vulnerability.

SHAME, AGGRESSION, AND SEX

When a man feels crushed or disempowered by shame (or by being shamed), he's likely going to try to get as far away from it as possible, escaping, for example, into the compensatory power he feels through aggression. And why thus escape? Because shame is such a squirmingly uncomfortable and contracted emotion—especially when it is directed not just at our behavior, but also at our very being. Quite understandably, we want to get away from it as quickly as we can, ordinarily doing so by shifting into other states, such as numbness, exaggerated detachment, or aggression.

In females, such aggression is more commonly directed at oneself; but in males, it is more commonly directed at others. Men tend to counteract the self-deflation that is felt through shame—falling short of what's expected of them—with the self-inflation they feel by being aggressive (getting righteously pumped up). In such aggressiveness toward others—passive, dominating, and otherwise—we usually feel more powerful, more in control. What more potent antidote to feeling crushed might a man find than feeling his readily activated, adrenaline-fueled capacity to crush others (as through verbal abuse or physical violence)?

Often, statements like "be a man" or "be man enough" not only catalyze shame but also drive a man to *prove* himself—a drive put into high gear when our shame shifts into aggression. The "proving" behavior that possesses so many males—and that starts at an early age—needs to be deglamorized and not so unquestioningly equated with masculinity. But this can't be effectively done without addressing and working with the shame at its root.

Aggression can make us feel better by beefing up our everyday sense of self: we're not down, but on top, or closer to the top, of the pecking order. Even if we're low on the ladder, under some unpleasant others, we can usually keep ourselves above some others who are lower in the pecking order than we are. We can also fantasize, perhaps very aggressively, about overpowering those who are above us in the hierarchy.

And what else can make us feel better in a hurry, especially when we haven't been feeling so good about ourselves?

Sex.

All the pressure and shame of trying to be a certain kind of man, all the anxiety and tension that can go with that, often can be briefly but potently eased very quickly through sex. And so too can the sense of not having much power, or of not being very important. So whatever feeds men's sexual appetite, whatever amplifies it, whatever keeps it front and central, can easily take on an exaggerated emphasis, as is so lavishly illustrated by our culture's sexual obsession. How easy it is to burden sex with the obligation to make us feel better or more secure or more manly!

Pornography has become one hell of an epidemic, sucking vast numbers of men into its images and ejaculatory dreams, hooking up mind and genitals in dramas that turn relational connection into a no-man's-land where sexual arousal and discharge reign supreme. The power that so many men give to pornography—and to what it promises—not only cripples their capacity for real intimacy but also keeps their underlying wounding cut off from the healing it needs. Pornography flattens and emasculates men, obstructing their ability to evolve into a deeper manhood. However, merely condemning pornography is not the solution, any more than being overly tolerant of it is (as if any restriction on things sexual were somehow an infringement on our freedom). We need to *outgrow* our "need" for pornography, including using it as a "solution" to our pain and unresolved wounds.

In their unhealthy forms, shame, power, and sex are at the core of male dysfunction, simultaneously possessing and crippling many men. Shame that crushes and shrinks, power (especially in the form of aggression) that inflates and dominates, sex that compensates and distracts—this unholy triumvirate usurps the throne of self in a great number of men, obstructing them from taking the journey that can restore their integrity, dignity, and capacity for real intimacy.

TOWARD TRUE MASCULINE POWER

Many men are at war—at war with life, with each other, with themselves—consumed by the fight to win at work and elsewhere.

Bloodless war is still war, still an arena where the battle is fought with whatever weapons are at hand. A victorious athletic moment may feature not just some full-out exultation, but also a sense of standing over the defeated team as if on some bloody battlefield. Our entire culture is permeated with the language of war: the war on drugs, the war on cancer, the war on poverty. We don't just die from cancer, but lose our *battle* with it. Warfare is all about oppositional extremes, as is much of conventional manhood, with its endless list of things to conquer. What a burden! And what a diversion from embodying our full humanity.

What could be more packed with excitement (both positive and negative) than war? After all, it includes huge drama, high stakes, tremendous challenges and risks, primal encounters, great danger, unusual camaraderie, and the extremes of playing at the edge. I once worked with a highly decorated Vietnam veteran, an officer of the highest caliber who'd done plenty of time in battle; after a few sessions with me that took him to the core of his emotional wounding and required a deep vulnerability on his part, he said that such work was more difficult than anything he'd had to do while in the military—and that he didn't want to stop doing it. It asked more of him, it gave him more, it further deepened him, bringing out in him a different kind of warrior: one whose vulnerability was an obvious source of strength and relational intimacy, a crucible for breakthrough healing.

True masculine power happens when courage, integrity, vulnerability, compassion, awareness, and the capacity to take strong action are all functioning together. Such power is potent but not aggressive, challenging but not shaming, grounded but not rigid, forceful but not pushy. Again, it requires head, heart, and guts in full-blooded alignment.

I sometimes tell men who are venturing into the work of accessing their true power that the journey they're beginning is one that requires a courage no less than that of real battle, and that calls forth from them a warriorhood as rooted in tenderness and relational openness as it is in facing and integrating one's monsters and shadow-places. This is a true hero's journey of healing and awakening, connecting the dots of past and present emotionally as well as intellectually, encountering all that we've been and are. Along the way, we cultivate an intimacy with *everything* that we are—high and low, dark and light, masculine and feminine, dying and undying—for the benefit of one and all. This is the primal odyssey pulsing in every man's marrow, whether he embarks on it or not.

There is a huge need for us to take this journey, not as one more "should," but out of service to everyone. My aim in this book is to illuminate and support this journey as much as possible, provide navigational guidance for us to step more fully into our own authenticity, and help deepen our capacity for taking wise care of ourselves and our environment.

I have seen many men suffer by shutting themselves off from their own depths, stranding themselves from what would enable them to have truly fulfilling relationships—not just their empathy, vulnerability, and capacity for emotional literacy, but also their true power and resolve, their authenticity, their capacity to anchor themselves in real integrity. There is a deeper life for men, a life in which responsibility and freedom go hand in hand and level upon level, a life in which happiness is rooted not in what we have but in what we fundamentally are. It is to such a life that this book is dedicated.

PART I

Orientation and Groundwork

Staying present with your shame takes far more courage than converting it into aggression. Neither indulging in your shame nor avoiding it furthers the authentic warrior in you, the one who can step into the fire of deep challenge and remain present, without numbing himself or emotionally disconnecting. Being present with your shame takes guts. It also deepens your capacity for vulnerability and compassion, and therefore also your capacity for being in truly intimate relationship.

1

Tarzan Must Also Weep
Manhood ReEnvisioned

I GREW UP assuming that being a man meant looking strong and being in control, fortified against the display of any feelings that might suggest weakness or softness, as so well modeled by my father. Television gunfighters were big heroes to me, especially the ones who didn't kill unless they were drawn on first; they met every challenge with clean-cut determination, their eyes and mouths unwavering slits. How I longed to possess their expressionless resolution in the face of adversity!

My heroics got no further than gunning down Marshal Matt Dillon at the start of each episode of the television Western *Gunsmoke*. I'd stand before the black-and-white television, my prepubescent legs spread wide, my eyes narrowed, my hand menacingly hovering over my holstered toy revolver, waiting for the towering, grim-faced marshal to draw his revolver. When he did—in the prelude to each show—I'd whip out my revolver, making a sharp *kkkhh* sound to indicate the firing of my gun. Matt never fell, but I knew I'd gotten him. My mother sometimes remarked that my father resembled Matt Dillon.

But my main hero was Tarzan. He was invincible. Again and again, he'd be captured after a mighty struggle—all alone against a brutish horde—and then taken before a haughty, alien queen, who would immediately be attracted to him. And how could she not? Was he not manhood at its impeccable and brawny best? Eventually, in a packed amphitheater, before the queen and her uncouth subjects, Tarzan would face a hulking monster of a warrior in a fight to the death. Effortlessly, he'd hoist his massive opponent overhead—the queen's breath quickening as he did so—and fling the flailing brute into the stands. Tarzan could outwrestle the mightiest gorilla. He could always, always rise to the occasion, with endlessly photogenic grace. No shame for Tarzan—he was, unlike me, established in a position where he could not be shamed.

In my adulation of Tarzan, I practiced tree jumping—leaping with outstretched hands from branch to branch of oaks and Douglas firs—and pounded my bony little chest, screaming out "Tarzan Tarmangani!" (just as Tarzan did in the books). In his noble perfection I basked, finding a thrilling escape. Tarzan was a flawless performer, unerringly heroic. Matt Dillon and Paladin (the suave gunslinger of *Have Gun—Will Travel*) were almost as good, for they rarely failed to gun down the villains they faced each week. And something else arose in me at the same time: I began secretly cheering for the bad guys, for many of them were just as stoic and invulnerable, just as tough and manly as the good guys. I was concerned not with the morality of what was going on but with the raw power being demonstrated—and my desire to overcome or overpower my father was starting to surface more and more insistently.

By my early teens, I began to wonder why Tarzan was never shot to death, for in many episodes he had to face unscrupulous white hunters who carried guns. How could they continue to miss the ape-man? I gradually began longing for his death; his Teflon impeccability was becoming more burden to me than inspiration. Still, I clung to what he epitomized, setting excessively high standards for myself, losing myself in the excesses of performance, both academically and athletically. Tarzan's life was a myth that both enriched and impoverished me. Through him, I not only contacted my dormant courage but also made a virtue out of invulnerability.

As I navigated my gypsyish twenties, riding the testosterone express and adventuring worldwide, I didn't fully leave Tarzan behind. For a long time, I was occupied with trying to conquer my environment, both outer and inner, infusing myself with more sophisticated versions of my Tarzanesque ethic, until an overwhelmingly painful relationship breakup in my late twenties (closely followed by my first experience in therapeutic group work) brought me to my knees with such pronounced impact—cracking my emotional armor—that I had to change course. So I started to reenter the very tenderness and softness that I had so desperately fled as a boy, rediscovering my heartland, finding and gradually embodying a power that served something deeper than my egocentric ambitions. Being vulnerable was scary, but at the same time made me feel more alive and connected, opening doors that had been closed tightly since I was a boy. And though my armoring didn't disappear, it loosened up and thinned, ceasing to be my go-to strategy whenever pain arose.

LONGING TO BELONG

When I was eighteen, my father found me a government job as a surveyor's assistant. The job was to last two weeks in Victoria, British Columbia, and then two months in the far north of Canada. It was my first paying job, other than strawberry picking. I puffed up a bit—having a job meant that I was more of a man, or so it seemed. My three coworkers were older than I, and much more worldly. They claimed they drank huge quantities of beer—frequently bragging about their prodigious barfing—and apparently had had countless girlfriends. Neither was true for me (I hadn't had a girlfriend yet nor been drunk even once), and I was unable to pretend otherwise. When we'd lounge around between work stints, sometimes for hours, I felt horrible, not knowing how to include myself in their exploit-recounting conversations. I was too fearful of their judgment to remove myself from these talks—or to even consider challenging what they were saying. I mercilessly judged myself as a weirdo, a misfit, a social failure, letting my inner critic shame-slam me.

Their bragging and snickered asides about how they'd like to "get into her pants" or about how they wouldn't "throw her out of bed for eating crackers" left me numb. The ubiquitous "her" was out of my reach. I couldn't participate in my coworkers' world any more than

I could in that of my high school friends when they would talk for hours about carburetors, mag wheels, and huge engines. I blazed with self-consciousness, my strained efforts to fit in only fanning the flames. Even so, I was determined to stick it out—was I a man, or wasn't I?

Two days before we were scheduled to fly north, a foreman, at least twice my age, approached me and, without looking at me directly, muttered, "You're canned." Before I could say anything, he turned away and left. I asked one of my coworkers what *canned* meant, and was told "fired." Fired! In shock and shame, I walked to a nearby park and sat on a bench for an hour, trying to choke back my sobs; it was the first time I'd cried since I'd entered my teens. The words "I've failed! I've failed!" pounded accusingly through me, a jackhammer refrain that hogged my attention. A short time later, I sought out the government official in charge of my job and was informed that some of my coworkers had said they could not get along with me.

My shame was immense.

What would my father say? Predictably, he was enraged, not so much at me as at the government; he, against my wishes, would have gone to see the official to try to get my job back, if I hadn't that very day found another job. His concern was not for me but for his pride—someone associated with him had conspicuously failed. I felt very unmanly, hating my vulnerability.

It was not until years later, when I'd done a substantial amount of deep emotional work, that I recognized that my vulnerability could be a source of power. Tarzan had not taught me this; nor had any of the men in my life. I saw that the strength it takes to lose face, to soften, to make room for our weaknesses is a strength truly worth cultivating—because its presence empowers us to stand our ground when we're emotionally shaken, without locking ourselves into our armor or fleeing our hearts, remaining relationally available.

WHEN POWER GETS DERAILED

Rarely are men taught that stepping into their power actually *includes* stepping into their softness and vulnerability, but such inclusion is a central component of what constitutes real power (*power* meaning the capacity to take action). The seeking of power, especially *power-over* (whether of oneself or others), is a common trait of conventional manhood—and, at the same time, a confession of already existing powerlessness. Quite often, men pursue a sense of power, of reliable potency, through membership in a male-dominated group—be it a work crew, an army, a team, a political organization, or a bunch of friends with a common ethic. (The group need not even be a physical reality; it might be no more than a particular ideology, whether radical or conservative, materialist or spiritual, sophisticated or crude.) Such membership provides a sense of security and commonly held power. The price is steep—personal integrity usually being peripheral to fitting in—but for most, this matters little, at least at the time.

Men who thus involve themselves become "one of the boys," which offers them a secondhand sense of power. In so doing, they get to shift much of the responsibility for themselves and their choices onto the group, just as they did in childhood when they submitted to parental expectations and regulations. So in becoming "one of the boys," they remain firmly entrenched in the boyhood they never really grew up from, a boyhood big on doing and acting grown-up, a boyhood lacking heart and empathy, turned away from the unmanliness of softness and vulnerability.

During my midtwenties I worked on a railway labor gang in the northern steppes of British Columbia. I'd taught high school for a year (in a small coal-mining town where my teaching meditation had been banned because some parents opposed it), and wanted to try something completely different. The gang lived in train cars and worked an average of twelve hours every day. All were male. My job, which I quickly ceased to romanticize, was swinging a sledgehammer and shoveling gravel.

Most mornings I awoke with my hands cramped into rigid claws, as though gripping the shaft of an invisible sledgehammer. The gang was gripped with equal rigidity by its code of manliness: complain upon awakening (usually a chill hour before dawn), swear whenever possible, talk in an unrelentingly loud voice, slow down when the foremen were looking the other way, show absolutely no sign of vulnerability, refer to women as sexually and brutally as possible, be tough, look tough, and talk tough. The main insult was: "Suck my cock!" In other words, "Submit!" Aggressively demanding one another's submission masked their submission to the gang's ethics. Alcohol was the sacrament.

One day some of the men started stoning a bear cub while others cheered them on. I watched from a distance, disgusted at them—and at myself for not stepping in to stop them. Suddenly the mother bear appeared, immediately charging the men, her teeth bared. They frantically fled, barely escaping her wrath, as I secretly cheered for her to catch a couple of them.

I remember childhood times with three or four of my friends, all boys, when I also obeyed a group ethic not to interfere with displays of cruelty. One boy would torture a cat, or mash in a snake's head, and the rest of us would watch, transfixed, desperately trying to appear as indifferent, as manly, as possible—learning to be *bystanders* in the presence of appalling male displays of power. We expected ourselves and each other to bear these sights without showing emotion—we could laugh or joke, but only to demonstrate mastery over the situation. We watched each other for signs of shakiness or fear. Only once did I actually participate, when I helped kill a snake. I felt disgust, fear, guilt, and a brief thrill.

When I was alone, I sometimes killed tent caterpillars, ritualistically mashing their heads. I did this on my own because I feared that my friends would laugh at me—for them, caterpillar killing was unmanly, something anyone could do. In my teen years, I watched, on two or three occasions, a friend throw live mice into a running tractor engine, laughing his loud hard laugh as the engine spewed out blood and fragments of flesh. In such situations I learned to numb myself, disguising any feelings that weren't supportive of the displayed cruelty.

When groups of males look down upon or injure that which is small and vulnerable—"boys just being boys" some would say—they're just revealing their repression of and dissociation from that which is small and vulnerable in them. *But not to thus armor and harden oneself doesn't necessarily propel one into authentic manhood.* The New Age male (the postmodern or spiritualized version of the nice guy), the sensitive, readily empathetic male, often makes such a virtue out of softness and tenderness and noncompetitiveness that he becomes just as rigid as those whose hardness he deplores; he institutionalizes sensitivity and vulnerability. He can cry, he is not enemy to his helplessness, he is in touch with his softer dimensions, but he *dissociates* from his raw power, his forcefulness, his more powerful passions. He is a stranger to his guts.

Such a male tends to live from the heart up, dividing his feelings into positive and negative; much of the time he'd rather rise above his "negative" emotions, be they anger, jealousy, shame, or fear, and simply focus on his "positive" emotions. However, this only renders his love and joy and humor lukewarm, stagnating in the flatlands of overdone niceness, impoverished by the lack of force that he's enforcing from the heart down, unable to make and take a real stand.

At worst he is a pushover, a must-be-positive man presenting himself as a paragon of spiritual values, self-consciously impaled upon his high-minded standards. His model of manhood is basically a reaction to the conventional model. Both suffer from a righteously upheld repression of feeling (anger for the "sensitive" male, sadness/grief for the "insensitive" male). Both are armored, one with hardness, one with softness. Both avoid shame. Both are at war with themselves; one projects his inner conflict onto his environment, thereby disowning any responsibility for it, and the other tries to transform his inner conflict from the safety of distant sidelines, treating it as a kind of unfortunate implant, thereby disowning any responsibility for it.

But manhood is not a matter of repression, of subjugation of what we fear or don't like about ourselves, nor is it a matter of transcending such qualities. A healthy man neither hides in nor abandons his maleness. The power that comes with maleness is not his to decry or apologize for, but rather to harness, to ride, to enjoy, and to use responsibly. Claiming his full power does not make a man less of a man, but permits him to embody his real nature, in all its depth and wildness. Power asks only for a discerning hand, a taking of the reins that is both loose and firm, both fierce and gentle, both daring and tender, both muscular and sensitive.

SEX AS AN INITIATION INTO MANHOOD

What does it mean to be a man? To answer this more than superficially, a good place to begin is to explore what we were taught about it, and to what degree we absorbed—and perhaps are still absorbing—this.

One such teaching that's very pervasive equates having sex with being a man—an adult male who is still a virgin tends to be seen by other men as being less than a man (lacking as he apparently is when it comes to potency). Think of the protagonist in the film *The 40-Year-Old Virgin,* a nice but dorky guy whose buddies conspire to get him laid—as if they're doing him a huge favor, helping him make the transition from dorkdom (or the geeky fringes of emasculated living) to real manhood. As if once having had sex, he'll suddenly have the qualities of a real man.

In 1972 I was on the road (the colorful, nonconventional adventuring of which fit my notion of manhood back then) proudly carrying nothing but my backpack, spending some time in the Goreme Valley of central Turkey. From the rolling plains of the valley rose hundreds of towering stone phalluses, many thirty to forty feet high, each topped by an oval head much larger in circumference than its supporting column, all shaped by nature's hand. This thrusting landscape—a congregation of hard-ons erected by a ten-million-year infusion of cosmic Viagra—seemed to my twenty-four-year-old imagination to be on the verge of exploding, of impregnating the sky.

Within a local home a prewedding celebration, to which I'd been invited, had begun. Only men were there. With arms over each other's shoulders, we danced long and hard and noisily, eating hashish and drinking copious amounts of wine and *raki,* an industrial-strength liqueur. The groom was no more than eighteen or nineteen. Unlike the rest of us, he was wearing a suit. The bride was elsewhere, not to be seen until our celebration was over, and then only by the drunken, advice-saturated groom. When dawn came, he was expected to go to his bride and copulate with her. I imagined her fear and discomfort; I was told that she was a virgin. The groom looked ill at ease despite his alcoholic intake, his writhing hands speaking a language none seemed to hear. There was no tenderness around him, no softness, only leers and winks and intoxicated backslapping (akin to the encouragement of the "experienced" men in *The 40-Year-Old Virgin*).

Across the groom's face, peeking through his drunken bravado, flitted the shy smile of a little boy. He appeared eager to please his older fellows, to do whatever he had to in order to fit into their world. Finally, loudly propelled by them, he stumbled out the door to where his bride was waiting.

I was also drunk for my first sexual encounter—with a minimal depth of connection to the woman. You're now a full-fledged member of the human race, I told myself shortly afterward, as I parachuted into sleep—now you belong, now you are a man! I felt tremendously relieved; I'd reached a goal I had long yearned for, and now that I had attained it, I felt a sense of lofty victory, as if astride the highest plateau of some great peak, not seeing that I stood only at the foot of the mountain. Through the unknowing crowds and past the oblivious buildings I walked the next morning, flushed and euphoric, a walking erection. My heady inflation didn't last long, but it did signal an initiation that was every bit as significant for me as was the wedding celebration and its aftermath for the young Turkish groom. Not that our actions were admirable—what mattered was that we were now men, or so it seemed.

Being truly a man is not such a simple matter. It is not so much a successful meeting of cultural standards and expectations as it is an integrity-generating, compassion-deepening *outgrowing of them,* an open-eyed, fully embodied passage through the very patterns and expectations that underlie and generate each culture's—and subculture's—notions of manliness. Far too often, manhood gets reduced to obedience to a group ethic, in order to be "one of the *boys*" (an unwittingly telling phrase). Such initiations, whatever their defining rituals, can dumb men so far down that it looks like up to them, especially when their behavior snares the rest of the group's approval. When sex is reduced to a display of power or a sign that one is indeed a man, all involved are impoverished, and whatever underlies such "prowess" is left unexamined.

NEITHER REJECTING NOR SUCCUMBING TO THE DARK SIDE OF MALE POWER

Being a man has very little to do with *trying* to be a man, and a lot to do with being present and trustworthy, grounded and transparent, and showing up as a warrior of integrity and intimacy, compassionately cutting through the roots of whatever is obstructing one's well-being.

When manhood takes shape as a largely desensitized, emotionally shallow construction—housing a gang of prefabricated, invulnerable behaviors—whatever humanity is left huddles in a no-man's-land haunted by the muffled cries of wounded boyhood, however hidden this may be by outward shows of sucking-it-up toughness. Men who are in such a position, hard-armored and far from empathetic, may seem to be able to take quite a punch with minimal flinching or upset—other than getting darkly aggressive. But they are, in fact, suffering immensely, marooned from real happiness and relational satisfaction.

I recall a dream I had many years ago: I'm in a large room with many men. They are talking and smoking, wandering around, looking very tough. They're wearing black leather jackets, and don't let their sneers stray very far from their faces. One of them is sprawled on top of my possessions. When I ask him to move, he growls unintelligibly. I push him aside, and he immediately attacks me. We fight, and I pin him down with an armlock, threatening to break his arm if he doesn't leave my stuff alone. Eventually, he mutters agreement. His buddies encircle me menacingly; the air quivers with the threat of violence.

Suddenly I feel very solid, very grounded and alive. Waves of compassion pour through me. Looking into the eyes of the man who had attacked me, I see not just his cultivated toughness, but also his faraway sadness, his grief, his fear—a bewildered little boy seems to crouch behind his defiant stare. I tell him what I see and what I feel. I speak of my own capacity for violence and of my fear of it, and how acknowledging its presence has helped me to express and use it in non-violent yet still powerful ways. As I speak, I sense that the man and his buddies don't really understand what I am saying, but that they like, or at least respect, the way in which I am speaking. I leave the room, and the dream ends.

The males' toughness in my dream is none other than my own toughness. At first, I'm polite, as I was when I was the obedient young son of my often-abusive father. Then I fight, as I did when I sought to best other males, including my father. My winning only makes things worse. As I see that I'm literally encircled by the situation, penned in by it, I break through my context of either giving in to or fighting the other men, and simply become fully present. My attacker is a blend of all the boys and men I've known, including myself, who wouldn't befriend their vulnerability. I see what he won't see—his pain, his lovelessness, his isolation, his darkness. What I see is the barrenness of a world dominated by excessive self-control, hardness, and unilluminated power. And I can see this and speak this only because I know another world, one in which I am intimate with qualities that don't qualify as manly in the conventional sense.

Without my vulnerability and tenderness, I am crippled, stranded in a wasteland populated by hypermasculine shadows. As I become more deeply established in my softness without abandoning my raw male power, finding in my vulnerability the strength to be my full self, I am less and less concerned with proving myself, with having to demonstrate my manliness to the dark inner sanctum of male unfeelingness, the black leather jackets of my dream. However much I'm disgusted by their behavior, my heart goes out to them. They loiter in me, dark and hard. I have struggled to discard them, to finish with them, even to transcend them, especially as I reclaim my more tender feelings.

My competitiveness and forcefulness have often seemed to be in the way of my growth. But these qualities, these "male" attributes, are just as much me as my tenderness or softness. It's easy to keep them in the dark or reject them, dressing them up in black leather jackets, but not so easy to cultivate intimacy with them, bringing them into the circle of my being, reclaiming and integrating their energies without, however, taking on their viewpoint.

It's so crucial to encounter this dimension of maleness without robbing it of its passion and fighting spirit, allowing it to full-bloodedly expand, permitting it to further energize and awaken the quintessential man in us. With rough grace, he becomes increasingly alive and present, embracing his forcefulness even as he remains sensitive to his impact on others and his environment. Without diluting its intensity one bit, his power becomes stripped of its aggression and infused with compassion so that it is for him a way of sharing himself, of revealing himself, of saying an unqualified yes to the seemingly more primitive aspects of his maleness. Such a yes is at the very heart of being a man, supporting whatever stands are necessary to sustain integrity, depth, and love.

2

Navigational Pointers
Things to Consider for the Journey

WHILE MAKING YOUR WAY toward a more empowered man-
hood, it's helpful to have some knowledge of what to consider or do
when things get rough or bumpy. What follows in this chapter are
navigational pointers—teachings in brief—that you can refer back to
when you feel stymied, stuck, or off track. I begin with shame because
of the often unseen and unacknowledged power it has to determine
a man's course (as mentioned in the introduction). The remaining
topics are in no particular order, all being equally worthy of your
undivided attention.

All that matters for now is that you begin familiarizing yourself
with these pointers, getting a preliminary feel for them. Some may be
relatively obvious to you, and others won't. Everything on this list is
expanded upon and fleshed out later in the book.

SHAME

WILLIAM is really angry at his wife. She has just questioned, not
unkindly, his handling of a tax issue they're having. His anger is over
the top, and he knows it, but feels justified in continuing. As she
pulls back from him, he gets even angrier, demanding that she "meet"
him. What he doesn't recognize is that in this situation his anger
is secondary, with his primary emotion being shame. He was put
down a lot as a boy for not being more competent, and so his wife's

questioning of his competence has triggered his old wounding over being shamed for not doing things better. And this shame has very quickly mutated into anger—and then into aggression—without him being aware of such an emotional shift. He has not yet recognized that his aggressiveness is an all but automatic strategy to avoid or bypass his shame. ▪

▪ Shame is probably our most hidden and misunderstood emotion. It's also the one most likely to motivate men to stay away from the help they need—and need to admit they need—which can range from psychotherapy to addiction programs. Performance anxiety is driven by shame; so is the drive to overachieve; so is the pressure to man up. Shame is behind the scenes much more often than you might think.

▪ Some shame is healthy—activating our conscience and capacity for remorse—but a lot of shame is unhealthy or toxic, flattening and slamming us with the message that *we* are defective, degrading us for not making the grade.

▪ It's essential to know your shame well enough to be able to stay present with it when it arises, instead of letting it mutate—as it very commonly does—into aggression or emotional withdrawal. Much of our aggression and relational disconnection is simply an unskillful solution to our shame, a way of avoiding it or not having to feel it directly.

▪ The point is not to get rid of shame—an impossibility—but to develop enough intimacy with it so that it cannot crush or run you, regardless of its intensity.

VULNERABILITY

ALLEN sometimes tears up while watching a movie, but he has not cried for many years. He's heard that it's not good to keep one's emotions undercover, but feels compelled to not lose face under any conditions. His friends describe him as a nice guy. He grinds his teeth while he sleeps, often dreaming of a young boy hiding in a dark bathroom, a boy he wishes would just go away. Allen has never told anyone about this dream. When he was a boy he was severely bullied; whenever he cried, he was hurt even more. It took a while, but he learned to numb himself in order to present a stoic, friendly-looking front. Pure survival. He equates showing any vulnerability with danger, and views it as a signaling of weakness. He doesn't see how this contributes to his difficulty in having relationships that possess real depth. ■

- Vulnerability—unguarded openness—does not have to mean weakness or a lack of masculinity. It can be an act of courage. And a *source of strength*.

- In vulnerability there's a transparency and capacity for self-disclosure that can help deepen our connection with others. Becoming more vulnerable asks that we stretch beyond our comfort zone, but the resulting increase in depth, vitality, and connection make doing so worthwhile.

- Without vulnerability, there's no intimacy.

- Vulnerability doesn't always mean leaving the door wide-open; for example, if it doesn't feel right to drop your guard but you know it's safe to do so, openly admit that you're guarded—such admission itself is an act of vulnerability. Or if you're with someone you know you can't trust with your vulnerability, don't "should" yourself into being vulnerable. Be discerning with your vulnerability.

- Vulnerability can be a risk, especially emotionally, but not doing what we can to access it is a bigger risk.

EMPATHY

JOE is an empath. He doesn't try to emotionally "get" others; it just happens. Even with people he doesn't particularly like, he very quickly finds himself standing in their shoes. He gets easily magnetized to others, unable to pull himself away when he starts to feel drained by being with them. He appears to be a very good listener, but the undivided attention he gives to whomever is speaking to him is not so much a chosen activity as it is an automatic one. Joe opens easily, loves easily, connects easily, but his personal boundaries are all but missing. Saying "no" is very difficult for him, so his "yes" lacks authenticity and real conviction, existing mostly as a means of not displeasing or upsetting anyone. Joe's work is not to be less empathetic, but to develop healthy boundaries. ■

By contrast, DAVE is far from empathetic. If his wife tells him she feels hurt and starts to cry, he gets very uncomfortable. He tells her she's too sensitive and needs to be more rational. Seeing her tears doesn't move him. When she tells him that she wants to feel him feeling her, he has no idea what the hell that means. He wishes that she'd just accept the fact that he's not into getting emotional, and often says to her, "Why can't you just accept me the way I am?" ■

- To be empathetic is to emotionally resonate with what another is feeling—we're in their shoes, in their skin, in their position. We get them.

- Empathy cuts through our isolation, generating a network of interconnection. Empathy brings our heart out of the cold. Empathy makes compassion possible.

■ But empathy also needs an empathic boundary, meaning an on-tap capacity to not get overly absorbed in or identified with others' emotional states—standing back just far enough to keep them in clear focus, *resonating with what they are feeling without losing ourselves in it.* Being empathetic doesn't mean putting up with bullshit just because we feel what others are feeling, but it does make it very difficult to dehumanize them, regardless of how strong a stand we might need to take with them.

■ Empathy helps keep us from getting numb, heady, or overly detached. It begins with and reinforces vulnerability.

EMOTIONAL LITERACY

FRANK doesn't like being asked what he's feeling. If pressed to answer, his usual response is: "Nothing." When his girlfriend presses further, he'll either stay silent or tell her to get off his back. When he doesn't feel so good, he likes to drink or indulge in a little porn. His girlfriend has been distant with him for a while, especially in the bedroom, so porn has become even more of a draw. How does he feel about this? He says he doesn't care, that he's tired of all this talk about feelings. Frank talks tough, acts tough, but is really hurting. When he was a boy, his father often said to him, "Don't cry or I'll give you something to cry about." Frank quickly came to view emotions (other than anger) as things best kept out of sight. Now, as there's more talk of men getting in touch with their feelings (an expression Frank hates), he feels shame that he has such a hard time identifying what he's feeling, not even recognizing that he's feeling shame. He's emotionally illiterate, and is afraid to admit this and do something about it. ■

■ Emotional literacy blends emotional sensitivity, understanding, and savvy. It means knowing what you're feeling while you're feeling it, and being able to both contain and openly express it.

- One of the first steps in developing greater emotional literacy is uncovering whatever shame you might have about your lack of such literacy. Many boys—and men—have been taught, however indirectly, not to lean in the direction of better knowing their emotions, as if so doing is something only for girls and women. Unfortunately being emotional is still commonly equated with being female, and being rational with being male.

- Emotional illiteracy has much of its rooting in the historical devaluation of emotion relative to cognition. Thinking clearly is often associated with a muting of our emotions. But rationality and emotion *work best when they work together.*

- To develop and deepen emotional literacy, we need to cultivate *intimacy* with our emotions, getting close enough to them—all of them!—to know them (and our ways of handling them) from the inside.

- Each of your emotions is worth getting to know very, very well—its nature, its purpose, its expression, its containment, its value, your history with it, your use and misuse of it. (My book *Emotional Intimacy* covers all this very thoroughly.)

TURNING *TOWARD* YOUR PAIN

WILL lost his job a month ago. He still feels a lot of pain about this. His friends have listened sympathetically to his complaints, but are now tiring of doing so, encouraging him to move on. But he keeps on complaining, losing himself in his sense of entitlement, going over and over the same material, hyperfocusing on it. He's just making his pain worse, even as he takes the edge off it by drinking and exhausting himself with his internal ranting. Even as he reinforces his pain, he keeps himself away from it. What he has not considered doing is turning toward his pain, letting himself fully feel it, and ceasing to dramatize it. ■

- To turn toward your pain is to face it and take your conscious awareness *into* it, sensing it from the inside, letting yourself truly feel and be with it without trying to distract yourself from it. This means, in part, relating to your pain as an explorer relates to new territory.

- Turning toward our pain is an enormously important step in our personal evolution. It doesn't matter how small the step is, so long as we take it, and keep taking it. Because we are conditioned to turn away from or avoid our pain, turning toward it may feel counterintuitive, at least at first.

- Distinguish between pain and suffering. Pain is basically an unpleasant sensation, an inevitable part of life, but suffering is something that we are *doing* with our pain, dramatizing it to the point where we lose ourselves in it.

- *To end your suffering, enter your pain.* This means getting to know it and its roots, exploring it deeply, moving through it slowly but surely. You can't emerge from your pain unless you enter it, and this begins with turning toward it.

- Have compassion for the you who fears doing this, holding him the way you'd hold a frightened boy, not letting him drive the car but keeping him close to you, both cared for and protected, as *you* drive.

DISTINGUISHING BETWEEN ANGER AND AGGRESSION

When BILL feels angry, he doesn't say so, but just gets sarcastic. If his target is upset by this, Bill lets them know that that's their problem. He doesn't notice that in his sarcasm, he's lost all care for the other. Being sarcastic allows him to remain intact, makes him feel more powerful, helps him put up a wall between himself and the other. Through his sarcasm, he is expressing not anger but aggression. He is not trying to get through to the other, but to diminish and degrade them. However softly or jokingly conveyed his sarcasm may be, it is nevertheless an attack. ■

- Anger and aggression are often taken to be the same thing, but they are not.

- Anger does not attack; aggression does.

- Aggression dehumanizes the other; anger does not.

- Anger is vulnerable, but aggression is not.

- Anger is often seen as a negative emotion, something to be muzzled or muted, something destructive. But is anger itself harmful or negative? No. But what we *do* with it may be harmful or negative, such as when we get aggressive.

- The key to not letting our anger turn into aggression is maintaining at least some caring for the other while we're angry at them—not so easy, but definitely doable.

DISTINGUISHING THOUGHT FROM FEELING

JASON is arguing with his wife, telling her she's being unreasonable and that she's not there for him. She fights back, saying that she feels he's not hearing her. His response is that he feels he is hearing her, but that she's not hearing him, and that if she were, they wouldn't be having this argument. And so on. They've had this disagreement many times, without any resolution; it usually ends with one of them storming out of the room. What they don't realize is that, though they're saying that they *feel* this and that, they in fact are not saying what they're actually feeling. If they were to simply say, "I feel sad" or "I feel angry" or "I feel hurt" (statements that are not arguable) and not get busy justifying why they feel thus, they'd have more of a chance to establish at least some connection at a deeper level than their he said/she said dramatics. They are both making being right more important than being connected, distancing themselves from their vulnerability. Telling her that she's being unreasonable is far less skillful than telling her that he feels hurt or angry or that he misses her. ■

- Sometimes when we say what we're feeling, we're actually saying what we're *thinking*. For example, "I feel that you're not hearing me" is a statement of perception or opinion, rather than of actual *feeling*, a statement that's debatable (unlike a straightforward statement of real feeling).

- If you follow the word *feel* with "like" or "that," you're probably expressing a thought or perception rather than a feeling.

- When you say "I feel . . . ," practice following this with the actual emotion(s) you're experiencing. Keep it simple: "I feel sad," "I feel angry," and so on, giving yourself and your listener time to let your statement of feeling fully register. Then say more about what you're feeling, if doing so feels natural, making sure that you don't lose touch with what you're feeling as you speak.

- Keep eye contact while saying what you're feeling. This lessens the tendency to get absorbed in your thoughts when you're trying to describe what you're feeling.

- Pay attention to your body and breathing as you state what you're feeling. The more aware you are of your physical sensations, the more likely it is you'll be able to accurately name what you're feeling emotionally. Soften your torso, especially your belly, noticing how doing so eases your breath and helps ground you.

- Practice stating what you're feeling without trying to explain or justify it, providing enough time to simply be with that feeling, allowing you and the other to settle into some degree of emotional resonance before you get into the details.

- If you can't figure out what emotion(s) you're feeling, then give data about what sensations you're feeling: "My stomach hurts" or "My heart is pounding" or "My forehead feels tight."

THERE'S MORE TO SEX THAN MEETS THE EYE

ED only gets erotically aroused when he's totally in control sexually (or is thinking about being totally in control sexually), able to come and go as he pleases. If there's any obstruction to this, he quickly loses his charge and distances himself. Not surprisingly, he was strictly controlled as a child, consoling himself with fantasies of dominating those around him—fantasies that he shared with no one. He thinks about sex a lot; his friends frequently joke about how horny he is, seemingly always ready to launch himself into sexual activity. But Ed's excitation is only *secondarily* sexual. What primarily turns him on (and has since he was a boy) is being in control, having the power, being able to dominate; when this is sexualized, he gets so amped up that it seems he's just being sexual, but in fact he is acting out a long-ago wounding in sexual contexts. Ironically, Ed gets aroused by being in control, but he is letting himself be controlled by such arousal and its sexualizing. ■

- Whatever's unresolved from your past will show up, however indirectly, in your sexual life. Your sexuality cannot be separated out from the rest of your life.

- Become more aware of whatever *nonsexual* factors (like wanting to be wanted or wanting to feel better) may be driving your sexuality. Our unresolved wounds can very easily direct our sexuality.

- Release your sexuality from being the go-to solution to make you feel better or more secure. If you don't, you'll tend to overly rely on sex for your well-being, making it too central in your life.

- Instead of expecting sex to create connection, come to sex *already* connected so that sex is an expression (and celebration) of already-present connection.

CONNECTING THE DOTS BETWEEN YOUR PAST AND PRESENT

PETER is raging at his sixteen-year-old son, yelling at him to listen. He presents a number of examples of how his son hasn't listened, the most recent being not washing off his dinner plate and putting it in the dishwasher, despite being told over and over to do so. His son, as usual, argues back; Peter gets even angrier, feeling an urge to pound his son into submission. Everyone else in the room—his wife and his twin nine-year-olds—are, as usual, quiet. Peter feels a moment of shame for what he is doing, but quickly lets it pass. Yes, his son hasn't done what he'd agreed to do, and yes, he is arguing back, but Peter has lost all contact with his own heart, treating his son as if he doesn't care about him at all. Peter doesn't get that he is being reactive, forgetting that his father used to roar at him to pay attention, to stand straighter, to stop being a crybaby, knocking him into submission. Peter's solution back then was to keep quiet. He hasn't dealt with any of this, and doesn't see how the dynamics of that time are still occupying him. His past is dominating his present, and his family is paying the price. Not that he shouldn't take a stand with his son, but doing it reactively only makes things worse. Once Peter connects the dots between what his father did to him and what he's doing to his son, he'll be far more able to communicate with his son in ways that don't do damage. ■

- Much of your past may still be present, in the form of automatic/reactive behaviors that were shaped long ago. Just because something has already happened doesn't necessarily mean that it's in the past.

- Our go-to actions—our behavioral defaults—when things were very difficult when we were young likely will be what we resort to when things are similarly difficult now for us.

- Our past will remain present—and will largely determine our future—if we don't face and work with it. Begin with connecting the dots—between your past and present—mentally, and then do so emotionally. This will greatly help in cutting through your behavioral defaults. When we overreact, it's very likely that our old wounding is surfacing.

- A crucial part of knowing where you're going is knowing where you're coming from, and knowing it at a gut level.

- When you recognize that your past is invading your present—as when you are getting reactive—name it as such. Be your own whistleblower.

DE-NUMBING

Almost every time RICHARD has an argument with his wife, he shuts down, and gets emotionally numb. He knows he needs to say something, but he says nothing. His breathing gets shallow, his throat dry, his chest tight—it's as if he were paralyzed. He may look as though he's just hardening himself, but he is caught up in a powerfully gripping contraction. When he was a boy, the same thing would happen when his parents were fighting. Their battles, which were sometimes physical, terrified him. Loud, angry voices still make him jump. All his wife has to do is raise her voice in displeasure, and he starts to shrink. He associates expressed anger with danger, so he goes into survival mode when facing another's anger. He won't allow himself to show much anger, so when his anger arises he tightens up, enough so for the energy of his anger to contract into the energy of fear, even as he distances himself from the boy in him—the boy who longs for both love and protection. What he does not yet realize is that all this is workable, if he will but cease associating getting some help with being weak or unmanly. ▪

- Emotional numbness or disconnection is learned behavior. It's a survival strategy from our early years (and perhaps also from later trauma), and needs to be seen as such. Don't shame yourself for it, nor let others shame you for it.

- Emotional numbness is often portrayed as a masculine virtue, a badge of toughness—many a hero is shown as someone who displays little or no feeling, other than perhaps tight-lipped aggression or contempt.

- When you feel yourself starting to get emotionally numb, acknowledge that this is happening, and start taking your undivided attention into and under such numbing.

- Do whatever you can to de-numb. It's worth it. Thaw until you're raw. Being able to openly and fully feel is foundational to embodying your full manhood.

- Take care not to numb yourself to your numbness.

Go through this list again, soon.

■ ■ ■

As you make your way through this book, you'll very likely be able to extract more value from this chapter than in your initial reading. Don't hesitate to return to it. Many men tie their self-esteem to being able to learn things quickly, including the use of tools. Take your time here, making haste slowly. Give yourself ample time for digestion.

3

Working with Shame

From Humiliation to Humility

THE MOST POWERFUL emotional roadblock for men is shame.

It is also probably the most hidden, neglected, and overlooked emotion in men (and in psychotherapy). Vulnerable emotions like sadness or grief may be difficult to access and fully express for many men, but aversion to them usually isn't as compelling as is aversion to shame. "Man up!" or "Be a man!" are just two of the many shaming admonitions that men are subjected to, whether directly or indirectly.

As I mentioned in the introduction, shame often rapidly mutates into various forms of aggression—whether directed at others or at ourselves—or into numbness or an emotional shutting down, all of which serve as "solutions" to or distractions from whatever shame was just felt. (An example: a woman tells her husband to be more of a man; and he, feeling shame, responds with hostility: "Get off my back!" or just goes blank, shutting her out even more.)

Furthermore, when shame is actually noticed or even named, it usually gets heavily saddled with negative connotations, as if it's something we shouldn't have. So much shame about having shame! Shame can be crushing, crippling, or toxic—and is often viewed as nothing more than this. But there is, as we shall see, a healthy shame, a shame that's essential to our maturation.

So first, what is shame? Shame is the painfully self-conscious sense of our behavior—or self—being exposed as defective, with the immediate result that we are halted in our tracks, for better or for worse.

Central to shame is the felt sense of public condemnation, even if our only audience is our inner critic. Shame can be relatively benign and it can also be excruciatingly unpleasant, usually accompanied by an unmistakable loss of face and status, which can be devastatingly emasculating for a man, cutting him down to size in the extreme.

When shame arises, we not only sag but also shrink; and the more strongly it arises, the more we tend to shrink, as if we were attempting to get as small as possible, decreasing our visibility as much as we can so that our critical audience—outer or inner—cannot so easily see us.

But such shrinking away—such cringing retreat—runs counter to our wanting to step forward as men, to be more visible, to take up space and establish our ground, to assert our competency. No wonder we want to get away from our shame as quickly as possible! When we thus shrink, we also shrink from our power, and let our fear of being humiliated control us—unless we can skillfully face our shame, which begins with knowing the differences between healthy and unhealthy shame.

(Note: This chapter about shame is quite extensive because shame is so prevalent and so often overlooked or only superficially considered, and has such a huge impact on us, both personally and collectively. It is crucial that as many of us as possible understand it, and understand it very well.)

The better we know our shame, the more likely it is that we'll handle it well.

SIGNS THAT SHAME IS PRESENT

- We feel increased heat in our face, lose our poise, and find it difficult to think coherently, perhaps also becoming tongue-tied. Brain fog sets in very quickly, often leaving us with an inability to retrieve our vocabulary.

- Our inner critic is giving us a piece of its mind, and we're literally a captive audience.

- We look down and don't want to look up, feeling a compelling aversion to holding eye contact.

- Someone questions our competency, and we quickly withdraw from them or get aggressive with them.

- We fall short of a standard that we or others have set for us, and feel a strong loss of power and presence, internally collapsing and shrinking.

- We get defensive when we are not actually under any sort of attack.

- We are being excessively prideful.

- We are beating ourselves up.

- We are not tired but we're slumping, as if we'd taken a blow to the solar plexus. Our sagging shoulders (our *should*-ers) are rounded.

For all too many men, unexplored shame blocks the way to vulnerability, empathy, and relational closeness, existing as a barrier or layer that must be illuminated and passed through before such capacities can be significantly accessed. As such, shame is *the* dragon for many of us—of course we fear it, but this does not mean that we ought to stay away from it. It may be massive, it may make us cringe, it may redden our face with its far-from-friendly gaze, it may seem to dwarf us, but that's just its front, as the warrior in us knows.

HEALTHY AND UNHEALTHY EXPRESSIONS OF SHAME

It is easy to trash shame, as if it were nothing more than a negative or unwholesome state, something to condemn or eradicate.

However, unhealthy shame—commonly known, in its extreme, as *toxic shame*—is not an innate emotion, but rather something that is *done* with shame, something that dehumanizes. To make wise use of shame, it's crucial to recognize the differences between its healthy and unhealthy forms:

- Healthy shame is directed at a specific action, but unhealthy shame is directed at the *doer* of that action. (If, for example, I've broken an agreement with you, you can be critical of *what* I've done, without degrading me, perhaps catalyzing my remorse. Or you can degrade *me* for what I've done, emphatically putting me down, catalyzing not my remorse but my desire to get as far away from you as I can.)

- Healthy shame triggers our conscience, but unhealthy shame triggers our inner critic (which often masquerades as our conscience).

- Healthy shame includes remorse and some degree of atonement for any harm that's been done, but unhealthy shame does not.

- Healthy shame mobilizes us, but unhealthy shame *immobilizes* us. (In healthy shame we are stirred to set things right; but in unhealthy shame, we tend to freeze, making ourselves all but incapable of taking fitting action.)

- Healthy shame opens our heart—after initially closing it—but unhealthy shame closes our heart and keeps it shut.

- Healthy shame allows us to feel for whomever we've hurt, but unhealthy shame does not, as we put all our energy into self-constriction or beating ourselves up.

- Healthy shame features humility; unhealthy shame features humiliation.

- Healthy shame can coexist with compassion, but unhealthy shame cannot, since our empathy has been shut off—and without empathy, there's no compassion.

GETTING BETTER ACQUAINTED WITH YOUR SHAME

Many men get caught up in arranging their lives so as to minimize the emergence of any shame—or to numb themselves to it as much as possible—as if shame somehow indicates nothing more than failure. The mortifyingly uncomfortable, discombobulating feeling of shame is both a mark of its power and of the intensity of our urge to get away from it. I say "its power" because of the enormous impact shame can have on our lives, as when we turn away from pursuing a path we really love because we've believed the voices that told us we weren't good enough to go in that direction or that we should be going in a "better" direction.

The more our self-esteem is tied to our competency or perceived competency, the more debilitating shame will be for us, whether it's coming from us or from others. The more attached we are to standing tall or looking as if we've got it together, the more threatening shame will be to us—not that shame has to cut us down, but in its toxic form (when it is directed at our very being) it does. So it is crucial that we get to know our shame and our history with it very, very well, recognizing that we cannot get rid of it—any more than we can get rid of any of our emotions—*but that we can change our relationship to it.*

One of the first things I do when working with a man who is emotionally shut-down is to help him—nonshamingly—explore his shame and his relationship to and history with it. Together we address any shame he has about doing some healing work. Not surprisingly, such shame has much to do with feeling defective, incompetent, or "less than a man" for having to engage in some psychotherapy or counseling. It may not seem manly or at all admirable to ask for help or to admit relational and personal shortcomings.

And the humiliation quotient for "breaking down"—a fear men usually have more than women in therapeutic contexts—can be very, very high, regardless of how much potential the resulting break-through may supposedly have. In my own experience, it took me a while to stop fighting my surfacing tears, given how much shame arose for me in "falling apart" or "losing it" in full view of another. Think of how a boy who cries hard is generally treated or viewed as compared with a girl who cries hard; there's usually a more overt nonacceptance of his breaking down. And this difference is even more evident in adults. We, as men, often get more praise for keeping it together (usually meaning not losing emotional control) than for dismantling our armor. We need to remember that putting down our weapons won't render us helpless.

In the 1990s, a company sent me some of their male employees for psychotherapy. All of them insisted that we call what they were doing with me something other than psychotherapy or counseling—one of their favorites being "executive coaching." Not that I didn't include coaching in my work, but the emotional and psychological dimensions of their treatment were something that they didn't want to acknowledge outside of our sessions, something that they, at least initially, found quite embarrassing to admit was happening, despite how good they felt from becoming freer emotionally and having a clearer sense of their psychological makeup.

This sense of shame that many men have about doing psychotherapy—and having others know that one is thus engaged—is best addressed as soon as possible in therapeutic contexts. If it is not, or is left untouched, the therapeutic process will most probably remain in the shallows and stay overly cognitive, removed from the vulnerability and healing "loss of face" that usually is part of effective psychotherapy. (Starting the process of sharing the feelings of shame with a partner or trusted friend can make the entry into psychotherapy less daunting.)

Once such shame is exposed and understood, though, vulnerability and empathy become less problematic to access, allowing men to more fully embody their innate happiness and aliveness. I have seen many men fighting their tears, trying to brush them back or deny them, struggling to "hold it together" or "suck it up," tightening their torsos as their hurt and sadness surfaced, as if these arisings signaled some sort of error in the system. Their prevailing sense was that such things shouldn't be happening, and wouldn't if they had it more together. But when the shame over this—this apparent incompetence or failing or outright breakdown—was openly shared, clearly seen, and compassionately faced (often in conjunction with their boyhood history with shame and shaming), then there was more room for, and more acceptance of, their rising hurt and sadness and vulnerability.

Put another way, a man reaching this position of healing would stop rejecting the wounded boy in him, and turn toward that younger version of himself with enough care so that he could allow his painful feelings to emerge into the open. Then he'd realize that what he'd been doing to these feelings was precisely what he was doing to the boy in him (which likely duplicated the way he was mistreated as a boy), treating that boy as though he were little more than a problem, an inconvenience, an embarrassing somebody who just needed to man up.

SHAME AND PERFORMANCE

The pressure to perform can easily generate shame, and the presence of shame makes it harder to adequately perform, which just catalyzes more shame. Part of what's needed here is to know the particular origins of the pressure to perform. So many of the standards that men set for themselves come from long-ago expectations of parents, teachers, or coaches—expectations that may have been well-meaning, but that often did not take into account a boy's real needs and unique capacities.

There are a number of reasons why shame can be agonizingly difficult for men, beginning with the loss of face that shame can catalyze.

Such a loss, especially when made at all public, usually signals a loss of competence, a failure to meet an expected standard, a highlighted slip (or pratfall). This is devastating to men who have, since boyhood and certainly during their adult years, been expected to measure up, to man up, to not be a wuss, to not get emotional, to have sufficient prowess to perform consistently well in various settings.

When a man's performance fails to meet the standard he has set for himself, or that his circle or culture has set, he "looks bad" and, even if he doesn't overtly show it, he feels humiliated, brought not just to his knees, but knocked flat. He feels the loss of competence, the disappointment of significant others, the failure to not "get emotional," the *mortification*.

When we hear of someone being called a "bumbling fool" are we more likely to think of a woman or a man? The odds are that we're thinking of a man. Similarly, this happens with labels like "a screwup" or "a blockhead," or just about anything that indicates performance incompetence. Yes, there are an abundance of negative labels for women, especially regarding their appearance and intelligence, but in arenas of doing well at tasks, men arguably get even more humiliation-oriented labeling than do women. When the standard is set high, plenty of men fall short, becoming magnets for "bumbling fool" kind of labels as well as others that question their masculinity.

What appearance and being sweet are for most girls, performance and being tough are for most boys. The pressure to look and dress a certain way doesn't exclude the softer emotions and their expression—but the pressure to perform, to be "a little man" in various tasks, largely excludes the softer emotions and their expression. A sense of vulnerability may enhance a girl's "looking good" (the shadow of this being an attending disempowerment), but a show of vulnerability in a boy is all too often taken as a sign of weakness, of a loss of power.

An achievement-centered boy who displays obvious vulnerability—trembling, tears starting to surface, insecurity showing, shyness taking over—is a boy very likely to not only feel a surfeit of shame, but also to be shamed and/or bullied, as if he has somehow let down or betrayed the gang, the boys, the guys, the family, the tribe, the culture. What intense cringing this can induce, what self-shrinkage! What squirming pain, even to the point of wanting to disappear.

Disappear? Yes. After all, if I can make myself small enough, others will no longer be able to see me. In the excruciating extremes of shame, we may long for some place we can go that is dark enough to fully conceal us. Thoughts of suicide might become appealing—doing ourselves in (the final compensatory act of competence), vanishing, no longer "burdening" or disappointing others with our apparently shameful or shame-reinforcing presence. As melodramatic as this sounds, it might seem like the only "honorable" option for men living in cultures that are intolerant of shame (as if there could be no healing from and through it). Think of the disgraced samurai in feudal Japan, committing ritual suicide after he's been shamed, keeping his face as impassive as possible, while other expressionless men stiffly look on, seemingly on guard against any display of emotion, as if equating being stone-faced with upholding "honor," or some other hypermasculine badge of merit.

Shame has most men not only by the mind—in the form of a drill sergeant of an inner critic—but also by the balls. Its grip may be relatively light, but can tighten at any time, contracting the belly and sagging the upper torso. The droop and slump of shame, however much it might be camouflaged by the erectness of a compensatory pridefulness, then becomes a dominant structuring in men, subjecting them to its relentless gravitational pull.

Not surprisingly, most men put considerable effort into avoiding or minimizing situations that might stir their shame or elicit shaming from others. This is especially destructive in relationships, as illustrated by the following example.

RON realizes that his wife wants him to be more emotionally expressive, but he keeps showing a strong preference for activities with her (like watching TV) that don't require him to be thus expressive, since he knows he's "not good at showing feelings," and that his efforts in this area have only made things worse because "he wasn't doing it right." Such shame. He's started to avoid having sex with her because she wants him "to show some feeling" while he's being sexual; she also wants him to look in her eyes at these times, and he finds this very uncomfortable. So, even though he likes plenty of things about sex, the pressure he feels here drops his libido way down—at least with her. He has insisted to her that pornography no longer interests him, but its appeal has actually increased, and he's secretly returned to it. His use of pornography both eases him—providing a brief but pleasurably consuming break from his shame—and reinforces his distance from his wife, taking up much of the very energy needed to face his shame over falling short of her expectations. So his shame stays intact, and he stays stuck, trapped by his urge to escape his shame. ■

SHAME AND AGGRESSION

As I've stated, for many men the solution to shame is to move into aggression. Getting aggressive when we feel shame rapidly obscures our shame, seemingly supplanting it. Our focus on the target of our aggression, be it another person or a situation that incenses us, literally occupies us, dominating our internal reality. There isn't much room for anything else. And aggressiveness is very familiar to us. For example, our partner may have an entirely valid criticism of our behavior, but we instantly retaliate with a sarcastic retort. Compared with shame, aggression is hugely empowering: we are not lashing out in the context of failure, but in the context of going after whomever (or whatever) we deem deserving of our anger.

Shame deflates us, but aggression *inflates* us—this is a major part of its appeal, especially to those for whom being on top or in command carries great importance. In shame, our everyday sense of self gets slammed and shrink-wrapped; in aggression, it gets pumped up and enlarged, often righteously so. The more irate we are in our aggressiveness, the more consumed we are by it, and the more we legitimize it—and the better we temporarily feel, as it blocks out our shame.

In the heat of such dark ire, we feel far away from our shame, even though we are in fact being driven by it and our aversion to it. It's easier to fight than to be vulnerable, easier to attack the other than to openly state that we're sorry for what we've done to them, easier to do battle than to connect, easier to hold a grudge than to grieve together, easier to engage in warfare than in peacemaking.

It's easier to armor ourselves than to step out of our armor.

"The best defense is a good offense" is the credo of all too many men. Being defensive is often a kind of attack. Aggression remains the emotional default for many men, however indirectly or calmly it may manifest, and is their primary defense against—and remedy for—shame. In fact, the more shame we have (but may not feel as such) or the more shamed we are, the more justified we may feel in getting aggressive or even violent. Protecting our honor. Wars have often been fought in the name of supposed honor—you sufficiently shame me (or my tribe or culture or country), and I'll dehumanize you enough to feel justified in killing you, whatever the cost. This is not the "good fight," but the foolish one, the black-and-white one, the knee-jerk me-versus-you or us-versus-them battle that impoverishes and degrades all involved.

The sequence of aggression following shame—of letting shame mutate into aggression—must be seen through and broken if men are to step into their full humanity. *Staying present with your shame takes far more courage than riding it into aggression.* Staying present with your shame, neither indulging in it nor avoiding it, furthers the authentic warrior in you, the one who can sit in the fire of deep challenge and difficulty, and remain present without numbing himself or disconnecting from others. Remaining present with your shame takes guts. Doing so deepens your capacity for vulnerability, and therefore also your capacity for being in truly intimate relationship.

Aggression militates against remorse; its pumped-up righteousness binds and blinds us, dehumanizing those we are targeting. Shame—and I speak here of healthy shame—makes remorse possible, activating our conscience and spurring us into enough empathy to make fitting amends with whomever we may have hurt. Aggression closes the heart; shame, once fully felt and not turned away from, can open it.

DISEMPOWERING YOUR INNER CRITIC

The central agent of aggression against ourselves is our inner critic, a cognitive and energetic composite of the main critical/shaming voices we were subjected to as children. Our inner critic manifests as a heartlessly negative self-appraisal. It is the voice that toxically self-shames. What was done to us by those who most successfully shamed us is what we're now doing to ourselves when we allow our inner critic to have its "should"-infested way with us, as though it were the all-knowing adult, and we're just the child. But the power it has is the power we give it.

It's so easy to beat ourselves up (actually beating ourselves *down*) when life gets difficult for us. We all have an inner critic, but that doesn't mean we have to let it browbeat and shame us. It can take us down—degrading us for not making the grade—only when we give it an uncritical ear, giving our power away to it and its toxic shaming of us.

You can't get rid of it, but you can relate to it in a way that disempowers it by taking the following steps.

- Get familiar with the history of your inner critic, dating back to your early years. Recall what you were put down or shamed for when you were young, what you did at such times, and to what degree you're still doing so.

- Learn to recognize the voice of your inner critic when it arises, becoming familiar with its tone and messages to you. The messages it assails you with are usually very repetitive, as if stuck on repeat. Also learn to recognize which voices from your past are incorporated in your inner critic's voice.

- As soon as you become aware that your inner critic has arisen, *name* it—firmly and out loud if possible. You might, for example, say, "Here's my inner critic," or pick a one-word name for it that fits with how you generally feel about it.

- Learn to recognize your tendency to identify with it or to feel like a child before it, doing your best not to allow this. If, for example, your inner critic's message in a particular situation is that you are pitiful, say, "My inner critic says I'm pitiful," rather than saying, "I'm pitiful." If you feel yourself regressing to a younger self as your inner critic holds forth, take a few deep breaths and imagine standing resolutely between that younger you and your inner critic.

- Practice relating *to* your inner critic, talking to it not as a helpless child but in a way that honors your boundaries. This means not taking its contents as truth, but as simply the predictable venting of your internalized toxic shame. Let yourself be as fierce as necessary when doing so. This means saying, "No!" to it, and not letting its shaming penetrate you. If you find yourself asking it questions like "Why are you so hard on me?" change your question to *statements* like "I hate what you're doing to me!" or "Stop!"

- Simultaneously embrace and protect the part of you that feels powerless before your inner critic. Perhaps imagine yourself being a healthy parent who is holding that part of you in a protective embrace, preventing a bully from attacking. You might place a hand on the part of your body where you most strongly feel this aspect of yourself, and say something like, "I see you. I understand why you feel this way, and I'm right here. I've got your back."

- If you have a really persistent or vicious inner critic, not only name it immediately and withdraw your attention from whatever it's saying, but also bring your full attention to your breathing for at least ten conscious breaths, softening your belly as you do so and, if at all possible, letting your body move freely (however small the movements may be). Many of us hold still when our inner critic is messaging us, freezing up like a child facing the glare of a very angry parent, so conscious movement—in conjunction with deep, deliberate breathing—can be very helpful at such times.

HOW TO WORK WITH YOUR SHAME

- Do the preceding inner critic practices regularly, until your inner critic no longer holds sway over you when it arises.

- Become very familiar with your shame (both healthy and unhealthy) and your history with it. Look at the role shame played in your parents' life. Consider collective shame, especially with regard to the pressures of manning up that are so culturally pervasive.

- Identify shame when it arises in you, and name it (simply by saying "shame" or "here's shame"), out loud if possible, or at least audibly enough for you to hear. Also identify what you're pulled to doing as it arises (like withdrawing, going numb, shutting down, refusing to speak, becoming pleasing, or getting aggressive), and name that, again out loud if possible.

- Notice if the shame arising in you is directed at your behavior and/or at your being. If it's directed at your being, it's your inner critic on the assault and needs to be approached as such.

- Ask yourself how old you feel as your shame kicks in. If the answer's preadult, make sure not to further shame yourself for this.

- Practice sensing the part of you—the vulnerable boy—most strongly impacted by shame, and bring him into your heart as best you can, both embracing and protecting him. Imagine that one hand is on your heart, holding him closely, and the other hand is out in front of you, palm facing away from you in a STOP position, keeping guard.

■ If you feel shame over hurting another, stay with that shame until a feeling of remorse arises, and then make amends from your heart. If you're reluctant to do so, admit this, letting any shame over such reluctance further spur you into taking healing action. For example, you could start by saying to your friend/partner, "I'm feeling awful right now, and I can tell it's about the way I treated you, but it's really hard to talk about." Get to know the you who doesn't give a damn about saying he's sorry and won't say it with any vulnerability. Saying "I feel shame about how I treated you" can be very healing to both you and the other.

■ Neither flee from nor lose yourself in your shame. Stay present with it, feeling it as fully as you can, noting where in your body you sense it most strongly.

■ Remember that the more compassion and vulnerability you can approach your shame with, the greater the odds are that you'll handle it skillfully.

■ ■ ■

Turning toward your shame, feeling it fully without losing yourself in its viewpoint and contractedness, is one of the biggest and most courageous steps you'll ever take. Yes, doing so hurts, but such pain is secondary to the healing that you are making possible through your bravery, the healing that begins when you cease being a victim or denier of your shame. Shame can bend and halt us, and sometimes needs to—such as when we're mistreating or are about to mistreat another—but it does not have to break us.

4

Bringing Your Shadow
Out of the Dark

Facing What You've
Disowned in Yourself

TO BE ALIVE is to have a shadow.

The term *shadow* is becoming more commonly mentioned in psychological (and even spiritual) contexts, but still tends to remain a somewhat vague concept, especially in its depths. However, it can be defined quite directly. Your shadow is a composite of the elements and qualities within you:

- that you are disconnected from or out of touch with

- that you are denying, pushing away, or otherwise disowning

- that you tend to project onto others (as if they had a particular quality, but you don't)

- that you are keeping—or trying to keep—out of sight or in the dark

- that you describe with the expression, "That's not me."

A person's shadow is not just some archetypal concept, but an everyday reality that dominates those who are unaware of it—and also plenty of those who have only an intellectual awareness of it. Our shadow is the dimension of us that's occupied by what we can't or won't face about ourselves. A no-one's-land. Denying that we have a shadow is just another element of our shadow. (In this chapter, I won't be discussing the golden shadow—the disowning or denial of our very best qualities. Opening to and embodying such qualities is implicit in the shift toward true masculine power, as is described throughout much of this book.)

For many men, their shadow includes at least some of the following: their shame, their vulnerability, their violent thoughts or feelings or actions, their appetite for porn (or what's driving their appetite for porn)—namely, whatever they're keeping or attempting to keep hidden. Our shadow tends to be the trash-bin for what we don't like about ourselves, the bottom of which often contains our unresolved wounds. But no matter how pushed away or kept out of sight our shadow material may be, it drives much of our behavior—hence the need for shadow work.

Not knowing our shadow keeps us partial, fragmented, stranded from wholeness, stuck in old patterns, regardless of our achievements. Following are two examples.

JOHN rarely gets ruffled. His wife gets angry a lot, especially when he criticizes her for her anger. He rarely remembers his dreams, but when he does, they usually feature him being pursued by hugely aggressive beings, human and otherwise. His anger is part of his shadow; he denies and disowns his anger, keeping it in the dark, projecting it onto others, be they dream-beings or his wife. She is expressing not only her own anger but also much of his. ■

WILLIAM feels very uncomfortable when his six-year-old son, David, cries. He doesn't tell David to stop crying, but he pulls back from him at such times, enough so that his own tears remain far from surfacing, and he doesn't lose face. William, however unknowingly, associates crying with getting in trouble, with the loss of love and with being shamed, and is transmitting this to his son. He is keeping his vulnerability in the dark, and creating a model for his son of being emotionally stoic or unavailable. ■

Whenever you find yourself being reactive, caught up in the same old patterns, or shutting down emotionally, you are in your shadow's grip. Whatever in you that you're keeping in the dark, whatever in you is unhealed, doesn't go away or keep quiet just because you don't see or hear or feel it.

Wherever we go, our shadow comes along. Pushing it away or ignoring it does not truly separate us from it. We may even float high above it (as in certain spiritual practices), but it remains attached to us, as if we were a kite and our shadow has a firm grip on the string, pulling us down again and again.

To the extent that our conditioning (our automatic go-to behaviors)—especially that originating in our early years—is allowed to run or operate us, it is our shadow. Or put another way, to the extent that we ignore our conditioning, it *is* our shadow.

When we are (1) aware of our conditioning and (2) not letting it drive us or dictate our direction, it cannot at such times be categorized as our shadow. However much we may still need to change how we relate to our conditioning, it's now out in the open, illuminated, and held in a significantly grounded awareness.

When we are acting out our shadow material—looking through its eyes and embodying its viewpoint—we usually don't know we're doing so. For example, we may be righteously condemning another for not listening to us (even though they actually *are*, but are not *agreeing* with what we're saying), while not realizing that we have not been listening to *them*—and that we're a poor listener in general. Our shadow here is the projection of our own shortcoming onto another, which we are doing with enough conviction to block ourselves from recognizing that we *do* in fact have such a shortcoming.

It's important to remember that just because we are projecting a certain quality onto another, like inconsiderateness, it doesn't necessarily mean they are not being inconsiderate! What matters is that we don't *solely* focus on what they are doing but *also* focus on what we are doing.

JONATHAN feels resentful when his partner complains about him focusing on his job too much, and his overworking. At such times, he gets angry, telling her that she doesn't appreciate him, and shuts her out emotionally. Part of his shadow here is that his ambition regarding his job is being driven by a fear of poverty, originating in a childhood in which there was a lot of suffering because of a lack of money. Imagine the effect on his partner if he were to vulnerably share his fear of not providing for her well enough, coupled with his connecting this to the painful life of poverty he endured as a child. ■

We must get to know our shadow, and not just intellectually—becoming intimate with its elements—bringing it back into the circle of our being in ways that can deeply serve us. There are enormous riches to be found here, but we cannot mine these unless we move *toward* our shadow and relate to it not with aversion but with curiosity and compassion, illuminating it with awakened presence, no longer treating it as something alien.

FACING YOUR SHADOW

If we don't face our shadow or, worse, if we deny its existence, it nonetheless persists, functioning largely beneath our radar, infiltrating our lives in all kinds of ways. *It's as if someone other than us were pulling our strings.*

But that someone, that stranger, that alien other, is actually none other than our self in disguise. We'll know this right to our core, once we have made the journey into and through our shadowlands.

When we're having an unpleasant dream, we typically want to get away from its disturbing elements. Though this mostly fails, we still tend to seek better conditions. Such dream scenarios are much like our condition when we're turned away from our shadow; our priority is getting away from what disturbs us rather than facing it directly. But face it we must, if we are to cease being a pawn of our shadow elements.

If you want to live a deeper life, you simply cannot bypass your shadow. Nor can you afford to only superficially approach it.

PRACTICE **Getting More Familiar with Your Shadow**

Following is a list of incomplete sentences. Out loud, finish
each one as spontaneously as you can, setting no limit on the
length of your response, and then write it out. (I suggest using
a journal here, so there is ready space if more writing comes
up.) When you've gone through the entire list, read each of
your responses and add anything to them that comes to you.

What I least want others to know about me is _____.

What I tend to have a disproportionate reaction to is _____.

The qualities of mine I often feel some aversion toward are _____.

What I most easily project onto others is _____.

The emotions I consider to be negative are _____.

The emotions I am the least comfortable expressing are _____.

In dreams in which I was trapped or being pursued, I was
specifically trying to get away from _____.

What I'm most scared or hesitant to openly express in a
relationship is _____.

Don't be concerned if you don't have clear responses to
these sentence stems. Just attempting to respond to them
brings you into the domain of your shadow, however slightly.
*Your answers indicate things that are probably part of your
shadow, things "housed," however partially, in your shadow.*
The lighting may be dim and your steps tentative, but at least
you are approaching your shadow. The very act of doing so
is a major step in your evolution, no matter how slight such
movement initially may be.

CULTIVATING INTIMACY WITH YOUR SHADOW

When it comes to our shadow, we have three options. One is to *avoid* it, in whole or in part—and we may spend much of our lives doing this—keeping ourselves so far away from acknowledging our shadow's presence that we act as if it weren't even there, and at the same time seeing its various qualities in others, and thinking *they* have the problem, not us! (What we dislike about others can often be a strong indicator of what we're keeping in the dark about ourselves.)

Another option is to *fuse* with our shadow, in whole or in part, absorbing ourselves in its darkness and its programming, and having no distance from it, including the distance needed to keep it in clear focus. For example, we may live without questioning why we avoid entering intimate relationship, telling ourselves and others that we're just not wired that way, instead of wondering (and exploring) why we fear intimacy. In both cases—avoidance and fusion—we are being run by our shadow, operating under whatever conditioning of ours that we are all but blind to or unwilling to take charge of.

The third option, the optimal one for handling your shadow, is to develop *intimacy* with it. This means getting close enough to it to see and feel it in detail, but not so close that you lose the capacity to keep it in focus. *So instead of avoiding or fusing with it, you get to know it very well.*

What is the purpose of becoming so close to your shadow? It's to reclaim all, *all,* of the disowned, rejected, and otherwise unwanted parts of yourself, welcoming and integrating them into your being. In so doing, you become more whole, more vital, able to live a deeper life, no longer needing to invest energy into keeping your unwanted or disowned elements out of sight. Then you're no longer run by the choices that your conditioning makes for you—you're shifting out of automatic.

This kind of shadow work does not leave us intact; it is not some neat and tidy process but an inherently messy one, as vital and unpredictably alive as birth—*and* just as rewarding, delivering us into a newfound wholeness. The pain such work brings up is the pain we've been fleeing most of our lives—the very pain that, once faced and skillfully met, helps catalyze an enormously beneficial healing. The openings that such work catalyzes are the precursors to hugely relevant breakthroughs.

ALEX is quick to judge other men for "taking up too much space" and for showing anger. He tries very hard to remain calm no matter what is happening, distancing himself from his own anger and need for attention—just as he had to do as the youngest of four children in a very volatile household. Any anger he expressed then brought on his siblings' aggression—with no protection from his parents. In a psychotherapeutic men's group, he describes the problem he has with expressing anger, feeling vulnerable and shaky as he does so. He adds that he doesn't feel good about taking up so much of the group's attention. The leader draws him out further, helping him by various means to access his anger, especially his anger at his siblings.

Alex is uncomfortable with this, but he is shaking so hard that he soon is really angry, and ceases caring about "taking up too much space." His anger is no longer in the shadows; his tears arrive, unbidden, and he starts grieving, even as his anger continues for a bit. A little later, he looks around at the other men in the group, feeling their care and support. He sees them with fresh eyes, not projecting his anger (or siblings) onto them, and is immensely relieved to be so out in the open and to feel safe in doing so. ■

The first step in cultivating intimacy with your shadow is to get acquainted with it. Start by revisiting your early history, noting what you had to leave unexpressed or express only indirectly (like certain emotions and needs), what facets of yourself you kept out of sight (like an interest that was disapproved of), what things you were drawn to but were not allowed to explore, and so on. The second step is learning to recognize the signs that your shadow is present. Your sentence completions in the "Getting More Familiar with Your Shadow" exercise likely pointed to some of these signs. Of these, perhaps the most common and revealing is reactivity, which can be defined as *activated shadow material.* So when you are being reactive (having a disproportionate response to something), know that your shadow has you in its grip. Note what behaviors tend to be almost automatic for you, especially ones that you later regret. Further steps are all about bringing what you've kept in the shadows (your shame, aggression, and so on) out into the open and working with it, as described in this book (and in my audio program *Knowing Your Shadow*).

As you cultivate intimacy with your shadow, you will inevitably find yourself in various situations that activate it, but you'll be far more likely to handle things with greater skill when this happens. For instance, you might get into a charged disagreement with your partner, you might have an upsetting encounter with a coworker, or you might be strongly triggered by a disappointment. But whatever happens, you'll be better able to take the situation as an opportunity to see your shadow more clearly and to make wise use of it.

Becoming intimate with our shadow frees us from being controlled by it and allows us to open to and embrace *all* that we are—high and low, dark and light, dying and undying. Such openness, such depth, such healing and awakening, such full-blooded aliveness and presence, is our birthright.

This is the reclamation project of a lifetime, an odyssey in which we encounter beasts, monsters, aliens, far-from-comfortable strangers, coming to recognize them as none other than ourselves in dark disguise, bringing them into the circle of our being. This journey necessarily asks much of us, both shaking and waking us, drawing us more and more fully into the quest at the heart of deep shadow work: to know ourselves fully and to live in accord with that in every area of our lives.

> Seeds grow in the dark—so do we.
> Let's stop making such a virtue out of the light
> and turn toward what's in the shadows
> and breathe it in, breathe it here
> meeting it face-to-face
> until we realize
> with more than mind
> that what we are seeing

is none other than us
in endarkened disguise

Seeds grow in the dark—so do we.
Let's not be blinded by light
let's unwrap the night
building a faith too deep to be spoken
a recognition too central to be broken
until even the darkest of days
can light our way

5

The Gift of Challenge
An Edge That Can Bring Out Your Best

CHALLENGE CALLS OUT the warrior in a man, the one who tests, hones, and refines himself through his encounters with difficult or unusual conditions. Challenge as such is more than a cocktail of testosterone, adrenaline, and manning-up pressures; more than a shame-driven opportunity to validate or showcase our manliness; and more than something done to meet someone else's standards.

As uncomfortable as challenge may be for a man, it can also be enlivening and deepening, presenting him with an edge that can bring out the very best in him, an edge that he's known in various forms since he was a toddler, venturing forth, however slightly, from parental safety.

Challenge is the part of our path that can most overtly build multidimensional muscle and strongly embodied presence, deepening our capacity to see, hear, feel, know, and act. It calls us to leave our comfort zone and venture forth into territories that may be far from familiar. As much as we may resist this pull—such resistance being natural—we know in our heart of hearts that it signals an adventure we must sooner or later take.

Challenge can take many forms—ranging from the most aberrant to the most ennobling—but its call to be met *and* how it is met are foundational aspects of manhood. Sometimes the deeper challenge is to reject or turn away from what's being presented, saying no to what others are insisting is right for us to pursue, so that we might more fully align ourselves with more worthy, more relevant challenges.

BEING AT YOUR EDGE

Your edge is the experiential zone where your deepest, most relevant growth happens. It is a domain of both trepidation and excitement, an existential threshold where you've begun to turn toward your fears, your pain, your grief, your shame, and your failings—everything you've kept in your shadow. Such encounters are what bring your edge out into the open.

Your edge doesn't have to be a place where meaning gets unraveled and rewoven, where your world undergoes foundational changes, where unsuspected realizations catalyze new directions for you; it can simply be a place where you say no when everyone around you wants you to say yes, or where you allow the armoring around your heart to melt. Whatever your edge may be, it is rich with life-giving risk, calling forth the very best from you. It is a marvelous developmental crucible for your true masculine power, an initiatory testing ground that awaits your full-blooded participation, serving your transition into a deeper manhood.

Intimacy with our edge is essential if we are to be our true size, embodying who and what we truly are. And such intimacy is not possible if we don't spend some quality time at our edge.

Our edge is the frontier of the known. It eludes preset cartography: our direct contact with it provides whatever guidance and navigational clues we need.

I vividly remember being in the far east of Turkey, over forty years ago, reentering a bus terminal and hearing my partner screaming just around the corner. A few seconds later, I saw her surrounded by a group of at least ten men; they were leering and grabbing at her, tightening their circle around her. She was terrified. Outraged, I burst through their circle, ready to do battle. Most of the men pulled knives.

Instantly sensing great danger with seemingly no way out, I shed my aggression in a moment, buzzing with an electric intensity. No thoughts intruded. Very quickly, I scanned the circle, meeting the men's eyes. One held my glance with less violent intent than the others, and I immediately began speaking broken French to him. (I spoke very little Turkish but knew that French was spoken in parts of Turkey.) He responded slightly, and I kept talking, slowly, establishing more rapport with him, drawing a few words from him. All this took place in a very short time. As our friendliness expanded, I felt the circle losing some of its tension. The knives were put away, and soon all the men left. I'd rushed in in a peak of fiery masculine force and immediately found myself at a perilous edge. What had worked, faster than thought, was my *softening* enough to make a crucial connection in an extremely brief time. Being at my edge brought forth what worked; all I had to do was not hesitate to cooperate with it.

If it's not a significant challenge, it's not your edge. If it doesn't require courage, it's not your edge. This doesn't mean that danger has to be present, but there is definite risk involved, whether it be losing face or speaking truths that might radically alter our life direction.

If all it requires is thinking positively, it's not your edge. If it doesn't, however briefly, bring up resistance in you—resistance that can easily toss aside or shed therapeutic and spiritual interventions—it's not your edge. If you think you're doing deep inner work while you sit relatively intact, it's not your edge. If it's easy, asking nothing much from you, it's not your edge.

You know you're at your edge when you intuit strongly that you need to go ahead regardless of how uncomfortable or fearful you are. This is very different from taking foolish or "should"-driven risks. A particularly challenging edge is that of opening to our core wounds, especially when we reach the point where we need to fully feel them without any "adult" dissociation or distancing from them. Being told ahead of time that this will be good for us doesn't have much impact; undertaking such an uncommonly vulnerable journey takes real guts.

Your edge, as always, beckons. Some say to look before you leap, and others say to look after you leap, but why not also look as you leap? Feel the intention to move a little bit closer to your edge, and slowly breathe into that intention, feeling it start to translate into action. Such action doesn't have to be big or ground-shaking, or even noticeable to others; all that matters is that you begin taking it with as little delay as possible once you intuit that it's time to do so.

Approaching our edge brings us more and more present, eventually taking us not just from here to there, but from here to a deeper here, from now to a deeper now. If this sounds like an adventure, it's because it is, both internally and externally. The very difficulty of this, the very dragons we meet along the way, the very self-restructuring we may undergo, all are but fierce grace, honing and refining and deepening us, helping forge a manhood that's a gift to one and all.

CUTTING THROUGH YOUR ILLUSIONS

I entered my early adult years with the conviction that opening up emotionally (other than by showing anger) was not something worth doing. Even when I'd had some experience that showed me this wasn't necessarily so, and had begun to recognize my conviction as an illusion, I still tended to avoid such opening up, needing to be at quite an edge before I loosened my hold on "keeping it together."

One of our biggest challenges is to break the grip our illusions have on us.

Cutting through what we recognize as our illusions—especially the ones central to us—is no small task, and it generally requires far more than sage advice or a gentle push. In fact, we sometimes may need to be at a perilous point before we'll cease clinging to our illusions—whatever lets us know right to our core that the stakes are very high. *Now.*

This is forcefully conveyed in the film *Instinct,* which features two very different men: Ethan Powell, a supposedly insane anthropologist, recently found guilty of murder; and Theo Calder, a well-meaning psychiatrist who attempts to get through to Powell. The two men are bound together through their opposing positions: the rational one and the irrational one, the civilized one and the uncivilized one, the got-it-together one and the not-got-it-together one, the law-abiding one and the outlaw. In one corner, rigid rationality; in the other, raw instinct.

As Calder sticks to his rational guns, continuing to keep himself sealed off from Powell's world, Powell suddenly seizes him—they're in a windowless prison room without any guards—puts duct tape over his mouth, and holds him in a position where he could easily kill him. Calder is very frightened, clearly in great danger.

Powell puts a pencil and piece of paper on the table before Calder, and says, "Now, this will be a very simple test. Pass or fail, life or death . . . Now, you write on this paper what I have taken from you, what you are losing."

Calder quickly writes: "My control."

Powell says, "Wrong. You never had control. You only thought you had it."

Powell then gives Calder another chance. He writes: "My freedom." Wrong answer again.

Calder is right at the edge, knowing he's in a life-and-death situation. "In the middle of the night," says Powell, "when you wake up sweating, with your heart pounding, what is it that has you all tied up, tied up in little knots?"

"I used to be you," adds Powell. "Okay, one last chance." And it's clear that he really means it. "Last try," he says. "Get it right."

Calder writes: "My illusions."

Right answer.

He didn't really have control or freedom in his everyday life, but just *thought* that he did. So how could he actually lose them?

Just a moment away from being killed—so existentially vivid a moment!—he realizes that he is, to whatever degree, starting to lose his illusions. About what? All kinds of things, especially those that he's taken as givens—like him being the sane one and Powell the less-than-sane one, or him being in control of his life.

For our illusions to begin giving up the ghost, we have to be, for starters, in a position where we can actually see them for what they are, and this is often a far from easy undertaking. Sometimes our eyes may truly open only when we are right at the edge of . . .

Big moments. Extraordinarily alive moments. Slivers of time when we're profoundly present, often featuring vivid proximity to immense danger. Or immense opportunity. Dreamt-of doors opening for just a very short time, through which we can pass only if we don't hesitate.

What is perhaps just as amazing as the appearance of such moments is our not letting our less spectacular times be similarly infused with wide-awake presence. When we deny such times their true significance, we pull back from the edge they present, settling for a partial aliveness, as though there's not much else we can do. It's as if we were pretending that we're not at an edge, not at the brink of something deeply significant—absorbed as we are in our habits—and at the same time, pretending that we're not pretending.

But our edge is nonetheless still very much here, moment to moment, ever inviting us to wake up to its presence and the opportunity it provides so that we might live more fully and authentically. In our core of being, we all sense our edge: we've been approaching it ever since we could crawl. It's been our real frontier—and still is—however convincingly we may have replaced it with lesser frontiers.

Like Calder, we don't drop—or even acknowledge—our illusions very easily, especially when our entire life is built upon them. We may have the illusion that we're free just because we are king or alpha male in our finely furnished cell; we may have the illusion that we're in control just because we're able to sit upon someone else or padlock the closet that contains our more undesirable elements; we may have the illusion that we are who we think we are just because so many others think the same way; we may have the illusion that everything is an illusion just because we're attached to a spiritual path that says this is so—except, of course, about itself!—and so on. And we may increase the degree of difficulty here by saddling disillusionment with a negative connotation.

Having the illusion that we are free does not mean that freedom itself is an illusion. It's just that we have an astonishing ability to delude ourselves, and an equally astonishing ability to cut through what's in the way of seeing more clearly. The first ability, which appears at every level of development, generates the very conditions that catalyze the second, conditions that feature enough suffering to grab our attention by the neck. However unwittingly, we invite in circumstances that, along with other conditions, bring our dissatisfaction to such a peak—or trough!—that something has to give, providing us with whatever rough grace is needed.

To cut through illusion, we have to get *disillusioned*—the more thoroughly the better—so long as we do so at a pace that allows for proper digestion of the shifts we're making. Before us stretches an array of digestive aids: there's the pill of sedation, and there's the pill of thrill, and then there's the pill that wakes us up in the midst of our dreaming and scheming. We don't need a prescription for these, since the inevitable challenges of life do such a great job of providing them.

Disillusionment is commonly taken to mean a kind of disappointment, a sense of being let down, but the very structure of the word speaks of something much more fundamental: being freed from illusion. This, of course, might sometimes feel far from pleasant, hence the darker connotations of disillusionment.

A crucial challenge is to stop treating disillusionment as a problem or something negative, and use it as an awakening force. To be disillusioned is to see through illusion, in conjunction with releasing its hold on us. We thus become *disenchanted,* no longer spellbound by our conditioning. And far more able to skillfully approach our edge. As such, disillusionment is a kind of sobriety, a catalyst for waking up, a great opportunity.

CHALLENGE AS A RELATIONAL PRACTICE

Challenging—and being challenged by—others is as essential for our growth as is nurturance, but this does not mean that relational challenge is always a good thing. Telling a man to grow a pair, to suck it up, or to be more of a man, is not helpful, even if the shaming in such statements spurs him toward taking the actions we think he "should" be taking.

If challenge is not delivered with at least some compassion, it will tend to overpower rather than empower, and it will generate either submission or rebellion. If it is too soft or indirect, it will likely lack in needed impact; if it is aggressive, it will more often than not be met with defensiveness, defiance, or a caving in that does no one any real good.

One of the most difficult things about challenge itself is that it is inherently *confrontational*—not in some melodramatic way, but in the literal sense of the word *confront,* "to stand in front of." Nothing sideways or devious or passive-aggressive about it. To confront is to directly come up against, to be face-to-face with. Unfortunately, this often carries some negative connotations, suggestive of hostility or pushiness. But compassionate confrontation does not have to be an oxymoron.

Regardless of its negative associations, confrontation can be a life-enhancing process, if we engage in it with strongly embodied presence, compassion, and clarity. This in itself is a real challenge, asking plenty of us, but not so much that it is not doable.

Healthy challenge is *not* an attack. It asserts, sometimes forcefully so, but does not aggress or violate. Nor does it shame the other, though it sometimes may—without trying to do so—elicit a healthy shame in the other that catalyzes their conscience regarding questionable behavior on their part, while helping draw forth the kind of vulnerability that makes heartfelt remorse possible.

The intention of healthy challenge, however fiery its expression might be, is not to dominate or diminish the other, but to clearly highlight and buttress life-giving possibilities, not leaving obstructions to well-being unaddressed. Men tend to be more at ease with the delivery of this than with the reception of it, so sometimes the greater challenge is not to let one's reactivity to being challenged get in the way of opening to it (assuming that such challenge is not abusive).

Healthy challenge does *not* ask for passive acceptance or mere obedience—like a "good" soldier unquestioningly following orders—but for a dynamic, vitally present listening. A hostile, sarcastic, or otherwise disrespectful response to another's healthy challenge constitutes not a real challenge back, but a kind of trashing, regardless of how we might rationalize or justify such pushing back. "Nicely" or "reasonably" deflecting, bypassing, or marginalizing such challenge is no better. Yes, speak up in response to a healthy challenge, emphatically or fiercely if necessary, but do so as consciously and caringly as you can, not losing touch with the humanity of your challenger.

Doing so with truly good intentions, but sloppily—as is sometimes inevitable—is not the same as lashing out at your challenger!

When we justify lashing out (as in "Get the fuck off my back!" or "Stop trying to control me!") as "our truth" in response to whatever challenge we've received, we're basically deluding ourselves, settling for making ourselves right instead of going for what is deeper, simply reinforcing the reactive boy and defensive adolescent in us.

In giving a particular challenge, it's important that we know, really know, where we are coming from—what our underlying motivations are—and that we fully take this into account when delivering our challenge, in conscious conjunction with our sense of the other's capacity to receive it.

Of equal importance is that we don't exclude our heart from our challenging of another—however strong that might be or might need to be—and that we remain as open as possible to however our challenge might be received. Much of our work here is not to armor ourselves with our challenge-giving—hiding behind its delivery—but rather to remain transparently present as we express it, not letting our passion or conviction obscure or dilute our sensitivity to our recipient.

So what are we, at best, conveying? Our succinct, well-grounded intuition, in as fittingly assertive and skillful a form as possible. And there's often a vulnerable piece here: through such challenge, we sometimes might risk our relationship with the other, even as we perhaps recognize that it's an even greater risk to not thus speak up.

Healthy challenge can be fierce and it can be gentle. It can be emotionally vital and it can be emotionally muted. But whatever its form, it is a *stand*. There is nothing meek or halfhearted or apologetic about it. Even when it is gently conveyed, it keeps its spine, with no downgrading or weakening of its message.

This stand needs to be delivered in a form that serves the best interests of the recipient. Doing so requires that we be attuned to that person, not through the assumption that we know exactly what's needed, but instead through an intuitive feeling *into*, feeling *with*, and feeling *for* her or him. If we deliver our challenge poorly (with a closed heart and mind), we're left shipwrecked on the reefs of our differences; and if we don't deliver it, we drift on stagnant seas, removed from not just the reefs but also the depths.

GREG let his friend Jack borrow a bunch of his tools a while ago; Jack promised he'd return them in two weeks. A month has gone by, with no word from Jack about the tools, and Greg's upset with him. Here are three options: (1) Greg calls Jack, and angrily puts him down for being so inconsiderate. He gets even more aggressive when he finds out that Jack has no excuse other than saying he forgot. Greg demands that his tools be returned immediately, and hangs up. (2) Greg contacts Jack, asks for the tools back, and Jack returns them. Greg makes no fuss, making nice, letting his relationship with Jack slip into the shallows. (3) Greg meets with Jack, and tells him, directly but not aggressively, that he's upset that Jack hasn't kept his word regarding returning the tools. Jack gets defensive, and Greg looks at him, without speaking for a short while, seeing past Jack's defensiveness, then says, "I'm not putting you down—I'm just feeling upset that this has happened, and really don't want it to get in the way of our friendship." He stops and waits for Jack to take in what he's just said. Jack softens, and apologizes for not taking better care of the situation. ∎

So what can we do to become more skilled at challenge? *Practice.* Find others with whom you can share healthy challenge on various levels; others who share your commitment to deeper, more conscious, more vital relationship; others for whom transparency, integrity, and emotional literacy go hand in hand. And don't make such practice something you engage in only when you're in the mood!

A great practice for getting more skilled at challenging others is to practice challenging *yourself,* seeing what happens—both externally and internally—and working with that in as grounded a manner as possible. Notice, and keep noticing, what you are avoiding challenging yourself about. Become more aware and less tolerant of your tendency to postpone what can and needs to be done now. Both enjoy the couch and get off it. Notice not only what you don't want to have seen by others, but also what your excuses are for this. Uncomfortable as this may be—abundantly supplied as it is with necessary self-exposure—it is an immensely rewarding process, bringing more and more of you out of the shadows.

There's no neat map or paint-by-numbers approach that we can consistently rely on when we are challenging or being challenged by another or by a particular situation. Every approach, in fact, has its own shadow elements, such as hidden motivations or desires for control. If we are not aware of this, we'll probably act out some of these elements, which will inevitably lead us astray, being, for example, too hard, too soft, too intense, too gentle, too caught up in the "right" way to do it. Here, a valuable check-in is to ask ourselves questions like, "Is my heart open, and if not, why not?" or "Am I being direct without being cutting?" or "What kind of impact am I having on the person I'm challenging?"

Healthy challenge is innately nourishing. It gets our blood going, opens up our body, sharpens our focus, broadens our understanding, clarifies and energizes the space between us and the other, breathes vitality into our step, deepens our breath, cuts through numbness, makes kindling out of relational deadwood, and brings together our anger and compassion, drawing our warriorhood out in an openness as potent as it is vulnerable.

The following are key factors in healthy challenge.

- Being assertive but not aggressive

- Staying in touch with your caring

- Being direct

- Being non-shaming

- Being sensitive to the impact your delivery is having

- Standing your ground without being rigid

- Not going for more than the other can handle

- Remaining compassionate without weakening your message

- Being nonreactive in your delivery

- Saying neither too little nor too much

■ ■ ■

Let us take on healthy challenge, allowing it to sharpen our focus, ground our heart, loosen our belly, anchor our legs, ease our shoulders, deepen our relationships, enliven and honor our very being. Do this enough, and challenge will become something not to dread or bear, but something to which we look forward, something that we cannot help but honor, regardless of whatever edge we are working with.

PART II

Power and the Modern Man
Anger, Aggression, and the Hero

If we don't recognize and have some degree of
intimacy with whatever in us can dehumanize or abuse
others—however "civilized" or "rational" its demeanor—
we pose a danger not only to ourselves but to others, no
matter how nicely we generally behave. What really matters
here is not so much the presence of this inner darkness, but
the kind of relationship we choose to have with it.

6

Fighting for Power

From Overpowering to Empowering

FIGHTING WAS A BIG PART of my life, even early on. As a preschooler, I spent long hours in rapt fantasy, having my toys noisily fight each other, never tiring of their full-frontal clashes, spills, and rapidly rejuvenating resurrections. These battles didn't have an end; when it was time to stop, it was just a pause until the fighting resumed—mirroring the struggle I felt with my father. I felt powerless before his rage and shaming of me, and hated my inability to do battle with him, especially when he was putting down my mother (who never fought back). All my longing to overpower him, to decisively defeat him, remained almost completely internal until I was in my teens.

I was a shy boy, ultrasensitive and dreamy, and I was also aggressive. I remember being pursued by two bullies every day after school when I was seven or eight; it was a mile walk home from school, and they'd usually be a short distance behind me, taunting and chasing me and throwing rocks at me, but not quite catching me. (This may have been the start of my high school track career.) But one day, they did catch me. I still recall the spot, a grassy area near the local store. It was the mid-1950s. I was terrified, feeling them upon me in a noisy chaos of fists and shifting weight, but I fought back. To my utter surprise, I defeated them both, outwrestling them and forcing them into submission, as though I'd been trained to do exactly that.

The rest of my preadolescent years included many fights, more than a hundred each year. The aggression in the schoolyards and surrounding fields was intense, and I mostly felt right at home in it. Indoors, I was ultracompetitive, snaring the highest grades with relentless consistency, exulting in being the best, year after year, even though I remained quite shy, and my goal of getting my father's approval never came about. Once I was outside, though, academics didn't matter; all that counted was physical prowess, especially in fighting.

My style was unusual; the other boys both wrestled and fist-fought, swinging wildly, but I would not use my fists. The very thought of striking another boy in the face did not occur to me, even though it would have probably brought a much quicker end to the fights. As soon as a fight began, I'd entangle the other boy's arms or grab his wrists, wrestle him down, and either put him in a choke hold or twist his arm behind his back or into an armlock, intensifying it until he said, "Give." (This meant clear defeat for him, and the release of my grip.) I took some pleasure in winning, but no pleasure in delivering pain. My aggression coexisted with something that was far from aggressive, which I did not understand, let alone think about. I had little empathy for others, viewing them as competition or someone to overpower; but at the same time, I didn't want to harm them.

For most boys, engaging in battle—and not just physically—gets very easily associated with manliness. And any mixed feelings a boy might have about doing battle usually get trampled by the pressures to not chicken out or get soft or feel any caring for the opposition. The battles we are in, and are culturally encouraged to be in, may be laced with notions like good sportsmanship, but nonetheless are still a kind of warfare, infused with an overemphasis on winning. In such a setting, defeat means failure (lessened only by "taking it like a man"), and victory is a grail that promises great satisfaction. Any questioning of this is taken to be a sign of weakness, a flight from manliness.

By the time I was fourteen, I could out-argue my father and best him in feats of physical strength. But this was a strange victory for me, for in order to reach it, I'd had to distance myself from the terrified, oh so vulnerable little boy in me, my adolescent heart frozen hard. My aggressiveness became mostly intellectual, and my competitiveness shifted into high gear, inflating me while my shyness deflated me. I physically fought very seldom in high school, with one notable exception: when the neighborhood bully, Darryl, a hyperaggressive, chin-out, seemingly tireless in-your-face confronter, challenged me to a boxing match.

He and I met on a small, sun-bleached field beneath a hazy evening sun, but we might as well have been in Madison Square Garden. One of those watching was my father; he'd seen very few of my fights, so this was unusual. He'd declared that fighting wasn't proper (probably ascribed to his job as a schoolteacher), but had privately encouraged me to demolish those who wanted to fight me. His presence elevated our battle to a spectacle; I was not used to getting any attention from him. I felt roped in. Darryl and I both wore full-size boxing gloves. He was far more aggressive than I. We boxed in silence, except for our breathing and thudding and thwacking. When we rested between rounds (my father announced the beginning and ending of each round), panting, the silence thickened, imbuing our desperate little arena with a strange significance. Darryl fought with unrelenting determination, trying to overwhelm me with his ferocity.

But neither of us had an edge. I was somehow able to stand my ground.

Suddenly, I began fighting as if in a euphoric dream, blocking most of his blows with unaccustomed ease, punching with a fluid confidence that didn't feel like mine, nor like my father's. In my dreams, I had occasionally turned on an assailant and fought until I killed him, or until he morphed into someone friendly to me—or even into me. Such dream-fighting was easy once I'd started it. With Darryl, as in those dreams, I was committed to fighting to some sort of resolution, and yet I didn't think of winning or losing. It was as if something bigger than my aggression—something for which I had no frame of reference—was present in the midst of that very aggression. I'd somehow shed my self-consciousness, which ordinarily plagued me. My father's presence became irrelevant to me. A compelling grace moved my body, directing my movements. Time slowed down.

Darryl kept pressing me, but I couldn't be intimidated. I felt both unable and unwilling to alter our course. If he'd stopped, I probably would have, but he kept going, with violent intent. I felt things coming to a climax. If I could have spoken, I might have said something like "This is ME!" Not the boxer, not the pained teenager, not the shy boy, but the very energy and presence animating them. This "me" was big enough to include within itself the boxers, my father, the patch of field, the lengthening shadows, the surrounding oak trees, the stalemated drama of my father and me.

Darryl finally began to tire. What followed has remained very vivid to me: I feinted to the right, and hooked a left toward his belly. As he moved to block it, my right slammed down over his arms, increasing their downward momentum. Then my left drove straight into his face, with the full force of my weight behind it. His scream punctured the silence. He fell heavily. His two upper front teeth were cracked. (I thought I'd broken them off.) In a moment, I was squeezed back into my usual identity, losing touch with the freedom I'd been feeling. Now, it was just a fight I'd won.

I had no context for what had happened; it was like a fast-vanishing dream, a dream for whose roots I had no soil. Darryl ran home, and his parents, irate over what had happened, soon called my father. I didn't know what they talked about, but I did know that my father was prouder of me than he cared to show. But I didn't feel proud of what I'd done; it was a victory, but I didn't feel at all like a winner. I felt sad, down, depressed, a stranger in a strange land, belonging nowhere in particular.

Though I wouldn't have labeled it as such then, I was experiencing some compassion for Darryl. I had been close to my true size for a short time, and now I was back in my cell, boxed in, my only consolation being the prizes my aggression had brought me—all the ribbons for my adolescent victories in the classroom and on the track tacked up somewhere behind my forehead. My momentary transcendence of my usual self—taking the aggressor out of the aggression—receded very quickly, and did not emerge into the foreground until a dozen years later, when I started breaking down my emotional armoring, finding my vulnerability and deep heart-hurt in therapeutic settings.

There was a long and unbreathing time
when I lived in an empty room
weeping without any sound
my teenage heart darkly bound
the trap mine and mine alone
echoing with a young boy's nightmare cries
his pain lost in the hardened fury of my mind

Down, down came the walls one long day
broken through by my hidden longing
from the inside of the inside
my grief breakthrough relief

Glad, glad am I to feel that boy
looking this way this and every day
resting in the heart of my stride
his shy slenderness smiling
unbound and so wide
inviting the man in me
to be here fully and fully alive
no matter where I might be

FIGHT CLUB: MEETING MASCULINITY IN THE BARE-KNUCKLED RAW

When we wake up in the midst of being aggressive, we may not step out of what we're doing, but we have the chance to do so—and the chance to use the energy of aggressiveness for more life-giving purposes. I'd had no frame of reference for my brief awakening during my fight with Darryl. But once we *know* that we can shift out of automatic when we're being aggressive, it becomes our responsibility to do so. The point here is not to *defeat* aggression (which would just be another kind of aggression), but to reroute its energies into something healthier, something that's of real benefit to everyone involved.

This is all about taking the aggressor out of the aggression—fighting without a fighter—thereby making room for a deeper sense of self to get behind the wheel. This may mean a cessation of what's going on, and it also may mean shifting the aggression into healthy anger so that what's being addressed continues being addressed with sufficient assertion to bring about the desired outcome—but without injuring, disrespecting, or dehumanizing the recipients. Here, wildness and compassion team up with a discerning awareness, catalyzing true masculine power.

If you're looking for a viscerally revealing window into aggression and contemporary masculinity's psyche, a film worth going a few rounds with is *Fight Club*. The narrator, young and wretchedly insomniac, is doing time doing his daily grind. He's deadened, emotionally castrated. Things are edgy. Eventually, he starts attending various support groups, where he finds some connection and emotional release. Then a deeper catharsis calls to him, right after he meets Tyler Durden.

Tyler is a wild man, anarchistic and spontaneous, cocky and unapologetically alive, immensely attractive to the narrator. Soon they get into pounding each other bloody in bare-fisted fights, in which the point is not to win, but to give everything—everything!—to the encounter. No gloves, no referee, no constraints. Soon other men join them, and an underground movement called Fight Club rapidly takes root, providing all-male settings where no-holds-barred fighting happens with primal intensity. The men are far from trained fighters, but they throw themselves into their battles with ferocious zeal. It's bloody, it's violent, it's riveting, and it's profoundly satisfying to the participants, whether they're being beaten or are delivering the beating.

Plenty of viewers were turned off by these scenes. But they need to be seen not as gratuitous violence—which they are not—but rather as ragingly raw depictions of an in-your-face fuck-you to an emasculating culture; a fuck-you that is neither romanticized nor a put-down. In their savage encounters with each other, the members of Fight Club are not battling an enemy but bonding, and not so far from doing battle against that which boxes men into the kind of world and life that, not so long ago, was the narrator's life.

The fighting is so bone-crushingly over the top, so violently visceral, that it allows us to see—and feel—its underpinnings, without any meaning-messages needing to be stapled to all the bloody poundings.

Eventually, the catharsis provided by Fight Club—which has rapidly gone nationwide, though remained undercover—leads not just to release, but also to a metastasizing organization headed by Tyler, called Project Mayhem. From club to cult. When things have really gotten out of control, the narrator starts to wake up to what is happening, is horrified, and takes a stand that undercuts the one he's taken up to this point, namely of assuming that Fight Club was a great thing, something to leave unquestioned. The narrator has gone from wimp to savage to empire builder to awakening dreamer, finally confronting himself right to his core.

Fight Club is commonly thought of as a man's movie, but I think it's just as much for women, if only because of the inside look it gives regarding the male psyche. Its blood sport is not a condoning of violence but an up close, intensely gritty illumination of it. Mix together postmodern alienation and stripped down savagery, and you've got *Fight Club*, breaking bare-knuckled through the schizophrenic fault lines of contemporary culture. *Fight Club* is about facing and starting to heal that split, which asks everything of the narrator—and of us.

Can a man heal without having faced, fully felt, and noninjuriously expressed his own primal maleness, however primitive that might be? No. The point is not just to get flat-out enraged but to also face and feel the savagery within, without castrating or crippling it. Much of a man's work is to reclaim the vitality and primal power of his wildness, without adopting its viewpoint or letting it direct things. This asks for a capacity for containment and contextual sensitivity, but it doesn't have to rob a man of any energy.

Wildness and compassion can coexist—and ought to coexist—in a man. Fight Club can easily become Project Mayhem if we don't get to the heart of our rage, keeping a consistently compassionate eye on it. Doing this in ways that are both life-affirming and discerning is work worthy of any man, work that helps bring us into the fully embodied, wide-awake present, work that truly empowers us.

A DEEPER EMPOWERMENT

Power is the capacity to act, to generate significant change, to impose our will on our environment (inner or outer), for better or for worse. We may take our power, step into it, avoid it, use it indirectly, abuse it, underuse it, refuse it, be seduced by it, give it away, hold on to it, hide behind it, keep it in the shadows, define ourselves through it, and so on; but whatever we do with it, whatever we bring to it, simply reflects our priorities, be they conditioned or not.

If we've been flattened or crushed by circumstances, an influx of power can resurrect us. This can expand us in ways that improve our lives and those of the ones around us; it can also inflate us, pumping up our egocentricity and selfishness. Nothing may be so clearly revealing of where we stand than how we use our power.

For many men, power is something hard; something commonly symbolized by a bulgingly flexed bicep; something carrying the promise of overcoming whatever obstacles may be in the way (this being the driving force of *Fight Club*). Such power can reduce the world to a battlefield, an arena in which others are there to be defeated or to be brought under one's command—and it can also provide the force to help bring about needed change, to shake up the status quo.

There is also a soft power. Think of a river pouring through a canyon, flowing around battalions of boulders, yielding in its rocky passage yet persisting in its course. When we are immersed in such power, we can get overly absorbed in flowing, in avoiding full-on contact, telling ourselves that something is not worth making a fuss over, making too much room for forces that need to be met with real impact. And we can also let such softness open us more deeply to our own core of being, so that our actions emanate not so much from part of us, but from our totality.

In my fight with Darryl, I began with hard power, thrusting my way forward, my fists iron extensions of my will. Not that this was wrong—for it allowed me to stand my ground, to survive, to not crumble. As the fight progressed, a softer, more fluid power emerged, through which a more panoramic view of the battle became foreground for me. I didn't let this take the fire out of me, nor did I simply see red. A further softening happened at the end, as my compassion (so unfamiliar to me at that time!) briefly showed up, stopping me from inflating myself, with the result that my defeated opponent lay not underneath me, but stood before me as a wounded teen, not really all that different from me.

What I didn't see then was that whatever I needed power for existed in a relational context. I had had power over my opponent and felt empowered through our fighting; without our relationship, odd as it was, this would not have been possible. Power arises in a field of mutuality, however imbalanced the dynamics may be, as exemplified by the power struggle featured in many an intimate relationship.

As a boy, I was overpowered by my father. As a youth, I was overpowered by my shyness and shame. In my twenties, I was overpowered by my passion for excelling in whatever I was doing. In my thirties, I started learning to share power, to enjoy cooperation, to fully feel my emotions. In my forties, sharing power took a backseat to my taking and being given a lot of power, despite all the work I'd done on myself; I let my strengths obscure my weaknesses, and hurt others in the process. In my fifties, I lost all interest in overpowering, seeing that the men I'd admired were arrogant and irresponsible and full of themselves—just like I was in my forties. As I had in my thirties, I shared power, but from a more mature place. And I also took joy in empowering others, having been humbled enough to outgrow my desire to be in a position of power. In my sixties, I've continued to relate to power as I did in my fifties, deepening my capacity to use it skillfully, and teaching this to others. I now feel all my earlier selves within, each with his own leanings, and I feel a tender compassion for all of them, without letting any of them run the show. Much of the power I now have goes into helping others heal, awaken, and become intimate with all that they are. (As an exercise, I suggest you write out your own history with power—at least a few pages—tracing the evolution of how you've used and been used by power.)

Power-over is all about dominating or controlling another or others, and is a key operational preference of unhealthy manhood, along with *power-under* (meaning finding a certain status or safety in submissively aligning with more dominant or privileged males). Power-over and power-under are foundational partners in many relationships, often constituting a cult of two—until the downtrodden one takes a real stand against the dominating one.

Power-to is a healthier approach in relationship, and is a shared undertaking that may not be particularly intimate, but makes for a more respectful mutuality, with the prevailing image being not one of opposition, but of side-by-side partnership.

Power-with is the most life-giving form of power. In intimate relationship, such shared empowerment deepens the partners' bond, helping to bring forth the very best from each, making it much more possible to share challenging things (like fear and mistrust) openly and vulnerably. Here, the needs of the partners and the needs of their relationship compassionately coexist. Here, power is an ally, with partners solidly behind each other, rooted in mutual trust. Their shared power deepens their love, and their shared love deepens their power.

True masculine power is full-blooded *power-with*—power that strengthens both our autonomy and our togetherness, power that is both hard and soft, penetrating and fluid, finely focused and panoramic, power that aligns head, heart, and guts. Such power, whatever its intensity, does not abuse, and protects what needs protecting. It brings out the very best in a man, backing him in taking needed stands, without forgetting his heart. True masculine power is not out to prove anything, but simply to support the living of a deeper life, a life of authenticity, care, passion, integrity, love, and wakefulness.

7

Anger

Tending the Fire

ANGER COMES with being human.

Its vocalization, however low-key, is a kind of battle cry. But what is the battle, and how is it being handled, and what is actually at stake? Whether such expression is thundering or muted, heartless or caring, destructive or constructive, it signals a challenge that draws forth our warriorhood. Anger doesn't go away just because we've matured or become more spiritual. The point is not to outgrow it, but to outgrow our dysfunctional ways of using it. Not to know our anger—and know it very well—is a dangerous choice, keeping us in the dark and in danger of being hostile or violent instead of just angry.

Anger is a heatedly aroused state that combines (1) a gripping sense of being wronged or thwarted and (2) a compelling pull to take care of this.

Anger's presence and expression, however impassioned, doesn't necessarily mean that we're off track or that we've regressed. Anger can be a tremendously beneficial force, a fieriness that provides both heat and light, helping establish—to take but one example—healthy boundaries. Just because it's easy to abuse our anger (letting it, for example, turn into ill will and violence) does not mean that it's a negative or unwholesome emotion.

Though anger can be reduced to reactive rage or hostility, it can also become wrathful compassion, a potent force for positive action in the world. And though it carries a sword, anger is essentially a vulnerable emotion, emanating, at best, not only from one's gut but also one's heart.

Anger is the emotion that is often the easiest to express for most men. And it's also the emotion that men most need to learn to express skillfully, especially in relationship. This doesn't mean repressing anger, any more than it means indulging in anger. Well-handled anger, however fiery it might be—or might need to be—does not feel threatening or dangerous, but builds more trust and safety, thereby helping to deepen intimacy.

However, as much as anger can be harnessed for life-giving purposes, it is much more commonly used to overpower, to dominate, to control, to frighten, to camouflage other emotions, and to squelch opposition. It can be saddled with being the megaphone and muscle for moral righteousness and tyranny, asserting a manhood that has gotten way off track, derailed by its aggression, egocentric ambition, and lack of compassion.

But the problem here is not anger per se, but what we *do* with it, as when we allow it to mutate into various forms of aggression. Thankfully, we can take anger in a very different direction, letting it and love coexist to at least some degree, usually in the form of a *fierce compassion.* There's no shaming or aggressiveness in such compassion, but there is fieriness in conjunction with care for the other. This, though, is an uncommon practice, being hugely overshadowed by unhealthy anger, anger that blames, shames, and attacks, anger that is little more than a tempest in a me-knot, a fist-in-the-face attitude, righteously lost in battles of sometimes extraordinarily tiny importance.

We talk of the fight-or-flight response—associating the fight part with anger, and the flight part with fear—but often do not recognize that anger can also be a flight. From what? Vulnerability, sadness, grief, fear, hurt, shame, remorse, responsibility. If, for example, we're really hurting, feeling a quickly surfacing sadness over a recent loss, we may get angry enough to obscure our underlying pain. Or we may feel some shame over what a significant other has just said to us and get aggressively angry at them to such a degree that we forget our shame, distancing ourselves from the discomfort of it through our immersion in our anger.

Anger has a bad reputation in many circles, being frequently associated or equated with aggression and violence. Voices raised in anger can easily become voices ready to attack or crush or humiliate. Many of us grew up in circumstances in which strongly expressed anger meant danger or rejection or the loss of love, and so tend to associate any fiery or forceful expression of anger with something far from good. We may also have been subjected to teachings, spiritual and otherwise, that slammed anger with a negative connotation, as if it were in the way of love, peace, goodwill, spiritual awakening, and other such virtues.

So it's not difficult to trash anger, to unquestioningly classify it as a negative emotion, something we'd do best to stay away from, or at least mute. Yet anger is central to self-protection, to guarding our boundaries and the integrity of our being, to standing our ground in the face of injurious or potentially injurious forces. Those who are cut off from their own anger almost invariably have weak or overly porous boundaries, and cave in all too easily in circumstances that require them to take a strong stand.

There's a raw intensity in anger that's central to masculinity, manifesting as a full-blooded muscularity of intention that roots our legs and expands our chest and increases the blood flow to our arms, providing us with an on-tap fierceness that helps underline what we view as needing to be done.

A man stranded from his anger is a man without power; but a man who is possessed by his anger is in no better a position, being a danger to himself and others.

ANGER AND AGGRESSION
ARE NOT THE SAME THING!

A big part of the reason why anger gets such bad press is that it commonly is made synonymous with aggression. But anger and aggression do differ, and differ considerably, regardless of similarities in surface appearance.

Many years ago, a man came to me for just one session—and only to talk. He told me that his wife was on the verge of leaving him because of his anger. He said he didn't scream at her, didn't threaten or hit her, didn't even raise his voice very much. He added that she'd wanted him to express his emotions, but when he did show his anger, she was really bothered by it. So what was he to do? As we spoke, it became clear to me that he was not just being angry with her, but *aggressive*, mostly through a "reasonable" sarcasm, cutting her down when she displeased him, emanating a mild but unmistakable hostility. I explained to him that anger and aggression—defined by me as an *attack*, however indirect or soft-spoken—are not the same thing. Simply hearing this—and understanding that his sarcasm was a form of aggression—made a huge difference to him. He very quickly stopped acting aggressively toward his wife, and this had a dramatically positive impact on their marriage.

So how do we distinguish aggression from anger? Here I'm speaking of skillful anger, anger that doesn't shame, blame, or dehumanize, regardless of its passion. Aggression attacks; anger does not. In aggression, we're emotionally hardened, whereas in anger—whatever its heat—we're vulnerable, to whatever degree. You could say that aggression is anger stripped of its heart and care, dehumanizing the other to the point of disrespecting, putting down, or violating him or her.

Regardless of its passion, aggression is not an emotion per se, but something that *we are doing* with an emotion, namely anger. To slip into aggression is to strip anger of its heart and arm its expression with a dehumanizing hardness. Aggression is a choice, a result of how we're handling our anger. Anger is not the problem; our letting it mutate into aggression is.

If we're angry and want to remove ourselves from its innate vulnerability—perhaps because we feel some shame about showing any softness in the midst of our anger—we can retreat into the armoring and mindset of aggression, finding expression there in a number of ways, ranging from the twisted niceties of passive-aggressiveness to the disrespectful digs of sarcasm to the unleashing of violence.

Aggression unquestioningly reduces the offending person to a mere "it." Any care we had for them is glaringly absent—they are simply our target, whether we jab, pound, hammer, steamroll, or blindside them.

In both anger and aggression, we can say a strong "No!"—but where anger simply is a forceful intensification or emphatic underlining of that word, aggression adds a hostile edge, often imbued with some degree of threat, its very tone cutting into the other.

Once we've let ourselves become aggressive, dehumanizing the offending other, we're on a very slippery slope, in danger of sliding into violent behavior. When we lose touch with the basic humanity of the other, we feel more justified in reducing them to a bull's-eye for our aggressiveness, losing ourselves in shooting them down, or otherwise giving them what they "deserve."

Males are not just biologically more prone to aggression than females, but are also more socialized in that direction. Consider how we have far less flattering labels for women's anger than men's. By giving men's anger a bigger stamp of approval than women's anger, we're more likely to okay extensions of anger in men, like aggression or violence, perhaps resorting to notions such as, "it's just part of being a guy" or "maybe he was just trying to knock some sense into you" (violence being spun here as tough love or even altruism).

An angry woman may be deemed less feminine because of her anger, but an angry man is not deemed less masculine because of his anger, and may in fact be viewed as more masculine, more of a real man when he gets angry (indicating that he "has balls" or is "kicking some ass" or is "taking no prisoners"). The relative support or sanction that men may get for being angry easily morphs into support for being aggressive, however slight the provocation may be. When there's enough intensity—be it negative or positive—and some sense of justification, an energetic threshold is crossed, and aggression is but a breath away, set on attack mode.

Aggression may go no further than the "playful" jabs of mean-spirited joking, or it may cross into outright violence. Anger protects boundaries, aggression disregards and disrespects them, and violence trashes them completely. Violence, like aggression, is not a result of anger, but an abuse of anger (with the exception of situations in which getting violent serves a higher good, like saving the life of our child or preventing a worse violence).

MARK AND JASON are starting to escalate their argument, one that's been a recurring theme in their relationship. Mark is keeping his voice even, while Jason is getting louder and louder. Mark starts to smile smugly, and Jason blows his stack, to which Mark reacts with contempt (a toxic mix of disgust and aggression), saying that this kind of predictable behavior from Jason is exactly what is ruining their relationship. Jason cracks; his tears come, along with his shame that he's falling apart. Mark remains impassive, dismissing his own responsibility in the interaction, and says, "Here you go again." Jason hardens. They move apart. Jason may have looked like the aggressive one, but Mark, by goading and then shaming Jason, was actually more aggressive, despite his lack of loudness. ■

If, while in the midst of being aggressive, we were to feel some caring for the other, we'd be starting to shift from aggression to anger. We might still feel outraged, but would be dropping out of attack mode. This is a hugely significant shift, essential for our healing, as it returns us to a skillful and healthy functioning anger, the kind of anger needed to fuel the needed turnarounds in our life and culture. Nonviolence doesn't mean an absence of anger, but rather a life-giving use of it, and this is not possible so long as we continue to let our anger morph into aggression.

Anger and compassion can coexist, but aggression and compassion cannot. There is no empathy in aggression, and without empathy there is no compassion.

SHIFTING FROM AGGRESSION TO HEALTHY ANGER

The shift out of aggression is not a small or lightweight shift, being of the same magnitude as turning *toward* our pain. It is a U-turn, a radical shift, a life-enhancing emotional and behavioral conversion, both personally and collectively. We may feel a certain warriorhood in aggression, but in moving from aggression to anger, we are activating a deeper, far more healthy warriorhood.

This conversion is not a matter of draining or stifling the energy of our aggression, but of liberating it from its viewpoint so that its passion and forcefulness can, to whatever extent, coexist with compassion. In this context, the world needs not less anger, but *more* anger, anger that comes to a significant degree from the heart and is aligned with the greater good for one and all. This is the anger that clears the temple of moneylenders, the anger that fuels needed revolution, the anger that is but wrathful compassion in the raw.

We need our anger in order to move forward, to level what no longer serves us, to potently address injustice, to protect the sanctity of our being—and this will backfire if our anger gets funneled into aggression or is treated as something negative or unwholesome or in the way of true peace.

Though aggression might seem to be an inevitable outcome of anger, it actually is an *avoidance* of anger and the hurt and vulnerability that are part of it.

Viewing anger as aggression, or as the cause of aggression, provides us with an excuse to classify it as a lower or primitive emotion. Yes, anger does have a primitive side—a purely biological uprising—but it's far more than just a primitive phenomenon, despite the fact that our use of it is often far from civilized.

Our work is to take the direction of anger-to-aggression and *reverse* it, *converting aggression back into anger,* specifically an anger sufficiently awakened to coexist with compassion.

Anger can be very fiery, very intense, and still not shift into aggression. In the face of injustice, be it personal or collective, anger rouses us to take action—its heat is activist. Anger is not just fire but *moral fire,* its nature being to protect what is weak or vulnerable or broken in us. Anger catalyzes us into taking as fierce as necessary stands to guard what needs guarding, including the sanctity of our being. Our task, our sacred obligation, is to do our very best to ensure that this doesn't become an aggressive or violent undertaking, one more war in which to get absorbed.

An essential piece of work for men is to distinguish between healthy and unhealthy anger, learning to consistently choose the former.

Without developing the capacity for the healthy expression of anger, a man will simply stunt his growth, continuing to attach himself to the kind of power dynamic that does no one any real good and letting his anger funnel into hostility, mean-spiritedness, and violence, however indirectly. Part of the good news is that working deeply with your anger brings out the kind of warriorhood in you that's so badly needed in our world: powerful, gutsy, and heartful, protective of what truly needs protecting, able to deliver anger without getting lost in it or turning it into aggression.

It's crucial to know the differences between unhealthy (or unskillful) anger and healthy (or skillful) anger more than just superficially, especially when circumstances are such that we're veering toward the unhealthy expression of anger.

The following are some activities that characterize unhealthy anger.

- We busy ourselves blaming the other—we act as if it were their fault that we're acting the way we are, and we're sure as hell not going to admit otherwise.

- We lose touch with our caring for the other, commonly shaming, dismissing, or dehumanizing them.

- We are on the attack, becoming hostile, mean-spirited, or otherwise aggressive.

- We armor and arm ourselves without any regard for the other.

- We don't take responsibility for what we're doing and the impact it's having.

- We stay reactive and won't admit we're being reactive (except when blaming the other for our behavior).

- We have no perspective other than that of our own righteousness.

- We don't give a damn about the other's boundaries, feeling free to cross them.

- We fight dirty, and feel justified in doing so, as if the other deserves this.

- We would rather be right than connected.

Unhealthy (or aggressive) anger often arises from feeling shamed or criticized or disrespected, however slight or even imaginary this may be. At the coarsest levels, it might manifest as a jaw-jutting glare laced with menace: "Who are you looking at?" or "You got a problem?" This can be a reaction to a sense of being lesser than, a suddenly bristling defense in the spirit of "the best defense is a good offense." The glowering eyes, the pumped-up torso, the far-from-friendly face, are not in themselves problematic—for anger's appearance is also often fierce—but all too often show up only in the employ of unhealthy expressions of anger.

Imagine such an appearance coexisting with some degree of care and vulnerability—with the eyes clearly seeing not just red—and imagine this for yourself, and what happens? You still feel heated, amped up, ready to take strong action, but you can't lash out or speak cruelly because your heart is involved, and you see more than just someone to crush. You see and feel the other's humanity, which keeps you from getting aggressive.

In the healthy expression of anger, we resort neither to getting aggressive nor to shaming, we don't lose touch with our caring for the other, and we take responsibility for what we're doing while we're angry. Healthy anger is *vulnerable,* however forceful it might be, and doesn't make a problem out of its vulnerability.

REACTIVE ANGER

Most anger is reactive anger. (*To react* means to automatically act the same way again and again.) We can't do much about this, other than repress it, unless we are able to (1) recognize the signs of being reactive, and (2) stop playing victim to these signs, whatever they may be.

Waking up in the midst of our reactivity is not so easy, but it is nonetheless doable with some practice. Taking action that's aligned with such awakening is more of a challenge, but again is doable with some practice. It also helps to remember that *reactivity is the dramatization of activated shadow material,* which we are letting hold us hostage.

The following are some signs of reactivity.

- Disproportionate response, as if you were facing something much bigger or much more important than is actually the case.

- Repetitive use of the same phrases—hearing yourself saying much the same words as you said the previous times you were similarly upset (like, "You always do this" or "You just don't get it").

- Sudden influx of over-the-top emotional intensity.

- Sudden regression to black-and-white thinking.

- Absence of self-reflection or a refusal to access any self-reflection.

- Exaggerated attachment to being right.

- Overdramatizing what you're thinking and feeling.

- Feedback from your partner or a close friend that you're being reactive, and a refusal on your part to even consider that they might be right.

Once you can recognize that you're caught in reactivity (having become familiar with its signs), you can work with it. Let's say you're very angry and know that you're being reactive—your anger having little or nothing to do with what you're apparently upset by. Initially, all you have to do is say out loud, "I'm being *reactive.*"

Then, *resisting the temptation to justify your reactivity,* breathe more deeply into your belly, letting it soften, holding eye contact with the other, letting yourself see him or her through more than the eyes of your reactivity. Stay with this until you feel your connection with the other. You may then have the sense that you are compassionately holding the *reactive part of yourself.* If you find this difficult, know that you are not alone. This is not an easy practice! If your reactivity persists, make space for having a *conscious rant.* (See the appendix for a detailed description of a conscious rant, and make sure to read it carefully *before* you attempt one.)

BEING VULNERABLE IN YOUR ANGER

It's easy to stay hard in our anger, masking any vulnerability or hurt we might be feeling. But it's harder to feel and express our anger while maintaining at least some care for the one we're angry at, not letting our anger slip into reactivity and aggression. Probably the biggest challenge for men in shifting from unhealthy to healthy anger is that of being *vulnerable* in their anger, letting the heatedness and intensity of it coexist with some degree of heart, and openly feeling and showing whatever emotions are co-arising with their anger, like sadness or grief.

Such vulnerability is not an indication of caving in or a collapsing of personal boundaries, nor of downplaying or sidestepping what we're angry about; rather, it's a source of strength and resiliency, rooted in compassion both for oneself and the other, a refusal to abandon one's heart for very long in the presence of anger.

If anger is fire, existing as both heat and light, its heat manifests as its forcefulness, its energetic intensity and internal pressurization, its volcanic capacity. And its light manifests as its vulnerability and sensitivity, its softer dimensions, its concern for the other.

Being vulnerable—transparent, open, unguarded—makes empathy possible, and when empathy is present, anger is far more likely to remain clean. Vulnerability doesn't take the power out of anger, but keeps it from straying into aggression. Vulnerability can be scary or uncomfortable, since letting down our guard might seem dangerous (as it perhaps once was when we were younger); however, if we remain thus guarded during our anger, we'll block ourselves from connecting with the other, keeping them in an oppositional position.

So, how can you be vulnerable in your anger? First, *feel* your connection with the one you're angry at. If you can't do this, *remember* your connection with them and remember that you care about them—even a moment of this can infiltrate your anger enough to bring about some degree of vulnerability. Second, attune to whatever hurt you are feeling in your anger, and keep some attention on that hurt, feeling into whatever emotional pain may be just under the surface. And, last, be as aware as possible of the *impact* your anger is having on the other; if they look scared or sad or troubled, take that in, enough so to stir at least some empathy in you.

FOUR APPROACHES TO WORKING WITH ANGER

Most men see only two options when it comes to anger: keeping it in or letting it out. But in actuality, there are four options when anger arises.

Anger-in, the first of these, is often not much more than repression—a squelching or muzzling of anger, perhaps accompanied by the admonition (whether external or internal) to "suck it up." But sucking it up usually means that we're forcing our anger-energy up into our heads, perhaps to the point of granting excessive importance to rationality, logic, and being reasonable, often aggressively employing these capacities.

We can also "suck it down," forcing our anger-energy down into our pelvic bowl and genital area. This may over-amplify our sexual energy, often to the point where we become excessively focused on it—especially when it comes to needing some sort of energetic release.

Imagine a tube of toothpaste and visualize its center as your solar plexus and upper belly area. Imagine squeezing it there, hard, and seeing its contents either moving upward—to the top end of the tube, representing our head—or to the bottom end of the tube, representing our genital region. Or imagine it being squeezed so that its contents move toward *both* ends, connecting head and genitals, with not much in between other than a compressed no-man's-land too crushed out of shape to be a user-friendly or habitable zone.

When anger is left unexpressed and undigested (because its concerns have not been sufficiently addressed), it seeks an outlet somewhere, a place where energetic discharge can occur. If we suck it up, we blow off some steam through thinking—and thinking about thinking—slowly but surely exhausting ourselves in mental loopings and reconstructions and excessive self-talk. And if we suck it down, we may find some release of its energies through sexual discharge—perhaps assuming that we're just feeling really sexual, when in fact we may actually be quite angry, either masturbating away the charge of that anger, or reducing our sexual partner to little more than an outhouse for our accumulated frustration.

Anger-out, the second common option, emphasizes openly expressing it. This may seem a better practice than that of suppression, but mostly it is just as dysfunctional. We may be told that getting our anger out of our system is good for us, but the way we express it can make things worse for ourselves and the recipients of our anger, as when we merely unload it without any regard for them. And does getting strongly expressive with our anger really get it out of our system? No. Anger is not a something (a mass or indwelling entity) we can empty ourselves of, but a vital activity—far more verb than noun—that includes feeling, cognition, conditioning, and social factors. Discharging the energies of our anger does not necessarily mean that the anger itself has left our system.

The last two approaches to working with anger are less commonly known and practiced than anger-in and anger-out, but they are far more effective.

Mindfully held anger is all about remaining present to our anger—observing its presence and moment-to-moment qualities—without expressing it externally. So we stay aware of our anger without distancing ourselves from it, allowing it to move through us internally, keeping an ever-alert eye on it. This meditative practice can, however, slip into mere repression, as when we are not sitting with our anger but *on* it—so that it's no more than a spiritualized version of anger-in.

Heart-anger is an approach in which openly expressed anger coexists with care for its recipient. Such anger is the face of wrathful compassion, and does not lose touch with its heart, no matter how fiery its expression might be. Heart-anger is the epitome of vulnerable forcefulness, taking stands without standing over anyone. Even a trace of it can make a big difference in relationships, generating a sense of safety that helps bridge communication gaps and relational impasses. Not easy, but definitely worth cultivating!

PRACTICE **Anger-In, Anger-Out, Mindfully Held Anger, and Heart-Anger**

Find a comfortable place where you won't be disturbed for the next twenty minutes or so, and where you have enough privacy to raise your voice considerably. Settle in and bring to mind an incident that really angered—and perhaps still angers—you. Close your eyes and focus even more closely on this incident, imagining yourself in the midst of it, with your anger strongly surfacing.

Now imagine that your approach to anger is anger-in. As you zero in on the offending incident, slow down your breathing and start thinking about what you could have done differently. Remind yourself that expressing any anger won't help anyone. Keep telling yourself to calm down. Do your best to think positive thoughts. Bring the nice guy in you to the foreground.

Next, imagine that your approach to anger is mindfully held anger. Sit still. Be aware of each breath's movement through you, feel your belly rising (without any effort on your part) with each inhale, and falling back with each exhale. Feel your anger rising in you, moving through your body. Observe the thoughts that go with and reinforce this. Make no effort to get away from your anger and remain aware of your breathing. Don't identify with your feelings and thoughts. Hold the intensity and heat of your anger with as much compassion as possible, keeping it all internal. Stay with it until it subsides.

Next, imagine that your approach to anger is anger-out. Breathe deeper, tighten your fists, and stand with your knees slightly bent. Inflate your chest and tighten your jaw, let your teeth show and your eyes glare. Let your words pour forth, uncensored and loud and fiery. Don't hold back. Feel your whole body alive with anger, and keep unleashing it with full-throated intensity.

And finally, imagine your approach to anger is heart-anger. Deepen your breathing, expand your upper torso, and tighten your jaw. Let your anger out, but not so strongly that you forget your caring for the offending other. Be fiery, be intensely alive, be forceful, but don't slip into any aggression or name-calling. Maintain a degree of vulnerability. Let your fierceness and your compassion coexist.

■ ■ ■

To summarize, anger itself is not the problem. If there is a problem, it's what we're *doing* with our anger. Are we turning it into aggression, hostility, ill will, hatred, violence? Are we swallowing it? Are we using it to control or manipulate? Are we channeling it into sarcasm or passive-aggressiveness? Pushing anger away doesn't work. Nor does indulging in it. Nor does rising above it or treating it like some primitive relic from preliterate times.

The key is to wake up to our anger as soon as possible after it starts arising, stepping back just far enough from it—from its energy and prevailing viewpoint—so as to be able to relate *to* it rather than *from* it. This means not allowing it to flame or further flame into reactivity.

So it's crucial to understand anger and to know it well, to have enough familiarity with our history with it and our usual ways of expressing it to be able to employ it in ways that serve our best interests.

A man who is intimate with his anger and who can express it skill-fully is a man in whom forcefulness coexists with vulnerability and compassion, a man worthy of our trust, a man capable of deep intimacy.

8

Aggression Unveiled

When You Shift into Attack Mode

IS THERE ANY QUALITY more commonly associated with masculinity than aggression?

When we hear admonitions such as "be a man" or "man up" or "grow a pair," we are usually hearing a call to be aggressive, or to be more aggressive.

The notion of aggression carries more punch than does that of assertion, more overt forcefulness and weight, more of a capacity to intimidate or overpower. Assertion doesn't brandish weaponry, but aggression can (and not just physically), often in the name of establishing "respect" or territorial boundaries. Assertion does not get in your face, but aggression usually does, often emphatically. It might even grin as it does so, its smile being little more than a sublimated snarl.

Some might say that aggression is no more than a going-toward forcefulness, centered by a will to take strong action. But in this book, I'm defining it as an intended or acted-out *attack*, however mild or indirect it might be (as in verbal sniping). This doesn't mean that aggression is therefore always a bad thing, for there are times when attack is entirely appropriate, when heavy intervention is clearly called for.

It is common to equate being aggressive with being manly, and—in many circles—to assign this a positive connotation. Men who appear far from aggressive may be subjected to slurs, or made fun of for such apparent weakness, as exemplified by referring to them as females. The drill sergeant or football coach who calls his male charges "ladies" or "girls" is but one example, reinforcing the concept of males as dominant and females as submissive—dominance largely being measured by one's degree of aggressiveness.

"Are you going to take that lying down?" is a far more common challenge to males than females, equating being supine with weakness. Though major steps have been taken in the last half century regarding women's rights, being female is still often associated with being weaker or less in charge—that is, less aggressive or less capable of overpowering or dominating. There's also more permission—and even admiration—in contemporary Western culture for women to be aggressive in career contexts. I remember a lawyer telling me she got ahead by "outmanning" the men in her profession. And how interesting it is that, as aggression begins to lose some of its popularity as a go-to indicator of manliness, various qualities commonly associated with being female—vulnerability, softness, emotional literacy—are starting, however slightly, to become thought of as virtues for men, with the tacit implication being that men need to become more like women, but not vice versa.

Take away a man's aggression, and you're taking away his manliness, his balls, his credibility, his status as a bona fide male. Absurd as this view might seem, it still carries considerable heft outside personal growth and spiritual circles. And it's not just about taking away a man's aggression, but also about taking away or delegitimizing his potential for aggression: if he's without aggression or is expected to keep it from surfacing, what will be left of him? Will he just be a wimp, a pushover, an emasculated figure stuck on the sidelines of life?

Such loss is far from appealing to plenty of men, *but actually doesn't indicate a loss of power,* if it means that a man ensures that any aggression in him gets converted into healthy anger, anger that remains vital but does not attack, anger that serves rather than hinders relational closeness. Attack is far from assertion, being much more than just taking or voicing a firm stand. There's usually a hostility in attack, a willingness to do harm if doing so helps us get what we think we need—in this we arm and armor ourselves, retracting our vulnerability and care, establishing ourselves in "battle" mode, as if "going to war."

Aggression implies a battleground upon which we skirmish, where war metaphors abound. We may be under fire, bombed, or caught in the cross fire. We may be on the front lines or need to call in the troops. We might be in a foxhole, living in a battleground state, or taking up arms. The start of a big game may be conceptualized as "going to war." Professional athletes may say of a particular intense game that "it was a war out there" or "it was kill or be killed."

Culturally we always seem to be "making war" on something: the war on crime, war on drugs, war on poverty, war on terrorism, war on graffiti, war on cancer, war on religion, war on guns, war on science, war on war. In May 2013, the United States Senate majority leader stated that he was prepared to possibly execute "the nuclear option" (in reference to bringing about filibuster reform). *Nuke* has become a relatively common verb denoting unusually strong aggression.

And on it goes, aggression generating more aggression, with enough momentum to crush most dissent, commonly framing its opposition as emasculated, weakness incarnate, or of dubious quality. In this, there's no heart, no healthily detached perspective, no compassion, just runaway aggressiveness that needs to be emphatically derailed. This is an essential part of what men are called to do, beginning with them working with their own aggression until it no longer runs them, while learning to embody a healthy anger, an anger at once fierce and caring, capable of rattling the status quo so strongly that needed changes become more than just good ideas.

AGGRESSION AS INSTINCT

Some view aggression as instinctual, some as socially constructed, and others view it as both. Let's start with the instinctual view, which was most famously fathered by Darwin and Freud.

Darwin viewed aggression as a simple reaction to threat, a self-defending behavior, often signaled by characteristic facial expressions and physical mobilization—think bared teeth, flared nostrils, and bunched-up shoulders. Survival, it seemed, largely depended on the capacity to aggress. So aggression was a valuable behavior, and the most aggressive were the optimal ones to pass on their genes. (This made sex little more than a triumph of aggression, which is explored in the chapters on sexuality.)

Freud held a darker view of aggression than Darwin did and focused more on its destructive and violent tendencies. Man, he dourly observed, was not much more than a savage lurking beneath a flimsy veneer of socially acceptable behavior, whose inborn aggression threatened civilized society with violence, war, and disintegration. And to make matters worse, the instinct for aggression was unavoidably intertwined with the sexual instinct. For Freud, civilization meant a repressing of aggression and sexuality, best achieved through internalizing aggressiveness and enlisting it in the service of conscience. His notion of conscience was that it was *constitutionally* aggressive and needed to be that way to keep us under control—thereby unwittingly equating conscience with what we now call our inner critic.

His validation of such an internal shame-delivering taskmaster and our "need" for it (as though we were but children before an authoritarian parent) is something that all too many of us still do to ourselves, confusing our inner critic with our conscience (or innate moral sense). In so doing, *we simply legitimize our aggression against ourselves,* beating ourselves up, crushing ourselves with guilt, degrading ourselves as we try to reach expected standards. No love, no compassion.

So we transgress—it's our nature, declares Freud—and then aggress inwardly, dividing and therefore disempowering ourselves, so as not to present a serious threat to our prevailing social/religious structures. But trying to be good through repressing ourselves simply keeps what's not so good in the shadows and on the back burner, until it flames into the foreground, its capacity for destructiveness directly proportional to how much it's been kept from sight.

And the erotic plays in here: the pressure to keep our aggression under wraps naturally generates a craving to seek release somewhere, somehow, and what more quickly satisfying outlet is there than the sexual? If we get constricted too tightly in one area of ourselves, other areas can become over-enlisted in providing relief: a man whose abdomen is chronically contracted from aggressively shaming himself may suffer an excessive amount of energy/pressure in his head and/or genitals. If there's sufficient focus in both terminals, there may be a compelling—and often addictive—linking of cognition and sexuality, generating a powerful pull to primarily find sexual release through fantasy or pornography.

As we shall see, plenty of sex is but eroticized aggression, a compensatory solution to nonsexual pressures and expectation. The very *charge*—usually a negative excitation—associated with our unresolved wounds and mishandled needs can very easily become eroticized, meaning that we act out such old hurt (and simultaneously distract ourselves from it) through sexual contexts. (See chapter 21.)

Repression, Freudian and otherwise, provides a very unstable peace. It does no more than keep our aggression in the dark—more often than not tangled up with our sexuality—with the result that we don't see its roots, distracted as we are by our involvement with its by-products.

AGGRESSION AS SOCIAL CONSTRUCTION

Many view aggression not as innate, but as a *disposition* fueled and governed by personal and cultural conditioning. According to social learning theory, aggression is a self-serving *learned* behavior: we assume we need or deserve something, and we find that we can get it—and sometimes even more—through being aggressive, whether directly or indirectly (as when we manipulate another into acting out our aggression).

This starts early in life. Very young children can get aggressive simply through seeing others getting what they want through being aggressive. Not surprisingly, aggression is commonly imitated when it seems that it is justified. Such justification can be very primitive, being no more than a matter of "I want it; therefore it should be mine." The logic is starkly simple: if you have it and I want it, and I can take it from you through being aggressive with you, then I will, only rationalizing my doing so if I've reached a level of cognitive development where I'm capable of such thinking.

And very young children may not get aggressive just for *instrumental* purposes—grabbing that wanted toy—but may also get aggressive for *social* reasons. For example, the appeal of a certain toy may suddenly increase when another child wants the same toy; when the tussled-over toy is finally won (usually by the more aggressive child), it may be then discarded, having lost its desirable status once there is no more fight over it. Hierarchical or status-seeking behavior can also start at a very early age, supported by whatever aggression can be mustered—and by parental and social rewards for such behavior.

Social modeling can play a huge role in the arising and development of aggression, as shown through research indicating that witnessing physical abuse between one's parents is more strongly correlated to later involvement in marital violence than being hit by one's parents. The glorification of aggression—admiring those who claw their way to the top, blitz the opposition, run over the competition—makes non-aggression seem bland, flat, not very pleasurable, and not very manly.

Men who stand for peace are often most admired when they fight for peace, as if such aggression makes them more manly. A quarterback who shows no fear of getting hit when he's running for a few more yards is often more admired than one who takes a feet-first slide to avoid getting thus hit—the implication being that he's more of a man. A boy who doesn't challenge his group's bullying of others is generally more accepted than a boy who does challenge it; the first boy gets to be one of the boys, and the second gets pushed to the outer edge of the group or is excluded from it. For many men being "one of the guys"—playing by the group rules (including being a mute bystander) and supporting its aggression—is more important than speaking up and risking exclusion.

Aggressive behavior appears equally in girls and boys until about age three, after which boys become clearly more aggressive than girls. Some of this is genetic—think testosterone—and plenty is socially implanted. Boys not only are more inclined toward aggressiveness but are also generally given more encouragement in this direction than girls are; an aggressive boy is usually considered to be more masculine, but an aggressive girl is not so often considered to be more feminine, being commonly labeled a tom*boy*.

The aggressive man, the alpha male, the violence-delivering hero, the female-dominating stud, the mesomorphic bare-chested hulk with the big guns, the tough guy who kills with barely a blink of his narrowed eyes, the ruthless moneymaker—all of these, in various combinations, infiltrate a boy's consciousness, however peripherally, implanting the notion that a man is primarily here to fight, however bloodless his battles may be.

THE MANY FACES OF AGGRESSION

Following are just some of the many faces of aggression.

Hostility—Probably the most common expression of aggression, ranging from mildly edgy to snarling. Being on the receiving end of hostility can be not only very unpleasant but also sometimes scary, because we know that whoever is delivering it has us in their sights and out of their heart, with attack weaponry ready for reloading.

Sarcasm—A hostility-centered putting down of the other. Sarcasm is not just heartless but also cruel (however masked it may be by a show of wit or reasonableness). With it, we target something in the other to belittle or make fun of in circumstances that usually are far from funny. Sarcasm is a matter of not only being aggressively mocking but also *shaming,* building ourselves up by trying to tear down the other, often taking some pleasure in doing so. However short-lived it may be, sarcasm creates relational distance so that later on we might find that our "target" has put up some sort of a barrier against us, even if they're being otherwise loving toward us. This may not be an act of retaliation, but simply a result of feeling on guard or self-protective around us, especially if they've not received any genuine apology from us for our sarcasm toward them; the jab sticks. Left unattended, sarcasm is an intimacy destroyer.

Ill will—A wishing of misfortune upon others, one step short of hating them. Ill will can manifest in emotions like contempt, jealousy, envy, and schadenfreude (the emotion of taking pleasure in others' suffering). When we're carrying ill will toward another, we may not look aggressive, but we feel it and emanate it (however subtly), reducing our target to something less than human.

Contempt—Take one part disgust, one part anger, one part moral condescension, blend with some ice, and you have contempt. Contempt is crueler than sarcasm and more aggressive. Its presence signals not just a problem in a relationship but the not-so-far-away destruction of it. Of all the emotions, contempt is probably the most dehumanizing.

Passive aggression—A very common behavior, most often indulged in by those who repress or mask their anger. It is as indirect as it is deliberate. It usually doesn't look aggressive, but feels aggressive. Passive-aggressive behavior can show up in many ways, some of which are: being intentionally slow or sloppy while acting as if we're doing our best; being temporarily compliant but actually resisting ("I'll do it as soon as I can"); refusing to admit that we're angry, when we actually are; dismissively saying "Fine!" or "Whatever" when we're bothered by what's just been said to us; saying with an innocent expression "I was just joking," when we weren't at all.

Heartless criticism—Often masquerades as constructive criticism because of how helpful we might think we're being. But such criticism is mostly just heavy-duty shaming, delivered with zero compassion; the recipient, however young or passive, feels it. This is commonly excused by the one delivering it as "I'm just speaking my truth."

Violence—Extreme aggression. (I will explore this in detail in the next chapter.)

Defensiveness—Not always aggressive, but it often is. A common counterattack, however much it might be camouflaged with a show of reasonableness or innocence.

Harshness—An edginess of expression that crosses the line into being cutting, with no caring in sight. A harsh look or tone can obstruct relational closeness, including when the recipient acts as though everything were fine.

Mean-spirited or shaming-infused teasing—It's easy to both mask and express aggression through supposed humor. If others feel hurt or disturbed by this, we can say that we were just joking, implying that they don't have much of a sense of humor, thereby shaming them for not measuring up. This lets us off the hot seat, framing *them* as the ones with the problem.

Excessive competitiveness—Losing all touch with any care for one's opponent. The compulsion to win at all costs. Dangerously myopic.

Intimidation—The intent to overpower, especially by generating fear in the other. The leading edge of bullying.

Hatred—Aggression and deep hurt knotted together in black-hearted focus on another (or others). Stifling or bypassing it only causes it to fester, to metastasize throughout us. Going into and through our hate (including expressing it fully, right to its pain-saturated core in a safe therapeutic setting), without harming ourselves or others, is a profoundly healing process, helping pave the path to genuine forgiveness.

ANTIDOTES TO AGGRESSION

Aggression militates against intimacy, keeping relationships in the shallows, marooned from any significant healing and deepening. To get to the heart of aggression, to undo its armoring without stranding ourselves from our anger and capacity to take care of ourselves, is a great undertaking, at once vulnerable and empowering, made possible in part through devoting yourself to the following practices.

Empathy—The more empathetic you are with another, allowing yourself to truly feel or emotionally resonate with what they're feeling, the less likely it is that you'll get aggressive with them. (Teaching children from a young age to "imagine how you'd feel if you were treated like that or if that happened to you" can help foster a healthy empathy.)

Compassion—Having compassion for another doesn't mean that you don't hold them accountable, nor that you won't express any displeasure over what they're doing, but that you won't put them out of your heart. Anger and compassion can coexist, but aggression and compassion cannot.

Vulnerability—Being vulnerable (transparent and unguarded) opens you to another, making room for empathy and compassion, greatly reducing the likelihood that you'll slip into aggression.

Cultivating intimacy with your shame, fear, and anger—The better you know these emotions (all ingredients in the genesis of aggression), the more skilled you'll be in working with them when they arise. For example, not letting your shame morph into aggression, whether directed at others or at yourself.

Sympathetic joy—Taking pleasure in the successes of others.

No name-calling—This doesn't mean to never swear about certain situations, but not to insult, malign, or otherwise verbally abuse the other. Saying "what a pile of shit" about a bank notice you've received is very different from telling the other that they're "a piece of shit."

Skillful anger—Keeping your anger non-shaming, non-blaming, and vulnerable prevents it from becoming aggression.

Having a conscious rant—A very useful practice when you are feeling strongly pulled to becoming aggressive. (See the appendix for a detailed description and read through it carefully before you attempt a conscious rant.)

AN INTEGRATIVE VIEW OF AGGRESSION

Aggression is not just a matter of physiology or social conditioning, but a result of biological, psychological, and social factors operating in conjunction.

Biological reductionism (assigning *biology and genetics* too much responsibility for bad behavior) leaves unchallenged our habit of over-looking or vastly underestimating the power of our conditioning to determine our aggressiveness. This can easily lead to an overreliance on medication to deal with aggressiveness, as if all we needed to do to truly reduce our aggressiveness was take some pills.

Where biological reductionism looks at aggression and sees not much more than "chemical imbalance" (a questionable concept that's starting to lose its moorings), *environmental reductionism* (assigning external factors, such as family structure and cultural conditions, too much responsibility for bad behavior) looks at aggression and sees not much more than something simply requiring behavioral modification.

This is where we find the various strategies used by those who advocate anger-in: engaging in soothing self-talk, reinterpreting events, becoming more positive, bypassing any confrontation, and generally muting our anger (since that's what supposedly leads to aggression). These steps have value, but when we rely on them too much, we strand ourselves from the passion of anger, emotionally flattening ourselves, paying a huge price for trying to prevent aggression by shutting down our anger.

Some argue that aggression is a socially molded behavior that's generated by frustration. This means that the presence of aggression presupposes the presence of frustration. But does frustration always lead to aggression? No. Frustrating circumstances, highlighted by thwarted expectations or unexpected hassles, don't always generate aggression, but how we *interpret* them can.

Frustrating circumstances—like crowdedness, noisiness, or insufficient sleep—usually catalyze some sort of physical arousal. But such arousal, however negative or unpleasant, does not necessarily lead to aggression unless it is coupled with a compelling sense of justification (as when we've been deliberately provoked or ignored). At the same time, arousal itself, whether negative or positive, can trigger aggression, especially when it carries enough *sustained intensity* to overwhelm us.

That is, enough excitation can push us over the edge. Our system simply goes into overload—and aggressive behavior is a common reaction to and outlet for this. Consider extreme crowd excitation *and* stimulation at a major sporting event. However exhilarating, this can easily become crowd aggression when what's being watched veers in an unpopular direction or gets interrupted, simply because of an *already* existing, near-the-limit energy threshold.

The more aware we are of our tendency to become aggressive under certain conditions (whether through how we interpret things or through heightened arousal or through a lack of sleep), the greater the odds are that we won't let ourselves slide into aggression.

What's missing in both the instinctual and social constructivist camps regarding aggression is an approach that appreciates and takes into account the whole person—so that their aggression is seen and worked with in the context of their inherent wholeness, their personal history, and their circumstances.

In this approach, clear connections are made between our early and current experiences of anger and aggression, and not only intellectually; the emotional dimensions of such connections are also experienced. For example:

JOHN has been going to an anger management class to deal with his aggression; what he's hearing makes some sense, but when it comes to practicing it when he's enraged, nothing changes. The ideas he's hearing have no impact on him when he's gripped by aggression. He grew up with an older brother who taunted him and regularly beat him up, with no interference from his parents. So now, any sense of being shamed enrages him. Finding a therapist who helps him cut loose with his anger in context—fully expressing it while at the same time emotionally recalling his brother's abuse of him—leads him (along with some fitting awareness and integrative practices) to an internal healing regarding the pain of his boyhood so that he becomes less and less aggressive. During this process, he is able to fully grieve, finding a deep healing in doing so, gradually reclaiming the boundaries he lost as a boy, learning to have his healthy anger on tap. ■

Aggression cannot be reduced to physiology, nor to behavior, nor to cognition, nor to socialization, for it arises for each of us from a uniquely evolving weave of all these. In the midst of aggression, we have an opportunity to experience the instinctual and the conditioned, the reflexive and the reflective, the biological and the biographical, all happening at the same time.

We can begin with facing our aggressiveness; then unearth the anger that underlies it, developing more and more intimacy with that anger, eventually feeling deeply empowered, simultaneously vulnerable and filled with a healing courage. There's undeniable growth in such work, requiring both a keenly discerning awareness and a full "yes" to passion, bringing together heart, guts, and head in ways that serve our highest good.

9

Violence
The Brass Knuckles of Aggression

VIOLENCE SEEMS TO BEGET VIOLENCE, from generation to generation to generation. Its very long history, dating back to our origins, has a momentum that shows little indication of slowing down. It's as if we were caught in an unresolved and seemingly unresolvable blood feud, the vast weave of which connects and binds most of us, from tribal to nationalistic to planetary levels. We can look at the old feuds of America's South and almost chuckle at such anachronism, not fully seeing that the feuding that currently pervades the world makes no more sense than did those old family feuds. There may be talk of honor, but it's mostly just more fuel for the fires of violence and has nothing to do with real honor.

Violence is the brass knuckles of aggression.

In violence, we don't just consider injuring others but also give the green light to doing so, often with a forcefulness as unrestrained as it is self-justified. Vengeance, bloodlust, severe dehumanization, rape, torture, acting with extreme prejudice—whatever its form, violence is aggression with no restraints, further fueled by a mindset that adds an emphatic, not-to-be-debated stamp of approval.

There are plenty of views about what constitutes and causes violence, but any deep understanding of violence has to include our own capacity for extreme aggression and the dehumanizing of others, especially toward those who offend us. The more intimate we are with our own violent urges and their roots, the less likely we are to be irresponsible with such urges, and the deeper our understanding will be of others' violence. This doesn't necessarily mean that we'll then be more likely to excuse or marginalize it or look the other way, but we'll be able to more skillfully relate to it and its origins, getting a deeper sense of how to best approach and work with it.

As uncomfortable as it may be to bring our own violence or capacity for violence out of the shadows, we owe it to ourselves—and everyone else—to do so.

It's a well-worn—and far-from-difficult—slide from anger to aggression to violence. All that's initially required is viewing the offending other as unworthy of any care or mercy, an "it" deserving whatever "justice" we (or those whom we esteem) might consider fitting. Amplify such hardened quick-to-indict righteousness with sufficient adrenaline, testosterone, and forward momentum, and violence will be at our fingertips, ready to curl into steely fists and a harm-or-be-harmed mindset—more often than not in a very short time.

We then may let our minds be colonized by revengeful or retaliatory or first-strike fantasies, taking up whatever arms we think are needed, finding ourselves in combat mode, firmly and unquestioningly aligned with "our side." In this, we're likely going to gather and buttress ourselves behind whatever lends legitimacy and muscle to our side, thereby highlighting and reinforcing our opposition to the other side, the "enemy."

This is not just a matter of cognitive sniping, but a passionate undertaking—and *takeover*—consuming us as few other things can do. After all, the call to battle is an ancient thing, sounding through many millennia, its echoes ricocheting within us as our blood rises in anticipation of unleashed aggression.

If our very survival is at stake—or seems to be—our capacity for violence is probably going to approach its peak level and set up camp there, with a rigidly walled no-man's-land between us and our offending others. When we see others behaving thus, we may decry their resorting to violence, forgetting that if we were in their shoes, we might be behaving much like them. Being in a life-or-death mode puts us in a precarious position. If getting violent makes it possible for us to go on living, we may find that it is not such a huge leap to take, regardless of our misgivings about doing so.

Whatever its negative connotations, violence cannot be condemned across the board as always a bad thing. A great deal of violence is abhorrent to almost all of us—like child abuse and rape—but there is plenty of violence that we are divided about. One man's terrorist may be another man's freedom fighter. We may say that we regret the civilian casualties that occur when we attack our enemy's territory, but not let such "regret" prevent us from continuing to pursue our attack-centered agenda. We might severely injure or kill others in order to save our child's life. And so on. So in considering violence, we need to take into account its prevailing context, not to excuse or marginalize it, but to better understand it.

Many view violence as learned behavior, and learned behavior only. The literature on child development is loaded with studies about the aggressive milieu in which little boys are acculturated, the widely encouraged rough-and-tumble play, the inculcated competitiveness, the drive to dominate and be on top (games such as king of the castle). At an early age, boys learn to associate their self-esteem with their capacity to be on top. Being an alpha male carries considerable prestige in most circles. Winning becomes overly important. Cooperation becomes emphatically secondary to competition (as reflected by our economy), with the winners getting huge spoils—and too bad for the losers.

In this, however, there are no real winners. Sooner or later, everyone gets screwed, if only through being part of a damagingly divided humanity. Ultraviolent video games, misogynistic rap lyrics, a growing gap between the rich and the not-rich, and so on—all are expressive of a culture that rewards, glamorizes, and profits from violence, a culture that provides minimal care for those less fortunate, and marginalizes the poor, the unemployed, the disabled, the homeless, the PTSD-crippled veterans, the outcasts, the unwanted, the ones most heavily burdened by our collective shadow—all of whom are seeking shelter in a place that fosters violence, even as it preaches against violence.

But violence is not just learned behavior; for better or for worse, it is innate to us. Toddler hostility is common—and usually harmless only because toddlers are far from adept handlers of weaponry, other than perhaps their teeth—way past the point of being just learned behavior. The potential for such bare aggression, so quick to arise and so quick to attack, is wired into us. After just two months in the womb, the male fetal brain is flooded with testosterone, which shrinks the communication centers and hearing cortex, and doubles the size of the part of the brain that processes sexual matters.

Ordinarily, we don't have to have been encouraged to be violent in order to get violent with someone who's harming our child—this usually comes quite naturally to us, no matter how removed from aggressiveness we've been prior to such a circumstance. Does this mean we are sentenced to being violent? No. But we carry in us the potential and capacity for violence, and we are often violent toward ourselves in our inner warfare—as epitomized by how our inner critic may be allowed to mercilessly put us down. So we'd do well to acknowledge our own propensity for violence, getting to know it so deeply that we don't act out its desires, except under extreme circumstances (as when our safety or the safety of those close to us is being strongly threatened).

A HISTORY OF VIOLENCE

If one were to question how central violence is in contemporary culture, one would find the answer in the frequency with which violence occurs in film and television. Straightforward cinematic portrayals of violence reflect and reinforce black-and-white takes on it, as exemplified by older Westerns (classically represented by *Shane* and *Gunsmoke*), shoot-'em-up slaughter-fests (think *Rambo* and *Scarface*), and gore-bedecked slasher movies—nothing complicated, just tough guys being tough guys, going about the business of killing.

And there are more and more portrayals of violence that are not so straightforward. These reveal a more complex take on the rise of violence, holding enough nuance to make us partial participants, given that we are being pulled into the unfolding complexity and ambiguity of the protagonist's emerging violence. On television, this is exemplified in *Breaking Bad,* the raw, far-from-glamorous violence of which is filtered through the multifaceted, tortured character of the protagonist. In film there are many examples of multiple-perspectival explorations of violence, ranging from *Fight Club* (see chapter 6) to *Unforgiven* and *Crash*. One of the very best of these examples is *A History of Violence*, directed by David Cronenberg, the title of which invites a double take on violence: a consideration of its evolution in general and a history of one man's ongoing violence.

This film doesn't just feature plenty of violence, but also conjures, while we're watching it, our own unmistakable—and not easily acceptable—reactions, conflicted and otherwise, to violence. Scenes are set up to provoke a certain response from us, drawing on our assumptions and sympathies, and then are twisted or tweaked to leave us facing this very response from unexpected, and often uncomfortable, angles.

For example, we see a bully, an over-the-top mean teenager, get savagely beaten—and we may have been hoping, however secretly, for such a schadenfreude-suffused event. And then, right after our need to vicariously experience vengeance has been satisfied, we are forced to face the messy consequences of the "victory" in which we've just automatically and voyeuristically participated.

Our pleasure in witnessing what we take to be justified violence now lies before us, naked and not so comfortable, while we perhaps start reaching for something to cover it up, some quick reframing, some reassuringly comforting rationalization. But not before we have to sit, however briefly, with our very recent armchair-pleasure in a way that makes us consider it more than we normally would.

In another example, the two killers who are killed by Tom, the small-town, seemingly ultradecent protagonist, are shown at the beginning of the film behaving with such casual, conscienceless violence that we don't mind (and probably feel some schadenfreude at viewing) their bloody demise at the surprisingly able hand of wouldn't-harm-a-fly Tom—who'd be right at home in a Norman Rockwell middle-America painting—even as we perhaps wonder how such a mild-mannered, almost bumpkinish character could pull off such a feat. And we are given almost no time to rest in his heroics. Our discomfort grows, as we soon realize that our hero may not be who he says he is. Is he just a good guy rising to the occasion, doing his duty, or is he something else? And if he is something else, how do we then hold his heroism?

Does his undeniably heroic killing of the two killers become less of a noble thing as we start to question his character? Does a heroic act become less heroic to us if we find things to dislike about the hero?

Our initial embracing of Tom and his violence with the two thugs starts to feel uncomfortable, like a warm hug that takes on a clammy feeling. His relentless good guy presentation of himself starts to feel like America's mainstream presentation of itself to the world—a freedom-loving, straightforward, we'll-protect-the-innocent façade, behind which festers an abundance of not-so-caring, far-from-noble qualities, including violence that is framed as something other than violence.

The fact that Tom's heroic exploits have the power to simultaneously stir and repulse us brings us closer to the truth, the increasingly uncomfortable truth. Do we root for him to do what he has to do to stay alive? And if not, why not? Did we identify with him more—including in his killing the two hoodlums—before we suspected that he may have had a violent past? And if so, why?

The final scene is deglamorized and distilled to the raw basics, por-traying a humanity that is opening, however reluctantly or unhappily, to its inevitable violence, letting it take a place at the table, like any other family member.

HOW WE RELATE TO OUR VIOLENCE

What kind of relationship do we choose to have with our own capac-ity for violence? Do we let it enter our living space, or do we keep it caged in the outback of our consciousness? Do we engage with it, or do we keep it muzzled and mute? Do we include it in the circle of our being—the family of *our* qualities—or do we ostracize it?

Some of us may claim that we have no violent tendencies, but that's just a confession of how much we may have invested in playing the role of pacifist, peacemaker, somebody devoid of violence. If our children were being viciously attacked, and the only way we could save them was by being violent with the person attacking them, what would we do? Even the Dalai Lama has spoken of "virtuous violence." The point is neither to glorify nor to condemn violence, but to understand and recognize it in ourselves so deeply that when we have to use it, we do only what is needed.

Consider a group of pleasant, relatively nonaggressive nineteen-year-old males who have just been enlisted in their country's army. None of them have any history of violence. They begin boot camp, and soon are being seriously toughened up—desensitized, shamed, broken down, rendered capable of killing others. This is a big step, a largely dehumanizing transition that readies them to be functional parts of their nation's army. Once these young men have completed their basic training and have done some time in actual combat, they are far from who they were a year or so ago. They may think they are more manly now, not fully registering how much of their humanity they've likely lost. What is left of their humanity is probably being bombarded by stress and PTSD symptoms, which they may be loath to fully admit, because that would make them less of a man, or so they think.

So the question arises: is the able-to-kill-on-command capacity for violence that now possesses these young men learned behavior? It would seem so. Their environment has certainly set them up to be readily violent, but I'd argue that the violence they are giving themselves to was *already* there. Their training and combat experience has brought forth their ability to be violent and exploited it to the extreme, just as pornography reinforces our capacity for sexual obsessiveness and exploits it to the extreme.

This, however, doesn't mean that acting out our violence is necessarily natural or inevitable. The irony is that, if we deny our own capacity for violence and keep it in the dark, we increase the odds that, when it surfaces, we won't handle it very well, having, in a sense, violated it. Internalized violence is important to consider here, being that it is not so different from external violence. For example, we may treat a certain aspect of ourselves (like our lack of confidence) with such disdain and heartlessness that it is but an outcast "it" to us, a valueless something to be eliminated, bombed with rejection, or thrown into a windowless cell.

Let us not deny our own violence. Keeping it in the shadows, keeping it out of sight, leaves it unilluminated, increasing the likelihood that we'll handle it badly. Let us not get lost in playing the role of the good one, the one who has no capacity for violence, or who has transcended it. Let's take ownership of our violence, keeping a clear eye on it, taking full responsibility for what we do with it. To deny or disown our own violence is to violate it, to force it into hidden corners of ourselves where it may mutate into savage extremes of itself, extending itself beyond necessity.

Becoming intimate with our own capacity for violence—and with our history with violence—greatly increases the odds that we will use it only when, and if, it is *truly* needed (as when there's no other way to prevent a break-in or to stop a loved one from being violated). And even then, it is still our responsibility to use only the amount that's absolutely necessary.

THE MANY FACES OF WAR

Is there ever a time when a war is not going on somewhere?

Some wars go on so long that they slip into the background—or under the radar—even as they pile up their kill numbers and eat up funds sorely needed elsewhere. Despite its horrors, war easily gets normalized, as if it were just part of life, the number of casualties not registering with much more impact than the latest headlines about wardrobe malfunctions. Men being men, boys being boys, my gang against yours, my tribe against yours, my country against yours—all feature aggression in the extreme, with dehumanization being okayed or rationalized to the hilt. Justifications for ultraviolence bombard us left, right, and center, accompanied by the long echo of wars and battle-time atrocities stretching back before recorded history.

Most war is a kind of mass madness, a group ethic gone to hell, an us-versus-them organized violence wrapped up in flags and intimations of glory, and enough gore to turn a small country red. We sense its underlying insanity and brute logic and perhaps protest it, but all too soon push the bare reality of it into a hard-to-reach place, along with whatever else we'd rather not look at very closely. To really feel the madness of war, we need to get up close and personal with our own madness, our own zones of cold disregard, violence, paranoia, and imperialistic greed. And we're not likely to do that unless there's been enough dissatisfaction, pain, and disillusionment in our lives to make us tire of seeking yet more distractions from such suffering.

War has often been glorified through the reported (or poetically immortalized) heroics of its participants. But there is increasing cynicism in contemporary culture about such heroics, often centered around a suspicion that they have either been made up or politically photoshopped. Also, if we don't feel good about a particular war, how are we going to feel truly good about those participating in it, however noble or self-sacrificing their reported actions may be?

For most of us, war has become a kind of background hum—perhaps faintly and sporadically blast-punctuated—a distant fact coexisting with other not-so-pleasant facts, like unemployment rates and faraway natural disasters. And this hum, this blunted sound of war drums, resonates with the presence of our internal warfare, the chronic struggles between different aspects of ourselves, threatening to break like warheads into the foreground of our consciousness when certain circumstances arise. We can get so inured to war that we become numb to it, reducing it to little more than a video game or a news headline—except when it involves us directly.

War may bring out the best in some men, but it brings out the worst in a lot more. Becoming numb enough to kill on command, even when there's no danger to us, is far from healthy. There's no way we can simply shut this numbness off and, a short time later, become sensitive, emotionally literate, vulnerable men who can be fully present in relationship. And when a war is over, it's not necessarily over for those who fought in it, as is shown by the high occurrence of reported PTSD symptoms in veterans, whatever their age. And these are just *reported* numbers; it's highly likely that many more are also suffering such symptoms, but not reporting them, in many cases probably being ashamed to admit such supposed weakness (which exists in glaring contradiction to their soldiery toughness and emotional levelheadedness). The deep scars left by war are too often left unattended or only superficially faced (just like the deep scars left by abusive childhoods) and worsened by the expectations—whether from ourselves or others—that we should just "get over it," like "real men" would. After all, does the hero let some rough patches in his life hinder his deed doing?

When it comes to war, what are we fighting for? Who decides? What's really at stake? And in this, what kind of violence is acceptable, and what kind is not? Such questions pale beside the bloody reality of war, but if left unaddressed, leave us deeper in the muck and madness of such mass violence, pervaded by waves of heartbreak and shock and grief and collective trauma that roll through the centuries unresolved, reducing almost everything to some sort of battleground.

War has been viewed—and in many ways still is—as a rite of passage for young men, something promising approval from iconic alpha males who gaze upon fresh-faced recruits or would-be warriors with steely-eyed presence, using shame as a weapon, an emotional cattle prod, with the potential flicker of a smile for those who have the balls to make the passage into wimp-free manhood, weapons expertly held aloft, their sweetheart on one arm and a bunch of medals on the other. Think of the old US Army jingle: "Be all you can be"—and consider the appeal of this, the manly promise, to young men bereft of any strong male mentors, wanting to belong to something bigger than themselves, something at once noble and challenging, something that'll help them truly be all they can be, initiating them into a longed-for manhood, a not-to-be-questioned bravery.

Think of contemporary rituals that are suggestive of entering or being initiated into manhood: getting laid; getting royally drunk and behaving stupidly but arguably bravely; walking past your friends with the hottest female draped on your arm; getting hazed by older boys; making some serious money; having your own car; and finally, joining the armed forces. Think of how important cars and guns are for many men; we have far more iconic images of men in the driver's seat than women, especially the man behind the wheel of a hot car, sitting erect and proud, ready to floor the accelerator and leave the competition in the dust. How easily we associate this with freedom! Just as cars can be seen as extensions of the feet, and computers as extensions of the mind, guns—so important to so many men, and often close at hand—can be seen as extensions of the penis, long steely erections with explosive power, easily triggered and harder than hard, beyond any possible flaccidity.

■ ■ ■

The number of casualties in war boggles the imagination—many millions. How do we digest that? How can we possibly conceive of that in more than just an intellectual way? Just one person close to us dying can overwhelm us, bringing us to our knees for quite a while—and if that person dies a violent death, as through war, we might be even more overwhelmed. If more than one person close to us dies thus, we might find ourselves at a very dark edge, lost in the deepest pits of grief. And yet if many, many more thus die but are not people we personally know, we usually are far less distraught—and the bigger the number, the less disturbed we tend to be, shifting into abstraction. A handful of people from our country dying violently gets to us more than a large number of people from another country dying violently; we may not know those from our country, so why do their deaths matter so much more to us? Because we feel some kinship or alliance with them, however superficially. Imagine feeling kinship with all people, imagine what that would take, and imagine what that might do.

To prepare men for war—for being able to kill others on command—they have to be not only hardened but also numbed; they have to have their capacity for extreme aggression deepened; they have to, as much as possible, believe in the rightness of the war they're being trained for; they have to view enemy combatants as something less than human; they have to emotionally disconnect themselves from civilian casualties on the other side.

Boys are often surrounded by the trappings of battle, of war, all too often suffering relatively small violences—like shaming or bullying—which easily slide along the continuum to larger violences.

Life as a battleground—there's always others to defeat, overcome, vanquish. Many video games feature brutal battles, often with extravagant amounts of blood. In the movies and in boys' collective imagination, the really tough guys effortlessly carry around huge weapons, gunning down those who oppose them with no more fuss than if they were taking out the garbage. Business as usual. Not that such phenomena cause a boy to *become* violent, but they do take whatever aggression is already there and, at the very least, reinforce it, glamorize it, normalizing its extremes. Vicarious participation in brutality initially stimulates, but soon dulls us, eviscerating our capacity to really feel the hellishness of what's occurring.

War is exciting; peace boring—or so it seems in much of contemporary culture. It's not so much that war itself is exciting, but that our excitement and raw vitality can easily get channeled into war or warlike activities, plugging us into larger-than-life, dangerous dramatics, not letting us stray too far from the adrenaline high of being near such a hazardous edge. But what if we were to channel the very same energy into facing our own darkness, healing our core wounds, and taking on the challenge of being in truly intimate relationships? Would not this call to the very best in us invite forth uncommon bravery, and contribute hugely not just to our well-being but also to that of those involved with us, both directly and indirectly?

We don't stop war by giving speeches about peace; we stop it by facing our internal warfare and disarming it without robbing it of its vitality and diversity—not an easy labor, but one that we must fully engage in if we are to wean ourselves from being part of external warfare. Nor do we stop war by eliminating anger—an impossibility—but by becoming so intimate with it that we no longer unresistingly let it mutate into aggression and violence.

As we take care of our inner wars, we decentralize war, stripping it of more and more of its power and appeal, if only because we cease being drawn to supporting or participating in it. There may always be a war somewhere, but we have a chance to make war an anomaly rather than a dominant presence in our lives. What we need to do is face our interiorized wars and oppositional mixes, and compassionately contain them without getting lost in their dramatics, not taking a side in whatever internal war is going on, but instead holding both sides in an embrace as caring as it is conscious. In so doing—and also in ceasing to overassociate being masculine with being warlike—we move toward a healing integration, a sense of wholeness that does not allow any of its parts to dominate the others.

WORKING WITH VIOLENCE

Much of the concern about violence is what to do when faced with it. Sometimes the best thing to do is get violent back—not because we're savages, but because without fighting back, we could be facing a worse future than if we were to fight. Imagine a half-dozen peaceful tribes, trading rather than warring with each other for centuries; then one tribe starts to get very aggressive, attacking the others, taking their land and either enslaving or murdering their members. What the peaceful tribes can do is at the very heart of any consideration of justified violence—theirs is an opportunity for a virtuous violence, one that does no more than what is necessary to bring the aggressive tribe into line. This, of course, can be a slippery slope, littered with the debris of justified violence that has crossed the line into barbarity, losing its humanity along the way.

The heroic warrior of the great myths battles with adversaries, human and otherwise, often to the death. No wonder it's so easy to associate heroism with battle skill and bravery. Yes, we can certainly imagine a hero who doesn't have deadly weaponry, but the hero who gets our blood stirring is usually armed. Generally he is as powerful as he looks; he may not have a bodybuilder's biceps, but his muscularity dramatically exceeds that of everyday men. His physical prowess is as legendary as it is awe inspiring. And he is an adept with his weaponry. Not someone to mess with!

The archetypal male warrior traditionally shows little emotion, other than steely rage and perhaps a flicker of a smile for selected women, his entire being focused on the task at hand, namely facing and defeating various adversaries. The less emotion—especially fear—he shows, the more he tends to be admired or envied. His violence carries a dark beauty, if only because of his not-to-be-defeated powerfulness. There may even be a certain nobility to his violence, as if he cannot help but cut off heads or pierce hearts.

There's a healthy warrior within us all. And there can be a healthy relationship with our own violence. Our own capacity for violence doesn't have to reduce us to savages. The primal energy of it, if divested of its viewpoint and dehumanizing tendencies, can be of immense benefit, fueling our entry into a deeper life. So, given that violence is part of us, however much it might remain deactivated, what can we do with our own capacity for violence (and for violent fantasy)—besides suppressing or indulging it—that serves our well-being and that of everyone else?

Steps to Working with Your Capacity for Violence

The first step is to recognize and acknowledge its presence. So long as you keep your capacity for violence in the shadows, you'll tend to either deny its presence or to treat it in ways that only increase the odds of edging into hostile or violent behavior when you're angered. You don't have to let it out as it is, but you do need to recognize it and name it for what it is. As you do so, you'll likely see what else you've stored in its vicinity: the roots of your anger, your shame, your tendency to dehumanize others, your rationalizations for doing whatever it takes to get what you assume ought to be yours. If you have trouble recognizing your own capacity for violence, think of someone very dear to you, and imagine them being horribly hurt by another who can only be stopped if severely injured or killed by you.

The second step is to move toward it. This means bringing more awareness to it, getting close enough to it through such focused attentiveness to see its details, its intentions, its history, its ways of showing up in your life. Its ways of showing up? Yes, as through hostility, mean-spiritedness, ill will, passive-aggressiveness, an absence of empathy—whatever leaves us close-hearted and unresistingly aligned with another getting hurt or injured. Through such activities we may not be showing overt violence, but we are operating in the spirit of it. So bring your undivided attention to your capacity for violence, relating *to* it rather than giving yourself to or identifying with it.

The third step is to bring it out of the dark. This doesn't mean unleashing it or letting it run wild, but illuminating it and, slowly but surely, bringing it into the open without, however, taking on its viewpoint and/or acting it out. In this, you are no longer relating to your capacity for violence as a distant "it," but rather you are beginning to relate to it as something to be integrated with the rest of your being instead of being treated as an outcast or an error in the system. Here, we are cultivating intimacy with our own violent leanings, getting to know them so well that they cannot sneak up on us or act out their endarkened agendas. (I strongly recommend getting skilled guidance with such work.) *This is the essence of real shadow work:* bringing what we've disowned, ostracized, or otherwise rejected in ourselves, out of the shadows and integrating it with the rest of our being, no longer projecting it onto others. (For more on this, revisit chapter 4.)

The fourth step is to not let it out of our sight. Just because we're now able to more skillfully relate to our capacity for violence doesn't mean that we can sit back and let it run free. We need to sense its arising—its shift out of latency—as close as possible to its inception; it's far easier to deal with it then than when it is full-blown.

From the very start of doing the preceding four steps, make sure to also engage in the following practices:

■ Work deeply with your anger and shame. Getting more in touch with what you've been really angry or shamed about (starting with your early childhood) is crucial, as is working with that anger and shame. Shame can easily mutate into anger, and anger into aggression, which is but the shortest of distances from outright violence. Learn to acknowledge your shame and anger as soon as they show up, straightforwardly admitting their presence, relating to them with enough presence and care to keep them from springing into harmful action. Reread the chapters on anger and shame, 7 and 3 respectively, in this book.

■ Learn to let anger and compassion coexist. This takes plenty of practice, but is doable—and is essential if you are to make wise use of your capacity for violence. Sometimes this will mean that your compassion has a fiery or fierce quality, a heatedness that helps deepen the delivery of your message. Compassion can be a great force, at times very soft, but not meek, and at other times not so soft, but never hardhearted. Practice both. Tenderness and forcefulness do not have to be mutually exclusive.

■ ■ ■

The more intimate we are with both our capacity for violence and its roots, the more likely we are to handle it responsibly, keeping a clear eye on it and on whatever fuels it. This is a task we all share, a labor to fully give ourselves to, both internally and externally, both alone and together.

10

The Hero

Courage, Pride, and Embodying Your Natural Heroism

THE MOST STRIKING and enduring figure embedded in men's consciousness is the hero. The bravest of the brave, the ultimate performer, the one who sacrifices himself for the greater good, the one who perseveres no matter how daunting the challenge—such are some of the many faces of the hero. Whatever shame and self-doubt a man might be carrying, the presence of the hero abides—perhaps pushed into the background or covered by the debris of accumulated failures, but still there, still arising, if only in fantasy or dreams, a beacon of quintessential manliness, anchored in unflinching courage.

An essential part of a man's self-work is exploring his relationship to whatever constitutes his sense of heroism, and turning that relationship into one that helps him heal and deepen his life. In so doing, a man evolves beyond submissive and vicarious orientations toward his inner hero, no longer letting his admiration of that one fuel any sense of self-shaming, inadequacy, or apathy.

HEROISM IN *AVATAR:* A FULL-BLOODED AWAKENING

The body through which we show up when we're asleep and dreaming allows us to navigate and interact with our three-dimensional dreamscape. Regardless of how bizarre the scenery and context may be, we generally adapt to it fairly quickly, much like Jake, the protagonist in the film *Avatar,* does when he finds himself embodied as a native of the alien world called Pandora.

Sometimes we realize that we're dreaming while we're in a dream. Jake finds himself in a situation akin to this, knowing that he's "really" in human form in a sleeping state in a high-tech pod, even as he immerses himself in the world of the Na'vi, the indigenous people of Pandora. He is fascinated, blown away by the beauty, but not fully. At first, he keeps himself removed from the hypervivid, pulsing beauty that surrounds him, sticking to his role as a good soldier, a conventional warrior, a man who doesn't question what he is being told to do by his superiors. *The hero in him is dormant, asleep.*

Jake initially looks at Pandora as nothing more than a place to be exploited for a higher purpose (read: more profitable); but before long, Na'vi reality (our deeply interconnected, full-blooded natural state) becomes more real to him than his normal state. To step into a deeper, more connected manhood requires that we, like Jake, wake up from the shrinkwrapped dreams of conventional manhood. *The hero in him has begun to stir.*

Avatar moved and shook many of its viewers quite deeply, mostly because they were potently reminded not only of their own primal core of being, but also of their adult disconnection from it. For many of those who saw *Avatar,* there was a simultaneous sense of deep opening and deep loss, a more-than-intellectual recognition of having lost touch with something essential, something at once raw and awakened, something suffused with the felt reality of interconnection, level upon level, on every scale.

The more Jake lets go of his old way of being, the more he is rooted in ground that resonates with his depths, ground that gives him the very base from which to take life-affirming leaps, requiring no bypassing of his essential humanity. He steps into a deeper and fuller manhood, starting to embody a strength that's not cut off from empathy and softness, a strength rooted in body-centered knowingness. *The hero in him is arising.*

His is a warriorhood that relies not on armoring but on highly sensitized aliveness and balance and deep connection. There is great risk in this, but even greater risk in staying put. The mechanical, military warrior he was (the man emotionally disconnected from his world) has become a very different kind of warrior, one awakening from the dreamland of conventional manliness and blind soldiering. *The hero in him is fully alive, fully present, wide-awake.*

Jake's greatest flight is *initially* a descent, as he free-falls—and he has no choice but to thus fall—onto the back of Pandora's mightiest, most feared flying creature, an enormous scarlet bird-dragon held in fearful awe by the Na'vi. Once upon its back, he rides to a Na'vi assembly, impressing them enough to lead them in battle. Is this, some might ask, just another version of the white man being the hero, the savior, *the* man, for a tribe of in-trouble indigenous people? Or is it a heroic leap born of extreme necessity, a leap by which Jake transcends his usual self, both human *and* Na'vi? Some might have seen a stereotype here, but I saw wild, at-the-edge heroism, feeling it right to my marrow, as if I were not just taking the leap, but were *inside* the leap, completely aligned with it. No thinking, just pure action, guts and heart and vision operating as one. *The hero in him is but pure action in the service of what truly matters.*

To manifest such a leap fully, to truly live such an ancient but everfresh passion, its opposite must be faced and deeply encountered, not pushed into the shadows. The final battle is an ancient one, externally played out over and over in myths and comic books and the halls of ecological illiteracy. But this does not mean that it is necessarily stale or banal, because this very battle, however mildly armed, is going on *in* just about all of us, and not just now and then.

Many of us think we have to pick one or the other side. But how about being at home both in primeval forest and executive office? How about making ecological sanity a profitable business? How about cultivating a second innocence, an awakened innocence, rather than regressing to a naive innocence or hiding out in cynicism and irony? How about getting so deeply in touch with our environment, outer and inner, that we can no longer desecrate or numb ourselves to it? If men want an arena that calls forth their full heroism, this is it: to heed the call to face our planetary disasters and disaster-making with huge resolve and stamina and compassion. Imagine all the energy that goes into armoring and overprotecting ourselves (overbudgeting for defense) instead of going into truly facing and cleaning up the mess we've made of our home—and our own inner terrain.

Many of us are out of touch with our Na'vi-like capacities, and do not find adequate compensation for this loss through our gains in even the finest things that contemporary culture can offer, trapping ourselves in our very "freedoms."

In *Avatar,* we witness the encounter of two opposing archetypal masculine forces. Early on, the rigidly armored male force (centered in capitalist militarism) is very close to being fully formed and clear about its mission. But the nature-immersed and interconnected male force (in the person of Jake) is barely formed, being not much more than embryonic, hardly having the legs to survive. Eventually, the latter force, personified as the true hero, matures and flowers, becoming capable of taking the kind of stand needed to potently meet its opposition.

The destructive forces *Avatar* dramatizes are eating away at our world (and also eating away at many of us from the inside). They call not for some compensatory fantasy of Bambi with a submachine gun taking down all the villains, but for an open-eyed—and *we-centered!*—courage from each of us, a collective brave-heartedness that carries enough fierce compassion and power to effectively counter the ecological insanity, greed, and numbness that pervades so much of our planet. This stand, fully taken, is that of the true hero.

COURAGE: HAVING THE HEART TO PERSIST REGARDLESS OF YOUR FEAR

Courage is perhaps the central attribute of the hero.

The word *courage* is derived from the Latin *cor,* meaning "heart." (In French the word for heart is *coeur.*) We say of a brave man that he has heart; we speak of a fighter's heart; we say of a man who has given up that he's lost heart. In courage, our blood may run cold for a while, but it is running—and as we persist, it'll heat up, flowing more and more strongly, heartening and en*cour*aging us.

To truly be a man has long been linked to being courageous. *Andreia,* the ancient Greek word for courage, carries the literal meaning of "being manly." The Latin word *vir* means "man, hero, man of courage." In turn, the connection between the words *virtue* and *virility,* both derived from *vir,* has a long history, infused with courage regardless of its less-than-ennobling manifestations.

Courage is all about facing what we're scared to do, and doing it nonetheless.

Its opposite is cowardice; its shadow recklessness. Courage is not fearlessness, but a resolute refusal to be paralyzed by fear, a deliberate turning and moving toward the dragon, step by conscious step, an activation of our will to persist in difficult conditions. It is the very heart of heroism. Courage may falter and lose steam, but it does not quit, unless quitting is the more fitting and courageous choice.

Without risk there is no courage. Without fear there is no courage. Without challenging circumstances, there is no courage.

To be courageous is to be brave and to persevere in that bravery, moving *toward* our edge in a particular circumstance, navigating the discomfort of doing so with resolve. However much we might bend with the challenge of this, we don't collapse. We may want to give up, but we don't. Though no one else may see or recognize our struggle, we go on, even if we're on our hands and knees. Courage doesn't always look like courage—at least as it's commonly portrayed—but when we're being courageous, we don't care how we look. We just keep going, again and again finding the optimal pace.

To have courage is to have not only heart, but also guts, intestinal fortitude, spine. As such, courage is about taking embodied action no matter how much our knees might be shaking. And there's a kind of love implicit in courage, the love of our own integrity, our standing up for what really matters. However small the impact of our courage may be, it nonetheless radiates out, touching more than we can imagine.

Wanting to be seen as courageous is very different from being courageous. Many men have a vicarious relationship with courage, especially spectacular courage. But courage is mostly far from spectacular, often taking shape in the form of activities that may seem mundane to others, not worthy of more than a fleeting glance.

Courage is activated resolve in the face of scary or threatening conditions, a moving forward despite our fear. It is never brute intrepidity, but a vulnerable undertaking, a choice to put ourselves in a position that part of us may be screaming to get away from.

Courage can occur in the simplest of actions; it can be quite easy to overlook or undervalue everyday acts of courage. Getting out of bed each morning is easy for most of us, but for some it is a huge challenge, a real edge. For some, parachuting from a plane is no big deal, but being emotionally honest with their partners is terrifying. We each have our own edge under various conditions, calling forth our courage.

Courage is an essential attribute, for without it other highly valued qualities, like compassion and integrity, would lack the strength and resolve needed to shift into action.

And there are many different kinds of courage. Here are some.

Physical courage—staying present and uncollapsed when you are physically hurting. Physical pain can be overwhelming, agonizing, exhausting, relentless. Relating to it, without getting lost in it, takes stamina.

Emotional courage—letting yourself speak with real feeling when you're afraid of the possible consequences, such as rejection or ridicule.

Moral courage—taking needed, value-based stands in the face of strong opposition or possible ostracism.

Existential courage—facing the bare reality of existence, without clinging to meaning; proceeding even when familiarity fades and personal identity seems to be the flimsiest of constructions.

Spiritual courage—awakening to your true nature without any dissociation from or denial of your humanity; cutting through *spiritual bypassing* (the use of spiritual practices and beliefs to avoid dealing with painful emotions and unresolved wounds).

Relational courage—sharing what you're scared to share; letting your relational closeness be both crucible and sanctuary for your woundedness and unflattering states; being your own whistleblower; keeping your connection to significant others alive and well.

■ ■ ■

"To be or not to be?" Courage chooses "to be." Courage does not allow for retreat into not-being, or any lasting shrinking away from what needs to be faced. Courage says "yes" on every scale, including to its own "no" regarding many things. Its faith is that of a radical trust in life, even when there are no apparent signs to justify this. Courage endures, including when it has to change course.

Courage is life-enhancing warriorhood, heart-centered heroism, a matter of not abandoning what's young and tender in you as you let courage's path rise up to meet your stride, not necessarily knowing what's coming next, and being okay with not knowing.

Courage is innate to us. Much of it is everyday heroism that doesn't result in medals or applause. Make as much room as possible for it, getting intimate with its rhythms and flow, breathing it into your heart and belly and right down to your feet, looking through its eyes at what is before you, and saying "yes" to the intention to take the necessary steps, holding and protecting the fearful you while you move forward.

KEEPING A COMPASSIONATE EYE ON YOUR PRIDE

Taking pride in what we (and others) have done can be a beautiful part of honoring ourselves and others. There's often a feeling of exultation in such pride, a swelling of our heart, without a swelling of our head, a celebration of the hero in us and others. Your son has just won a big race, working very hard for his victory, and you're bursting with happiness for him, feeling yourself both touched and uplifted. You're proud of him, without feeling any need to diminish his competitors. Or, you've just had a major success at work, and you're not being modest about it, but allowing yourself to be openly proud of what you've achieved, without indulging in any sense of superiority over your coworkers.

Pride can also be a far less honorable state, rooted in arrogance and a sense of superiority, existing mostly as an antidote or solution to shame, exalting itself through diminishing or disrespecting others. To be caught up in this kind of pride aligns us with a narcissistic heroism, featuring a blown-up version of "me" at the helm, a massively myopic individualism.

What a sense of incompetency is to shame, a sense of competency is to pride.

Shame has many men by the balls, its grip tightened by their failure to measure up to or maintain an expected standard. Pride may be employed as a remedy to this, providing a sense of self-enlargement and upswelling that can offset the sense of self-shrinkage and sagging that characterizes shame. At such times, the originating shame is left unaddressed, left to fester in the dark, existing as part of pride's shadow.

Where shame deflates us, pride inflates us.

This is not to say that pride is something necessarily unhealthy or neurotic. Just as shame can be healthy or unhealthy, so too can pride. A little boy's radiant swelling of pride for what he's just accomplished can be a thing of beauty, an out-front testament to the kind of achievement that celebrates his growth. Taking pride in something that we've accomplished (the bare pleasure of obvious competency!) doesn't have to be an occasion of egocentric engorgement, but can simply be an exultantly contagious acknowledgment, a vitally visible "yes" that's being shared for the sheer joy of it.

Where shame sometimes morphs into aggression, pride sometimes *is* an expression of aggression, as when we, swollen with self-importance, view others disdainfully, reducing them to attackable objects.

Pride can get conflated with arrogance, machismo, or overestimations of competency. It can pump and puff us up so much that we lose touch with our ground, hovering just above our everyday reality like over-swollen balloons, oblivious to their upcoming popping. Carry this further, sucking out any remaining trace of compassion and sensitivity, and it's not hard to find the kind of pride that's one of Christianity's seven deadly sins. Such pride is aggressively me-centered, leaving us not only standing over others, but also invested in having them remain "in their place," whatever the cost.

Shame's pressure often squeezes much of the life out of us, as if we'd taken a heavy blow to the solar plexus and were, for a short time, in a straitjacket. By contrast, pride's pressure squeezes life *into* us, as if from an air pump, expanding our torso from the inside, generating the characteristic swell of pride, sometimes to the point of overinflating ourselves.

Shame grips many men, and so does pride. It's not an easy grip to break, but break it we must. The point is not to be without shame and pride, but to align ourselves with their healthy forms. A man's pride doesn't disappear as he matures, but becomes an expression of his joy in what he's doing. His taking pleasure in or celebrating what he's accomplishing doesn't isolate him or hold him above others, but brings them into his circle of influence in ways that further them as well. This isn't the pride that's one of the seven deadly sins, but rather a virtue, part of the hero's self-presentation.

Healthy pride exalts not our egotism, but our basic individuality —our personalized essence—brightening what is uniquely ours, both in personal and collective contexts. (How unfortunate it is that in some very influential modern teachings ego and individuality are taken to be the same thing.)

Healthy pride celebrates what is best or most life-giving in our doings, without isolating us in our momentary specialness. Many become unnaturally humble in the face of this, self-consciously downplaying how well they've done, as if associating any display of pride with grandiosity. Yes, healthy pride often makes a noticeable splash, highlighting us for a vivid moment, but does not go over the top. In it, we walk tall but don't strut; as big as we may feel at such times, we don't look down on others, and are as open to celebrating their triumphs as we are our own, making room for an unabashed and happily contagious "yes" to spring forth from us in such circumstances.

Maturity doesn't mean an absence of pride—any more than it means an absence of shame. Rather, it's an outgrowing of egoic inflation and hubris, a letting go of the need for any "king of the hill" or star or role model status. We may be the captain of the boat and have some pride in our navigational leadership and skill, but we do not look down upon the deckhand, knowing in our heart of hearts that he and we are fundamentally in the very same position. Here, the sense of specialness central to pride does not obscure the fact that we're all simultaneously special and not special, being, as we are, in the same boat.

Pride can get in the way of our maturity, but it doesn't have to. Does pride go away as we evolve? Not necessarily. However, it can become very subtle as we stand on the highest rungs of accomplishment, perhaps manifesting as an almost invisible conceit over the position we are in relative to the rest of humanity. As long as we are busy being a somebody, we will experience pride—and we might also still feel pride when we have, in our spiritual ambition, become an apparent nobody. We can even take pride in not having pride!

In pride there's often a sense of being on higher ground, and therefore having somewhere to fall from. In shame, by contrast, we've fallen, usually flat on our face, often as if in an endarkened slapstick routine. The more shamed we are, the more important pride may become for us, both individually and collectively. A shamed nation is a nation that can be intoxicated by pride, beating the drum of aggression.

Part of a man's work is to not let his pride have him by the balls and mind, nor to let it be but a compensation for—or a strategy to avoid—shame. A key question to consider is: do you have pride, or does your pride have you?

Don't give yourself over to your pride; instead, feel it, riding its expansiveness and warmth, but don't let it occupy your headquarters. Keep a fiercely compassionate eye on it. Don't let it turn your competitiveness into adversariness; you can, for example, play full-out in a game of tennis, giving it your all, but you don't have to let its winner–loser dynamic separate you from your care and appreciation for the one against whom you are playing. Your pride can help keep you at your edge, but if you let it swell past a certain point, you may simply go over that edge. (And it's important not to reject healthy pride just because you don't want to appear arrogant.)

A man filled with healthy pride stands naturally tall, not defying the pull of gravity but flowing with it, at once grounded and uplifted, expanding in ways that include rather than exclude others. Such pride quietly celebrates the hero within. A man filled with unhealthy pride stands exaggeratedly tall, swollen with independence, so full of himself that there's no room for anyone else, other than unquestioning admirers.

Pride without compassion is arrogance, hubris, cocksure self-inflation, a hyperautonomous bubble, a hothouse for grandiosity. When pride arrives, welcome it, but don't let it take over the premises. Remain mindful of the sense of specialness that comes with pride, but don't let it occupy the throne of self even as you enjoy its fleeting presence, much as you'd enjoy the few seconds of a brilliantly hued butterfly flitting across your path.

THE PRESENCE AND EVOLUTION OF THE HERO

The figure of the hero—extraordinarily courageous, steadfast, and life-affirmingly proud—appears early in most boys' psyches, usually as an amalgam of various mythic figures and larger-than-life performers. Animated characters ranging over time from Mighty Mouse to Turbo have stirred the hero in very young boys; older boys have been similarly stirred by films ranging from *Shane* (in which the iconic gunslinger is seen through the awed eyes of a young boy) to those about Harry Potter. Teenage boys have often found the hero in much less clean-cut forms, ranging from Rambo to Batman to Wolverine, shifting from younger boys' fascination with films featuring young protagonists who play underdogs triumphing in difficult circumstances, to a fascination with heroes who are often little more than fighting machines, as epitomized by video game icons, commonly hugely muscled and armed, frequently solitary, often fighting impossible odds, and usually carrying far more darkness than their more human predecessors.

One example, straddling the end of the last century and the beginning of this one, was Spawn, a brooding, tortured comic book and movie figure who had arisen from the dead—having been a murdered special operations soldier and assassin—to do away with the scum of humanity, even as he remained aware of a cosmic struggle between evil and good, a struggle in which he was, however reluctantly, playing a key role. Spawn was ultraviolent, ruthless, more powerful than the human evil he was facing. And, he was still somewhat human, with occasional signs of having some heart—a complex character, reflecting the dark ambiguity of our times, not fully mainstream but still there, muscling into the corners of consciousness.

But even in our increasingly uncertain times, to a little boy the hero still stands tall, steady, and broad-shouldered, even when he's reduced to a plastic action figure; he is a *solid* he, an iconic masculine presence, usually as emotionally unperturbed as he is resolutely present. (I speak here not of the cute or funny or bantering hero, but of the one who elicits awe in a boy.) The wind may bend him, the heat cause him to droop, the sheer number of the enemy push him back, but he keeps taking his stand, picking himself up out of wherever he may have fallen, perhaps dusting himself off before he delivers whatever justice he deems necessary. The more he gets up, the more heroic he seems. The opposition simply cannot stop him for long. Even when he's knocked flat, imprisoned, handcuffed, tied up, or otherwise incapacitated, he finds a way to get up, get loose, get free, thrilling the little boy watching him from the sidelines.

That boy is not caught up in envy but in mesmerizing adulation, lit up with a fledgling sense of something to grow into, something profoundly empowering, something that belies his sometimes excruciating vulnerability and lack of power. When, as a young boy, I used to beat my fists against my chest in emulation of Tarzan, I did not experience my chest as tiny and skinny—in photos of that time, my ribs show prominently—but as big and broad, like the surface of a massive drum, with each pounding resonating through me.

Little boys commonly have their action figures act out battles large and small. After all, what is a hero without a battle in which to demonstrate his prowess? Imagine Achilles without the Trojan War, Muhammad Ali without Joe Frazier, Harry Potter without Lord

Voldemort, Frodo without the One Ring of Sauron, Batman in a violence-free Gotham City.

As a young boy, I loved to line up my tiny plastic cowboy and Indian figures and have them battle. The figures rose and fell, accompanied by my sound effects, never staying down for long, quickly resurrected for more action—regardless of the bullets or arrows my imagination plunged into them. And I continued this theme in my early grade school years, not using action figures anymore, but acting out good guy versus bad guy encounters (often outside) with such full-bodied abandon—playing both roles all-out, like a child's version of *Fight Club*—that neighbors called my mother, apparently concerned about my sanity. (Such Gestalt—dramatically going back and forth, including physically, between opposing positions—later became an essential part of the therapeutic work I did with others.)

These battle-centered theatrics were of course strongly influenced by what I saw on television and read in comic books (and by my repressed anger toward my father), but without these, I believe I still would have been pulled into various acted-out conflicts, my young boy dramatizations being perhaps less but, nonetheless, still aggressive. As I've discussed elsewhere, aggression is not just learned behavior; it comes with being human, and shows up quite nakedly before we're swamped with environmental factors that encourage aggression. Is there a more aggressive time than that of toddlerdom? When I was two, I was a very dreamy child, wandering openmouthed through the fragrant fields of my parents' farm, but I was also reportedly aggressive toward my six-month-old sister. (She'd supplanted me simply by being born, and needing the attention, which I wanted, from my mother.)

Children individuate through separation, not only from their parents, but also from earlier versions of themselves. They act this out in many ways, including through their play. The hero figures in a boy's consciousness aid in this process, clearly demarcating through their battles with bad guys a me-against-them dynamic that mirrors a boy's need to have a "them" against which to define his emerging self.

The hero makes this easy, because he so clearly stands out against his opponents. And he does it so well, so fully, that he—unlike most boys—cannot be put down or shamed for long, sending the message that if we achieve at a sufficiently high level, we'll be in a position where we cannot be shamed. (This is part of the reason why so many boys, and men, want to be king of the hill in their activities, removed as far as possible from the accusing finger of shame.)

Before the advent of video games, the hero didn't usually die. He could fall from a great height, be placed in dreadful conditions, but he stayed alive, decisively extricating himself, meting out fiercely satisfying justice to those who had dared treat him thus. With the advent of video games, the hero not only became more of a pure killing machine, but could also "die," again and again. Such dying was not the bloodless flattening of Wile E. Coyote or other cartoon characters (who popped back to life very quickly), but more often than not was a bloody spectacle, marking not any sort of felt death, but rather just signaling that one's mission had been terminally thwarted. "Fortunately," such dying was temporary; all that had to be done, in most cases, was resetting or restarting the game so that the player could have another chance to make his way through the opposition, usually leaving a bloody mess in his heroic wake. There can be quite an adrenaline rush to this, as anyone who's played a game like Halo knows.

There is a concern that playing such games—and there are a lot of them—leads to more violence, but the jury is out on this. My concern is that excessive time spent playing them can short-circuit our imagination, pulling us out of ourselves into a domain that reduces violence to a spectator sport that asks nothing more of us than an intensifying and narrowing of our attention. Yes, video games trivialize death, but so too do the very real conflicts and ultraviolence that continue to pervade humanity, providing far-from-optimal outlets for our aggression.

The contemporary conventional hero is aggressive (except when he shows up as the disadvantaged character that succeeds despite no one initially believing in him). He is usually armed, or has special powers. He morphs from the good guy par excellence of early childhood to the deliverer of righteous violence of late childhood and early adolescence, to the more-blood-the-better death-deliverer of adolescence, to the ruthlessly efficient überachiever of late adolescence and so-called adulthood, usually as quick with witticisms and cool asides as he is with lethal power. The aggression may eventually become more antiseptic, more ordered from a distance, but it remains, marooned from any vulnerability. (There are, however, some cracks in this for young boys, as masculine figures in popular children's movies are becoming increasingly powerless. And more and more heroines are showing up, drawing attention away from impenetrable male take-charge icons.)

For a teenage boy, the conventional hero often is a veins-apoppin' he-man, armed to the teeth—with weaponry and bulging biceps in photogenic proximity—a testosterone-saturated powerhouse whose attributes plenty of teenage males dream of possessing so as to offset their often excruciating sense of self-consciousness and the looming pressures of becoming an adult male. For them, the hero cuts through whatever's in the way, with an engorged confidence and resolute countenance they wish they had themselves. That such qualities are presented as being so closely tied to industrial-strength aggression tends to squeeze adolescent males into a very restricted notion of manhood, lessening the chances of them opening to a vision of being a man whose power includes his vulnerability and softer emotions.

THE ANTI-HERO

Our times vastly complicate the concept of the hero, at least once we're within a year or so of entering adolescence, for he has to coexist not only with the villain, but also with the *anti-hero*. So what is an anti-hero? The opposite of the hero? No, because that position is already occupied by the villain, the bad guy, the one with no redeeming moral qualities. The anti-hero exhibits some of the qualities associated with the villain, ranging from brutality to cynicism to an apparent lack of empathy, yet is capable of taking heroic action, albeit in a far less glamorous or admirable way than the hero.

The anti-hero is a shadow-infused hero, a tortured rebel, a brooding visionary, a morally complex revolutionary, a deeply flawed doer of good along with considerable damage. He is messy. He is, in part, our darkness unleashed with just enough light and care, seizing our attention and perhaps also our begrudging admiration.

Prior to the 1950s, there were very few anti-heroes, except in existentialist writings and Byronic poetry, which were far from widely read. Basically, there were good guys and bad guys, heroes and villains, with very few shades of grey between such pairings. Audiences knew whom to root for. The heroes were clear-cut, and so were their adversaries. It wasn't only television that was black-and-white. The bad guys were not in any sense heroic; they existed merely to highlight the virtues of the hero. Superman was simply the Man of Steel; Stan Musial was Stan the Man; Joe Louis was the Bronx Bomber. There was no significant awareness of the "shadow," except in a few esoteric psychological circles. Sure, there were brooding leading men, grizzled seen-it-all detectives, as perhaps most famously played by Humphrey Bogart, but these were only nominally anti-heroes, making a fuss only in a very small arena of activity.

But in the 1950s, certain iconic figures who were not exactly heroes or villains began to emerge, carrying enough charisma to fascinate many people. Such figures, epitomized by James Dean, infiltrated the popular imagination, reflecting a growing ambivalence regarding what had previously been regarded as an unquestioned good. The disaffected character, the outsider, the rebel without a cause, Albert Camus's stranger, took the stage with insouciant ease. In *The Wild One*, Marlon Brando's character is asked what he's rebelling against. He replies, "Whaddaya got?" without a flicker, all wrapped up and surly in his black leather jacket, his motorcycle waiting just outside the door.

The hero wouldn't just sit back, taking no action, nor would the villain; but the anti-hero might. His lack of participation, his cool or indifferent removal, his distance from ennobling action, all reflected a growing disenchantment with the direction things were taking culturally and politically and morally. This dropping out, whatever its quotient of laid-backness and Kerouacian abandon, made a statement that resonated with many, especially those in their teens and early adulthood. In *The Catcher in the Rye*, the protagonist is not an admirable character by any conventional standards, but nonetheless provided a sense of adolescence that resonated with many.

In the 1960s, the anti-hero started to go mainstream. Superman became more vulnerable. Authority was increasingly questioned. The concept of shadow began to edge into popular consciousness. Black-and-white thinking started shifting into Technicolor. Little boys still had much the same heroes, but older boys looked up to more complex heroes, ones who broke with convention far more than in earlier generations. The inner lives of cultural heroes came under more scrutiny, far from what it is now, but still significantly more exposed than in the 1950s. The clean-cut hero began yielding to the wilder, less conventional one. Consider the late Ken Kesey. He wrote *One Flew Over the Cuckoo's Nest* in 1962, not long after taking LSD a number of times as part of a government-sponsored study; and then, a few years later, he famously toured the United States in a wildly painted bus (driven by Neal Cassady, the legendary protagonist of Kerouac's *On The Road*) promoting LSD and a far-from-conventional lifestyle. So here was a seemingly all-American guy (Olympic-level wrestler, great novelist, and so on) wearing an American flag shirt and speaking a language immensely appealing to American youth. A hero? To some. A villain? To some. An anti-hero? To many more—made heroic through his very opposition to much of what constituted typical American values.

By the 1970s, the anti-hero had gone mainstream (helped in part by the strong opposition to the Vietnam War). "Bad" became an expression of approval. Thumbing one's nose at the powers that were became more and more common, signifying an adolescence not limited by age. Dirty Harry showed up. The anti-hero had become the new go-to man, often possessing some qualities not only of the villain, like brutality and lawlessness, but also some qualities of the hero, like standing up for the downtrodden or being morally offended by dehumanizing behavior.

So when boys entered their teens, what awaited their imaginations was a mass of contradiction, a heroism largely defined by ambiguity and internal conflict, a heroism suffused with what it was doing battle with. Perhaps the only thing that stayed uncomplicated was the reality and appeal of aggression. Films got bloodier, and violence got more graphic, providing a break from the increasing moral complexity of life. *Pulp Fiction* gave violence style. In the face of the hero as the "best" anti-hero, the hero as a straightforward aggressor took up more space, was more muscular, more steroidal, pumped up with anger and avenging righteousness (think Rambo), slashing through his opposition with a cutting ease that contrasted with the more tortured reality of the anti-hero (think Batman or Wolverine).

The appeal of the anti-hero—beyond his nonmainstream independence—has much to do with how much like him we are. He doesn't fit in, nor do we, at least inwardly. He's complex; so are we. He's not some remote and impeccable icon of masculinity; he's but a breath away from us, making it easy for us to step into his clothes and attitude. To truly integrate the anti-hero is to embrace his commitment to being himself at all costs, without, however, isolating ourselves in overblown individuality.

However cool the anti-hero may come across as, he is vulnerable; this may not show outwardly, but we feel it, and this often makes him very attractive, including to plenty of women (which, for many men, makes him even more attractive to emulate). The anti-hero stands for our ambiguity, our uncertainty, our courage to take unpopular stands. He presents us with an edge that can, when wisely approached, spur us into embodying our quintessential masculinity.

THE HERO AS HUMAN

So what is a healthy and whole vision of today's hero? The hero has become quite a complex character: he is more than an anti-hero, being far from cool; but less than the mighty heroes of yore, given his obvious and out-front limitations. The hero is not infallible, not always victorious, and far from being unemotional. He is starting to have more than a passing acquaintance with his shadow. His integrity is usually stronger than his appetite. He is respectful to men and women alike, and doesn't look the other way when they are being mistreated. And he does not pathologize masculinity.

Though he may not have enough heroic qualities to gain the sympathy of a large audience, he persists, ennobled by his intimacy with his flaws. He sometimes does the right thing in the wrong way—moral ambiguity is far from alien to him. He is not an unperturbed doer of admirable deeds, a Captain America of personal growth, a guru, a perfected being, a man of steel. He's seen the embodiment of heroism morph from a god to a demigod to a superstar to a human, and views this not as a downgrading, but as healthy evolution. He is not run by the boy or adolescent in him, nor does he run from them, choosing to be intimate with all that he is.

Heroism in a man is a matter of doing what it takes to bring forth the very best in himself, enough so as to potently align him with what really matters in any given situation. This is what true masculine power is all about.

When a man awakens deeply enough to embody his full-blooded maleness without any dissociation from what's tender, soft, and vulnerable in him, he is his own hero. Nothing special—just a man anchored, more often than not, in his core; a man uncommonly trustworthy, courageous, and emotionally literate; a man as grounded as he is open, not letting his flaws get in the way, and no longer haunted by the ghost of perfectionism or unshakable impeccability. A man who did—and continues to do—the work to make this possible.

PART III

Relational Intimacy

Not every man needs to go into conscious intimate relationship—for some may find sufficient evolution and fulfillment in other domains—but, for the sake of one and all, every man needs to wholeheartedly engage in the learnings and work that make such relational closeness possible.

11

Clearing the Relationship Hurdle
Some Preparatory Considerations

MANY MEN FEEL at a loss when it comes to intimate relationship.

And plenty of men live as though there's not much they can do about this; even when they know better, they tend to settle for much less than they could have. Why? Because of (1) what going for more—namely, genuinely intimate relationship—would ask of them, and because of (2) the shame that this would bring up, the shame of having their relational incompetence so openly exposed. Being competent—and even more so, being seen as competent—is a central component of conventional manhood, but if we let ourselves be held hostage by this, avoiding facing our less-than-competent areas, we narrow ourselves, missing out on so, so much.

Cutting through this bind begins with developing compassion for our weaknesses, viewing them not as liabilities but as diamonds in the rough. Consider emotional literacy, an essential part of authentic relational intimacy. We may know that we lack in it—being far from at home with our emotions—but once we stop shaming ourselves for this lack, and view it with some compassion, we can begin working with it, honoring ourselves for being beginners, rather than shaming ourselves for not already being competent in this area. As part of our learning here, we can take a fresh look at our history with emotional know-how, seeing how it very likely was given no significant priority at home or school. We probably were preoccupied with other seemingly more relevant hurdles than knowing our emotions, such as getting better grades or toughening up or impressing our social circle.

There are such riches in genuinely intimate relationship—and in doing what makes it possible.

There's work here that asks much of us, but it's a labor of love, opening us in ways that serve us deeply. A relationship that's truly intimate is one overflowing not only with remarkably deep love and connection but also with transformational possibility, providing an optimal environment for embodying our full manhood. In such relationship, wholeness is not a potential, but a vital, foundational reality.

THE VULNERABILITY AND CHALLENGES OF RELATING

The pressure of *having to* express their softer feelings or *having to* be vulnerable is far from appealing for most men, being one more "should" on the relational to-do list, one more shame-inducing expectation to bear, one more hurdle to somehow face and try to clear.

If a man doesn't know how to be openly expressive with his feelings, or attempts it reluctantly or begrudgingly, chances are he's feeling shame about his inadequacy in this area—a shame that may be both unacknowledged and magnified through how his partner is conveying the desire that he open up more. Though he probably realizes that he's lacking in the capacity to be emotionally open, he may feel a load of resistance to addressing and exploring this, defending himself by saying: "Accept me as I am," possibly with the implication that there's something wrong with his partner for not thus accepting him, thereby turning the focus back on his partner. (It's important to note that when we say "accept me as I *am*," we often mean "accept what I am *doing*.")

Such defensiveness may just seem to be a refusal to take responsibility for engaging in something essential to healthy relationship, *but underlying it is one hell of a double bind:* (1) the pressure to cultivate and make central the qualities that make great relationship possible (like vulnerability, emotional openness, and integrity); and (2) the *coexisting* pressure to cultivate and make central the qualities that supposedly make us real men, especially at work (like aggression, emotional stoicism, and driven performance). Trying to do both, trying to please both sets of standards, simply divides and, therefore, disempowers us.

Conventional manly qualities may bring success in business, but not at home. Trying to operate in a marriage in the same way that you operate in your workplace carries a very high risk of failure. Trying to bring the values of emotional repression and invulnerability—keeping it together—into intimate relationship is a recipe for failure. The aggression and overly detached rationality that might have helped you succeed in your career will not help you succeed in your relationship. (And it's worth noting that vulnerability and the capacity for relational closeness are being viewed as more and more of a value in more and more workplaces, with aggression being increasingly viewed as less of a workplace virtue.)

So what to do about this double bind? Step aside from it and its pressure. See both sides, sensing what is most valuable in each, deepening your relationship with that, taking it into your heart as much as you can. No shoulds. No bind or binding. The qualities of relating that are most important to you can be brought, however indirectly or subtly, into all your relationships. You may not be able to show certain aspects of yourself at your job, but you can stay in touch with them, allowing them an internal aliveness no matter where you are.

Track athletes talk of *attacking* the hurdles that face them in a race, but relational hurdles don't need an attack, but an approach that neither underestimates nor overestimates their height and solidity, an approach that asks for leaps in which we don't lose touch with our ground or heart. Failing to clear a hurdle is then not taken as a reason to give up, but as a chance to re-center and further ready ourselves, attuning ourselves to the right time to again take the leap.

It's essential for men to (1) become conscious of the double bind of successfully being a man in conventional terms and successfully being a man in intimate relationship; and (2) do what it takes to step into a different kind of manhood, in which strength and drive beneficially coexist with transparency, vulnerability, and emotional literacy. This is all about aligning heart, guts, and head—meaning in part that emotion and rationality get to work together—and finding the courage to cease submitting to the pressure to be other than ourselves. There is a deep dignity in this, an integrity of being that is inherently liberating.

It's very helpful to realize that *the things you need to do to have better relationships are the very things you need to do to further your own growth and evolution.* To work on yourself is, in part, to make yourself more available for the kind of relationship that you, in your heart of hearts, long for, a relationship in which whatever arises can be used to strengthen and deepen the partners' bond.

Having a relationship with others is not the same as having an *association* with them. Having an association with your partner—centered by negotiation and contracts—may create a certain flow, but is far from being truly satisfying because so, so much is missing. For an association to work, there usually doesn't need to be any vulnerability or deep self-disclosure, though it will probably function optimally if some heart is brought to it. But this simply isn't true for an intimate relationship. In an association, there may be a mutual agreement to have sex regularly, but how fulfilling is this when there isn't any mutual vulnerability or emotional rawness or undressed love? There's a much-needed transition for a man to develop the ability to be his integrated self—both soft and strong, both transparent and resolute—at home and at work. Though his surface self-presentation at work may be different from at home, he does not have to lose touch with his core integrity.

A man also needs to develop intimacy with the younger versions of himself, recognizing them when they show up, and compassionately relating to them without losing himself in their worldview. For example, Charles easily gets reactive when he thinks he's being shamed. He speaks quickly and in a higher than usual voice, and feels very agitated—just like when he was a boy being put down by his mother. He learns, during such reactive bouts, to shift his attention to the shamed boy in him, bringing that one into his heart as best he can, both holding and protecting him, without, however, turning into (or identifying with) him. So he feels and gets as close as possible to that part of him, while maintaining his adult perspective.

Doing such practices is not just great for deepening a man's relationship with his children, but also for deepening it with an intimate partner. Doing so also helps with friends and coworkers, because it allows him to see and connect with them more fully; even if he doesn't—or doesn't want to—meet them in any significant depth, his sense of their emotional and psychological whereabouts allows him to more skillfully navigate his interactions with them.

A man who can truly father himself is no longer at the mercy of unhealthy fathering, whether from his own father, other men, or the authoritarian dictates of various elements of his culture. He is in good hands. His ground is solid and true. He is capable of deep relationship.

What's mostly in the way of meaningful man-to-man connection is the investment that one or both men have in keeping up a wall between them—a barrier that, however soft, keeps them safe from losing face or being otherwise unpleasantly exposed to each other. The ethic of men's allegiance to keeping distance from each other needs to compassionately be laid bare, along with their fears of what might happen if that ethic were to be deconstructed—fears that range from being rejected (as may have happened during boyhood when they showed vulnerability) to being seen as gay (as if being gay means having less than manly qualities).

During group work, I have had many men sit facing each other in dyads. With a little guidance, it usually didn't take long for them to do so with presence, care, and steady eye contact, without any significant aversion to thus positioning themselves. It didn't matter if they were young or old, shaky or steady, straight or gay, happy or sad. They were settling into real connection, relieved at not having to put energy into keeping up a wall between themselves. And at the same time, they were maintaining enough of a personal boundary to not lose themselves in the dyad. They were sitting in an embodied awareness of their individuality while simultaneously expanding their boundaries to include the other. (This is very different from collapsing or abandoning our boundaries in order to be close to another.)

Such connection felt natural, easy, satisfying, respectful. That this could happen so readily in group after group means that it could happen far more than it does in other settings, in ways that take into account the dynamics of such places. The point is not to always sit facing each other in transparent openness, but to bring the possibility of such depth and relational openness between men out of the shadows.

This asks for more than just being drinking buddies, employees of the same company, business partners, or members of the same political party or gang. Something more deeply interactive is required, something that many men long for with other men, but don't approach, keeping not just a respectful distance in their meetings but also an emotional and psychological distance, a gap that is often also present in their relationships with women.

My hope is that a thorough immersion in the rest of this part of the book will help to bridge that gap.

Onward!

12

Relational Intimacy for Men

Relationship as a Sanctuary for Transforming Your Life

PERHAPS THE BIGGEST and most relevant challenge for men is doing what it takes to be established in truly intimate relationship. By *intimate,* I mean loving, cherishing, and being very close to another, and not just sexually, in ways that deepen both the partners' connection *and* their individuality. The commitment that centers this is not only to making relational closeness—whatever its form—a central priority but also the well-being and growth of the partners.

And what are the essentials for being in such relationship? Here's an initial list, in abbreviated form, much of which has been explored in earlier chapters.

- Loosening your conditioning's grip on you. This begins with understanding and exploring the relevant connections between your past and present, seeing what circumstances in your early life generated your current automatic and reactive behaviors. Ceasing to be run by your conditioning is very difficult to do on your own; most need skilled guidance in doing so.

- Turning *toward* your pain, including emotionally, rather than continuing to distract yourself from it.

- Not letting your anger or shame turn into aggression.

- Vulnerability.

- Empathy and compassion.

- Love, and a deeper love.

- Deep listening.

- Emotional literacy and openness.

- Not letting your strengths camouflage your weaknesses.

- Gut-level honesty.

- No longer being under your inner critic's thumb.

- Zero tolerance for disrespect and abuse.

- Knowing your shadow—and integrating it.

- Standing in your power without disconnecting from your heart.

- Outgrowing pornography.

- Freeing sex from the pressure to make you feel better.

- Accountability. Being consistently reliable, dependable, and trustworthy; making no excuses for your less-than-healthy behavior; being your own whistleblower.

- Integrity. Acting from your innate sense of wholeness; taking full responsibility for what you do, internally and externally; making your and the other's highest good your priority in whatever interaction you may have with them.

- Commitment to working on yourself—and the relationship—more than just intellectually.

- An abiding, ever deepening interest in and love for the other.

These are not things to reduce to "shoulds," nor ideals to harness yourself to. (You do *not* have to have perfected them before you enter into intimate relationship!) Treat them instead as gradually unfolding parts of a journey devoted to deep healing, awakening, and relational maturation.

Enter—and further enter—them in the spirit of adventurous exploration, moving more fully into a manhood that's eventually epitomized by cultivating intimacy with *everything* that you are, learning bit by bit to allow all things—high and low, pleasant and unpleasant, dark and light—to awaken, hone, and further you. Such is the edge and great challenge that brings forth, honors, and refines the deep masculine.

This is no small endeavor, again and again uprooting us until we stand truer ground, calling out our essential manhood—our soul-centered warriorhood—without any abandoning of our sensitivity and empathy and child-side. Aligning ourselves with the imperatives of this call, this deepest of invitations, is an immeasurably rewarding adventure, bringing our total being out into the open, making the richest, most life-giving kind of relationship more than possible.

Intimate relationship has been my greatest and most demanding teacher, having not only brought me deep happiness but also exposing my weaknesses, my zones of selfishness and unresolved wounding, my less-than-noble reasons for seeking such relationship. As a young man, I did little about this, other than acknowledging it in therapeutic contexts. It took me a long time to fully appreciate the opportunity I was being given to heal and awaken *through* intimate relationship. My bond with my wife, Diane, is not only the deepest, richest, and easiest

I've ever had but also the most challenging and full of growth. In the presence of her love, maturity, and capacity to really see me (including in the most subtle ways), I feel a permission to go fully into both my core wounding and my deepest dimensions, feeling at home no matter how shaken I might be. With her, it feels utterly natural to keep opening to all that I am, not only resting in our uncommon intimacy but also venturing forth with her into new territories, as well-seasoned elders. Not so long after meeting Diane, I finally let go of the fantasy of reaching a point where I wouldn't need to work on myself anymore, stepping instead into the happily humbling realization that this is a life-long process, lit by a sense of ever-evolving relationship with all that I am, proverbial warts and all.

Everything that precedes this part of the book can be seen as essential training for genuinely intimate connection with others, especially in the form of deeply committed relational closeness.

Not that every man needs to go into conscious intimate relationship—for some may find sufficient evolution and fulfillment in other domains, like uncommonly meaningful and/or creative work. But every man needs to wholeheartedly engage in the learnings and work that make such relational closeness possible, if only because through doing so he learns to fully and compassionately *relate to all that he is*—and therefore to *all* that *we* are—eventually healing himself so deeply that he renders himself all but incapable of dehumanizing others. Full-out intimate relationship is one of the most healing paths there is, including as it does all of our dimensions.

The healing between men and women—and men and men, and women and women—has the capacity to revolutionize relationship on a significant scale, but only if it goes to a sufficiently deep level. More than cosmetic shifts are needed, more than superficial gains, more than dips in self-help literature and seminars, more than attendance at men's groups.

Without a saner, deeper bonding between intimate partners, dysfunctional associations will continue to dominate the relational landscape, along with all the compensatory activity—ranging from apathy to violent acting out—that inevitably accompanies such dysfunction.

The shift needed is from fragmentation to wholeness, from frozen yesterday to fluidly alive now, from numbness to full feeling, from alienation to compassion, from reactivity to responsiveness, from gendered standoffs to mutually respectful coexistence—making full-spectrum intimacy possible. This is a worthy challenge, the very demands of which are precisely what men—and women—need to align themselves with and meet wholeheartedly, for everyone's sake.

Having a healthy, fully functioning relationship is not a luxury or something just for the rare few. It needs to become a reality for enough of us to significantly impact the majority.

If a man wants to be of real service—and I see more and more men who do, and not just when they reach midlife—and wants to bring forth the very best in himself, then the great testing ground, at once sanctuary and crucible, is intimate relationship, or at least doing what best ripens him for it.

Prior to the last half century, the relational demands on men were not that great; all they had to do—and I'm not minimizing this—was bring home the bacon, keep a roof overhead, perhaps make a bit of manly conversation, not beat their wives, and keep the kids in line. Things were much more black-and-white back then, with tidy delineations between good guys and bad guys, the man-of-few-words hero and his girl kissing chastely in the sunset, and the not-so-good stuff (like brutalizing the wife) kept out of sight. Heroes were clean-cut and square-shouldered, sat tall in the saddle or cockpit, and were courteous to the ladies. There was little or no suspicion of what they might be doing behind closed doors. If there was any trouble—a few bad boys—it usually was so far on the outskirts of society that it didn't seem to matter all that much.

Things are *very* different now. We seem as far from that generation —pre-Vietnam, pre-Beatles, pre-computers, pre-feminism, pre-LSD, pre-Internet—as we are from the Middle Ages. Intimate relationship is not something a man can engage in just because he's departed his teens. Women are no longer so compliant, so willing to play the backup or be just a support person. Now they want to be related to in ways that frighten many men, ways that bring up men's insecurity and concerns about not being enough. Yes, as women step more and more into the relational foreground, they have their work to do—like reclaiming their voice and establishing healthy boundaries—but men need to learn to take the increasingly voiced need of women to be *fully met* in relationship not as a problem but as a great gift, an incredible opportunity to embody their full manhood.

Intimate relationship is probably where men are most challenged—and invited—to be their full selves. And what an invitation it is! An invitation that will not go away, calling forth the very best from a man, but also often bringing up the very worst, not to be indulged in or acted out, but to be faced, healed, and integrated with the rest of his being. An example of this would be surfacing hostility being stripped of its aggressiveness until it is but healthy anger, perhaps still fiery, but infused with responsibility and compassion.

JOHN is close enough to his partner to be really hurt by her, and what she's just said wounds him deeply. He very quickly gets defensive, hardening himself and moving into attack mode. As his hostility escalates, he suddenly realizes (from the work he's done on himself) that he's being aggressive with her. Seeing this, and letting her know that he sees this, he feels some connection with her, as his aggression loses its edge and becomes anger. He stays angry a bit longer, no longer trying to shield himself from his partner. Soon they are talking, with mutual care and curiosity, about what's just happened, feeling closer to each other than they have for a while. ∎

Do you want to see what you don't want to see about yourself? Do you want to discover and face what you've been keeping in the shadows? Do you want to wake up to who and what you truly are, without bypassing your raw humanity? Do you want to find a deep alignment of heart, guts, and intellect? Are you looking, however reluctantly, for what calls forth the full you? Are you losing interest in settling for less?

Do you want to do more with your resistance to these questions (and such resistance is entirely natural!) than just give in to it or rationalize it? Are you, however indirectly, looking for an adventure that will make you fully alive, that will shake and take you to your core, and give you back more than you can imagine?

If so, choose to move in the direction of truly intimate relationship. This doesn't mean finding the "right person" in the very near future, but launching yourself—at the optimal pace—into the work that makes this possible.

If you don't do this, the odds are very high that your conditioning—with your unwitting permission—will continue to select your partners for you, repeating the pattern of leaving you in me-centered bonds that feature little more than two personalized sets of unresolved wounds interlocking and controlling the relational dynamics. To not remain mired in such relational automaticity is a huge step in developing the capacity for real intimacy.

ESSENTIAL STEPS TO AUTHENTIC INTIMACY

- **Know your conditioning inside out.** This means being very familiar with your personal history, recognizing whatever wounding you carry (and how you tend to compensate for it), seeing how and where your conditioning has made your choices, and how and where it is still running you. Breaking your conditioning's grip on you won't erase it, but will put you in a position where you're not at its mercy: being able to relate not *from* it, but *to* it. You'll likely need the help of a good therapist to do this well. A good place to begin is to take a reactive pattern you have and, when you're not feeling reactive, look at it objectively, tracing the raw feeling of it back to when it first arose in your life, noting what triggered it back then.

An example: To make him "behave," JEFF's mother used to criticize him in a shaming way. Now, when his wife starts speaking to him about something he hasn't done so well, even in the form of a loving observation or question, he usually explodes, ragingly accusing her of picking on or nagging him, not realizing how much he's projecting his mother onto her. His old hurt, still intact, must be worked on to reduce the inner charge he carries regarding being criticized. ▪

Another area to explore is that of past traumas, which we coped with as children through survival strategies, like dissociating, going numb, dividing ourselves, and so on. For many of us, these strategies remain our adult go-to methods when we face conditions that mimic our past circumstances.

An example: When SAM had to face his father raging at him, he learned to blank out (to vacate the premises, so to speak), having the sense of standing a few feet behind his body. Nowadays, when his partner challenges him with even a slightly raised voice, Sam goes blank, immediately slipping into a mental fog. He doesn't do this consciously; when his partner gets upset at this, Sam pulls even further into his fogginess. The solution is a compassionately guided journey into and through the roots of his going blank (best done under the guidance of a professional who is well trained in working with trauma). ▪

> ▪ **Turn toward your pain.** As natural as it may seem to turn
> away from or distract yourself from your pain, practice
> turning toward it, daily. When pain arises, acknowledge
> this as soon as possible, and then direct your undivided
> attention toward it, taking care not to turn it into
> suffering (meaning the over-dramatization of pain).

An example: When GERALD thinks he's not succeeding at work and gets discouraged, he watches a lot of TV. His new practice, when he's about to watch TV, is to name what he's feeling emotionally, saying it aloud to himself ("Here's shame" or "I feel sad" or "I'm afraid") and noticing where he feels this in his body, breathing a touch deeper, and allowing himself to simply *be* with that feeling. He can also include the sensations he's experiencing ("My upper back feels tight" or "My jaw is aching" or "There's a tingly feeling in my right hand"). Gerald is turning toward his pain and his discomfort, paying attention to what's making his watching TV so attractive. In so doing, he's beginning the process of being controlled by neither his pain nor by his craving to distract himself from it. ■

■ **Don't treat vulnerability as a weakness.** Practice being vulnerable (transparent and undefended and significantly softened) in safe circumstances, where the only "danger" is getting embarrassed by such overt self-unmasking. Vulnerability can be a source of strength. For example, your partner says something that triggers you, and you slip into aggression, getting defensive. But then, instead of continuing to "protect" yourself, you admit you're being defensive, adding that you felt hurt when you heard your partner's comment, avoiding the temptation to blame your partner for your hurt. As you drop your guard, you soften, making your connection with your partner more important than being right. This is vulnerability. Not so easy perhaps, but so potent in getting your relationship back on track.

■ **Bring your shadow out of the dark.** To the extent that you allow your conditioning to operate you, it *is* your shadow. Get to know whatever in yourself you have disowned or rejected, and know it very well, to the point where its energies no longer internally divide you. (See chapter 4.)

■ **Deepen your emotional literacy.** Become a student of emotions, casting both a finely focused and panoramic eye on them, and get to know them intimately. The more deeply and skillfully you can relate to your emotions, the more you'll be able to do so in actual relationship. (See my book *Emotional Intimacy.*)

- **Distinguish between anger and aggressiveness.** Aggression is an attack, however "nicely" it may be conveyed, but anger is not. When you feel your anger starting to shift into aggression, acknowledge this (at least to yourself) and don't allow it to do so, choosing to see the offending other with compassion. (See chapter 7.)

- **Practice opening your heart when you least want to do so.** Don't lose touch with your love when you are not being loved, and do so without collapsing or sinking into exaggerated tolerance. At times, this may mean opening your heart to your own close-heartedness. Opening your heart doesn't always mean you'll look loving, but the very intention to thus open is a potent context shifter.

- **Love and protect the boy within.** It's so easy to push away our inner child, that locus of pre-rational innocence, vulnerability, and softness, as if his presence somehow lessens our status as men. But a man who is out of touch with the boy within is a man cut off from much of what makes intimate relationship possible.

- **Face and outgrow whatever pornographic leanings you have.** This means healing the psychological and emotional wounding that originally drove—and still drives—us toward pornography. (See chapter 22.)

- **Release your sexuality from the obligation to make you feel better.** So long as you assign your sexuality to the labor of making you feel better or more secure or more manly, you'll overrely on it, preventing it from being a natural expression of *already-present* love, connection, and well-being.

- **Make your connection to your partner top priority.** If you are caught up in reactivity or battling for relational turf, you've very likely forgotten or marginalized your connection with your partner. At such times, do your best to remember your connection with her or him, and reestablish it as soon as possible, allowing it and your autonomy to fruitfully coexist.

■ ■ ■

You don't need to be an expert in all of the above before you can enter intimate relationship, but you need to be already committed to learning them as fully as you can, having at least some momentum in your practice of them. And of course, it's crucial that the other also be similarly committed, otherwise your relationship will be all about you trying to get your partner to "do the work."

And even if you don't end up in such partnership, the very steps you've taken to ready yourself for it will further and deepen your life immeasurably, including in all your relationships.

13

Deep Communication

When Dynamic Receptivity and Expression Work Together

PERHAPS THE MOST common complaint heard from couples who go for counseling is a lack of communication. Usually, they both have compelling arguments for their position, and both are strongly attached to being right. Increasing the volume doesn't help. Repeating one's position doesn't help. Fairly often there is unrestrained and growing disrespect for the other, often manifesting as sarcasm or disdain. Aggressiveness is common; so is emotional disconnection; and so is forgetting to make the *connection* with each other top priority.

THE WAY BACK TO CONNECTION

The way through such dysfunctional discord is not to summon up more convincing points, but to disengage from intellectual sparring and establish some *mutual emotional ground*—and to remain anchored there as much as possible when it's time to address the issue in question.

This doesn't necessarily mean emotional harmony or meshing, for there may be very serious conflict that's far from resolved, but *mutual emotional recognition,* a *noncognitive* knowing of—and being attuned to—each other's emotional state. Thus, what's going on emotionally for the couple is held separate from the *content* of their argument. Disagreement and quarrelsomeness are put aside, and what's going on emotionally for each of them is brought into the foreground and given full focus until they both can feel and acknowledge the other's emotional state.

This begins with each partner stating not what they're *thinking* or *perceiving*, but the emotion(s) they are *feeling* and nothing more, no matter how tempted they may be to say more, to justify their position, to make the other responsible for what's happening, and so on.

My wife, Diane, and I do such work with couples by having them face each other, holding steady eye contact and stating only what they are actually feeling. Saying "I feel that you're not present" or "I don't feel heard" are not feelings, but perceptions or opinions, and are thus debatable. Saying "I feel sad" or "I feel anger" are statements of feeling, and are not debatable. These statements are simply data, interpretation-free, and therefore not arguable. (If we're having trouble identifying our emotions, we can state what we're feeling at the level of simple sensation: "I feel tightness in my belly" or "I feel an achiness in the back of my neck" or "My breathing feels shallow.")

What's often most difficult here is resisting the temptation to say more after we've said what we're feeling. But when we *end* our sentence (which begins "I feel . . .") with the fitting emotion word or words (anger, fear, sad, and so on), and not continue it with "because . . . ," we are giving the other a chance to (1) let in the bare fact of where we are emotionally, and to (2) resonate with it at a feeling level without getting reabsorbed in or distracted by thought. Openly sharing our feeling state in this way invites empathy from our partner. We can easily argue with a perception or idea, but not with raw data. Simply stating that we're angry (assuming that we are indeed angry!) is not disputable, however much the other may be bothered that we're angry, or thinks that we should not be angry.

In a couples session, JASON is upset with his partner, Mary, repeatedly telling her that she needs to get off his back. She looks blankly at him, and says nothing. I ask him to describe what he's feeling, and he says, "I feel like she's always on my case, wanting to talk all the time." I explain that this is not a feeling but a perception, and take some time to clarify the difference. He responds by saying, "So I guess I'm angry."

He's about to add more, but I tell him to just stay with his anger, and breathe a bit more deeply, softening his belly. As this happens, Mary brightens. "This is okay, but I feel like he's hardly ever present." I ask her what she's actually feeling, and she tears up. "Sad, defeated, like giving up." I tell her to shorten this to "sad," having her remain with this; there'll be time later to go more deeply into her sadness, which shows signs of depression. I have him simply state his anger, and her, her sadness, guiding both into feeling and resonating with the other's emotional state more fully, breathing it in, helping them stay emotionally present. Several minutes pass. There is less tension between them. She starts to cry, and he looks sad. Now their relational impasse can be effectively explored. And no matter what the content, I'll continue to monitor their emotional state, taking it deeper when necessary. ∎

What we're being asked to do, as the recipient, is to *listen emotionally,* letting in the bare reality of the other's emotional state as well as their straightforward acknowledgment of it—regardless of our mental commentary. We don't have to agree or disagree with what we're letting in; there's nothing to argue about. Once both partners have clearly and openly stated what they're feeling—with nothing added and in a non-attacking tone—all they have to do is stay silent for a minute or so, making more room in themselves for the other's emotional condition. This often translates into some degree of empathy, with the contentious issues not being allowed to dominate the foreground.

Only when some mutual emotional recognition has been established should the original concern—the topic that was being debated—be addressed. Without the ground of some emotional co-listening and empathy, the concern in question will just get boxed into the same old back-and-forth arguments.

The point is to make emotionally centered communication more of a priority than intellectually centered communication. Both are obviously important, but relational flow and conversation simply work better when there's at least some emotional resonance. Once this is in place, the interplay of differing views doesn't dominate whatever communication is occurring.

WILLIAM and his partner Frank are busy arguing, caught up in mutual reactivity, emphatically making the same points they usually do at such times. The more they get into this, the more they stray into aggression and mean-spiritedness. There's plenty of emotion, but no emotional connection, no empathy, no real listening. In exasperation William says, "Here we are doing this again!" and is about to blame Frank for it, when he remembers their agreement (until now little more than confetti in the storminess of their reactivity) to "make their connection priority." He stops, says this, and Frank stops, too. "I'm so pissed!" says William; and Frank, on the verge of tearing up, quickly adds, "Me too!" Both sit down, gaze at each other, and say nothing until they feel some emotional reconnection and resonance happening. ■

This turnaround may not always happen so quickly—working with our reactivity can take some time—but it is always worth putting some energy and attention into, as soon as possible after it becomes obvious that reactivity is happening.

The process of stating what we're feeling—and keeping it at that—usually feels more natural to women (however challenging it might be to not say more). But with practice, it can feel just as natural to men. I've found that most men experience some relief once they've got the hang of this, enjoying the simultaneous simplicity and depth of it, especially as they become more emotionally literate. Stating only what emotions and sensations are primarily present relieves them of getting caught up in cognitive combat zones and let's-fix-it strategies, and provides enough space and time to settle in and get really grounded before proceeding with the issues at hand.

Communication doesn't work well when its emotional dimensions are not clearly acknowledged and shared. An argument can be very emotional and do no more than go in circles or drain us or be injurious. At such times, our emotional energy is just being used to underline our arguments. We might devalue the other's statements by telling them that they're being too emotional, or by telling them to calm down as a way of shutting them down, or by using our emotional intensity to overpower them.

Truly effective communication is as attuned to what's going on emotionally as it is to mental activity, staying empathetically present, listening both to what's being said and to what's not being said. This is about undivided attention, openness, compassion, and genuine interest, all working together.

DEEP LISTENING

Though listening may seem like a passive activity, it can actually be quite dynamic, requiring both alertness and ease. It is vital receptivity in action, taking in not just the speakers' words, but also their emotional state, their body language, their quality of presence.

As we listen, we become aware of what isn't being spoken but nonetheless still being expressed. We deepen our resonance with the other, becoming a kind of caring clearing for the full expression of what they are sharing with us. Such nonverbal attunement is especially valuable when the other is disturbed enough to be saying things that are easily categorized as irrational or even absurd. At such times, it can be best not to take what's being said literally, and to simply be present for the other. (That said, deep listening does *not* mean putting up with abuse or disrespect.)

JACK's partner is hugely upset about a difficult situation she's in. She yells dramatically at Jack that there's no point to going on, that she sees no reason to live. He knows she is not suicidal, and is about to give her a bunch of reasons to live, but he stops, resisting the urge to try to reason with her or go into fix-it mode. She keeps ranting, fighting back her tears; the more intense she gets, the more steady and present Jack gets, saying nothing except an occasional "yes" to her fury and sadness. He realizes that this is a very temporary state, having previously witnessed her tendency to express herself this way when she's upset. He breathes deeply and slowly, keeping his belly soft, giving her his wholehearted attention, inwardly reminding himself that she doesn't actually need him to jump in and caretake her. Within a few minutes she is calmer, settling into her hurt, becoming more aware of his presence, with any shame she feels about "losing it" fading before Jack's obvious care. Simply being listened to this way was all that she needed. ∎

Being nonverbally present with another's upset can be quite challenging, especially for those whose default response to such distress is to fix it as soon as possible. All too often, we get into fix-it mode, not so much to help the other, but to try to get them past feelings that we are far from comfortable with in ourselves. The quicker they're fixed, the better we feel—or so it seems. But our "helpfulness" here can easily backfire, as when we point out the other's irrationality or faulty logic. Even if we're right, we're trying to talk them out of being in a place where they may very well need to be, at least for a bit longer. And that place is emotional, perhaps very emotional, and needs to be felt, seen, acknowledged, held, related to.

If we can make compassionate room in ourselves for such expression from the other, their irrationality and faulty logic won't matter so much, and will usually recede quite quickly once they feel we are emotionally there with them. (Being familiar with our partner's personal history makes it all the more possible to do this for them.)

Simply being present—including emotionally—with another when they are feeling distressed or overwhelmed can be immensely helpful to them. When you thus "hold space" for another in a non-directive way, you are bearing witness to their process and generating a conducive environment for them to be with, and move through, their pain. Such "holding space" is not a dissociative, emotionally vacant, or passive witnessing, but a grounded, empathetic expression of presence, the boundaries of which have been expanded to include the other. When we are established in this, we can at any point shift into fitting action, the capacity for which the other can intuit—and this tends to make them feel even safer.

The more open, attentive, and curious you are when listening, the quieter your mind will be—not trying to construct a response—and the clearer your intuition will be. The deeper we let this take us, the richer the "we-space" between us and the other becomes, without any loss of our autonomy.

Deep listening requires:

- being wholly attentive to the other, without losing touch with yourself;

- being empathically connected to the other, without any loss or weakening of your boundaries;

- being patient with the other, but not passively;

- being present and consciously embodied (aware of your sensations, breathing, posture, intentions, energy level), no matter what you're feeling or thinking;

- being genuinely interested in the other, beyond what they're saying;

- being able to make compassionate room for difficult states in the other; and

- being able to listen to yourself as you listen to the other.

■ ■ ■

Communication works best when there is not only mutual emotional transparency and empathy, but also an established, well-anchored trust. Such trust provides a safe place to let go of playing it safe, providing a stable sanctuary for the deepest kind of sharing (including the timely sharing of distrust), however painful or risky that might be. (The trust I speak of is not one automatically given—because we think we should totally trust the other—but one that is earned through having witnessed that person's integrity, reliability, and trustworthiness over a period of time.)

In fully functioning communication, there is no power struggle, no investment in winning, no strategy to overpower. Being off track is seen not as a problem, but as a chance to get more deeply back on track.

When you and another are truly connected, emotionally and otherwise, the arising of emotional disconnection is not a problem because there's enough trust and safety to openly communicate and explore this more deeply, which almost inevitably leads to more connection, thereby reinforcing and deepening your trust. Simply saying, "I feel sad about our disconnection" or "I miss feeling our connection" can help catalyze emotional reconnection.

Communication, at its best, is communion and articulation functioning as one. It is the electricity and circuit board of relationship, optimally flowing when its emotional components are illuminated, respected, and fully connected.

14

Fighting *for* the Relationship

Transitioning to Shared Power

IN OUR COUPLES PRACTICE, Diane and I often find ourselves working with a couple caught up in a dead-end argument, with both partners making passionately articulated cases for their position. Yet, however novel their verbal fencing and reactive emotional infusions, it basically is just more of the same old I-said-you-said power struggle. When we initially clarify this and help them devote more attention to what's going on below and behind all the talk, their battle to establish who is right may still continue for a bit—the thrusts and parries are more spectral or veiled, but still have enough impact to keep the power struggle alive.

A war for control. Once again.

But as their core feelings emerge more openly and vulnerably, and transparency is allowed to play a more central role in their encounter, being right becomes less important to them than being connected and intimate. Feeling the other—an emotional resonance that includes feeling *into,* feeling *for,* and feeling *with* that person—becomes primary, and agreeing or disagreeing secondary.

Then, opening to and letting in the other—emotionally, mentally, energetically—signals not a loss of power, but instead a freeing up of power, with *both clearly sharing it.* Love and humor return, along with greater clarity about their mutual battle for power. The space they're in feels quieter, softer, looser, more spacious, no longer dominated by courtroom tactics and their corresponding thoughts. The war may not be over, but it has lost much of its appeal and much of its grip.

The point is not necessarily to stop fighting, but to fight cleanly—no blaming, shaming, or attacking, no name-calling, no losing touch with our caring for each other, no rationalizing of our reactivity, no excuses for remaining adversarial or hurtful. We can be fiery, fierce, confronting, and still remain compassionately present and respectful.

It's also important to remember that, at some point, just about all relationships grapple with—and frequently succumb to—power issues. And in most relationships where there's not an apparent power struggle, one partner has simply allowed the other to run the show; this, of course, speaks not of resolution, but of *resignation.* (And what is relational resignation, other than a kind of depression, a bypassing of the inevitable bumps and dips of relationship through flattening oneself? It takes energy to keep ourselves down, and if we do this long enough, keeping an unnaturally low profile so as to tune out or marginalize our partner's nastier side, we simply exhaust ourselves, leaving ourselves in the position of not having sufficient energy to challenge, or even leave, the relationship.)

In the presence of awakened intimacy, conflict is just shit auditioning to be compost. The shovels are supplied; all we have to do is use them.

Most couples don't fully resolve their power struggles, settling instead for a partial resolution, taking comfort in the common territory between them that's no longer under dispute; what hasn't been dealt with is then simply kept in a peripheral enough position so as not to threaten or seriously disrupt the relationship. Still, their power struggle exists, and shows up, if only in dreams or as an undercurrent of distress in one or both partners.

So how do we work through our power struggles with our partner? First of all, we need to see what we're actually struggling over. We can call it *power,* but what exactly is that? Autonomy? Noninterference with what we want? Agreement from the other person? Social strength? Taking a stand?

There are many ways of looking at power, but for our purposes here, let's just say that power is the capacity to act effectively, to generate significant change, to impose one's will on one's environment, human and otherwise.

And why do we need this power for which we are struggling? To stay on top? To not go under? To win? To be heard, felt, seen, appreciated, loved, known?

Whatever we need power for exists only in relational contexts. As mentioned in chapter 6, power-over is power held over another or others (or perhaps over something in us); power-with is power shared with another or others; and to be empowered is to experience power or an increase in power in the company of—or through—another or others.

I'm reminded of Jet Li's film *Fearless*. From an early age, Huo (the protagonist) is obsessed with defeating opponents, at whatever cost. This obsession had its origins in his being humiliated by another boy who had easily crushed him in a fight. No matter how great his victories are now, he is not satisfied; he is obsessed with having power-over, with being on top. When a rival martial arts master apparently wrongs him, Huo seeks him out and does battle with him, not just to win, but to destroy him—the hypermasculine epitome of righteous vengeance. Only with the great tragedy that follows this is he knocked off course, returned to the shame that he's spent his life fleeing, and deposited in a new life, one of unadorned ordinariness and natural humility.

In his broken, unguarded state, he gradually learns to flow with his new condition, eventually becoming very at home with it. His inner war is over so that when he eventually returns to combat—for a very different purpose than before—he is no longer seeking power-over, but rather a resolution that dishonors no one. As much as I've enjoyed watching mixed martial arts fighters strive to overpower each other, watching Huo do battle *after* regaining his integrity and spiritual core stirred something much deeper in me: the fully embodied taking of a stand that serves a greater need than that of vanquishing others.

It isn't wrong to want to overpower another under certain conditions, such as a fiercely competitive, yet still mutually respectful, game of tennis. Nor is it wrong to exult in our achievements at such times. But there's also a deeper game to be played, a game in which far more is at stake than our ego's status.

This is not about blind honor, wherein we're willing to trade our life or make enormous sacrifices for an ideal we've never properly questioned or examined. It's about doing what honors our very being. There is healthy renunciation in this, not repression, but *a "no" that deepens our "yes."* There is also tremendous freedom, the kind of freedom that is found *through* making optimal use of limitation (as in the best of intimate relationships). Early in the film, Huo is diminished by things not going his way; later, nothing can diminish him.

This kind of heroism—call it *being-centered heroism*—is timeless, and therefore always timely. When another embodies it, we are naturally touched, no matter how small, old, or frail that person may be. The image of spiritual sage Ramana Maharshi (from black-and-white footage shot in the 1940s) hobbling along on arthritic limbs, even as his whole being is smiling, comes to mind, moving me not because he is trying to be heroic, but because he is so obviously and so completely surrendered to the ultimate empowering act, namely the awakening of others to their real nature.

Back to our couple: their task and sacred labor is not to stop fighting, but to fight *for* each other and *for* their relationship. Theirs is an often humbling task that does not require them to hang their heads or dilute their energy, but rather—after calming down enough—to compassionately face their mutual wounds *together,* identifying what old patterns had surfaced during their argument, and discussing, as a team, how they might handle future similar situations more skillfully.

Power released from the labor of overpowering or controlling the other is shared power, power that can coexist with love, power that's an ally, asking only that we continue using it as such. Such is our responsibility and sacred obligation. In this, we do not necessarily stop fighting, but refine and illuminate our power, using it as discerningly as possible, especially when we're engaged in relational combat. To truly fight for the relationship is not an act of aggression but of love.

15

What Women Need from Men

An Invitation to Be a Full Partner

MANY MEN CONTINUE to misunderstand, neglect, or ignore what works and doesn't work relationally for the women they're in partnership with (or are considering being in partnership with). No wonder such men find women confusing! What follows describes some areas of concern regarding what women need from men in relational contexts, and what can be done about each. None of this is meant to imply that women don't also have work to do in these areas to deepen their relationships with men. (Note that what follows is written with the assumption that both partners want to stay together, and that their relationship is not abusive.)

Listen to her without trying to figure out solutions for what's going on, and listen with your whole being. Your job isn't to fix something, but to genuinely take in and resonate with what she's feeling. Stay alive and fully present in your listening, doing so not as a duty, but as an act of intimate interest and care. And don't be passive in this! If your interest wanes, or it's not good timing, don't pretend to be listening. Either refocus, or let her know, in a non-shaming way, that you'd like to continue the conversation later on when you can be more present, making sure you aren't using this option as a way to avoid listening!

Get more emotionally literate and attuned. Become a student of emotion and emotional expression, learning the lessons by heart rather than trying to get good grades. Take some quality time with my book *Emotional Intimacy.*

Don't give in to any neediness you feel, including sexually. Separate your neediness from its desperation and manipulative tendencies until you're in touch with the raw need (and emotional pain) that you're letting morph into neediness. Remember that neediness and sensitivity are not synonymous.

Spend more uninterrupted and undistracted time with her. Don't let short encounters become the norm. Don't let your only fully attentive time with her be when you're seeking or having sex with her.

Give her more real and unsolicited appreciation, including for the little things. Just because she's not saying anything about it, don't assume that she's fine with not getting unsolicited appreciation. And don't make her ask for it.

Cut through your tentativeness. If you're touching her, don't do it gingerly, as if asking a question or trying to see if she approves. No walking on eggshells, and no going to the other extreme (being pushy or aggressive). Be fully present in your touch. When you feel tentative, clearly say so, and tell her what's going on for you emotionally.

Be trustworthy, a safe place for her, protective but not possessive. This is not about being on your best behavior, but about working on yourself deeply enough to be incapable of betrayal or any sort of abuse.

Don't let the little boy in you run the show, but don't push him away. Get to know him very well, and make sure she knows him well, too. Keep him close to you, but not so close that his take on things becomes yours. If your relationship with him remains unhealed, you'll be crippled in your capacity for healthy adult relationship.

Stop making excuses for your crappy behavior. And don't run from whatever shame it might induce in you; stay with your remorse, and make amends as soon as possible. Explore the roots of such behavior instead of just promising not to do it again. Include her in your exploration.

Give her some unexpected affection and caring, and not just every now and then. Don't make her earn your affection and caring.

Cherish her, daily. This means, in part, not taking her for granted. Keep your gratitude for her and for being with her alive and well. And tell her how you feel.

Meet her fully. Choose to see her as she is, rather than her surface presentation or potential. Don't pull back from her when she expresses herself fully (assuming, of course, that she does so cleanly).

Let the entire relationship be foreplay, and not just in sexual contexts. Women are far more turned on by how they are spoken to and connected with than by some "romantic" moment. Pay special attention to connecting with her above the shoulders, meeting her eyes with wholehearted awareness and touching her face with tender, fully embodied presence.

Stop treating her like something to fix when she's upset. Put away your repair tools and do whatever you can to be a compassionate and grounding presence for her at such times, focusing not so much on her words as on her energy, keeping a solid but flexible boundary around her and yourself as her feelings pour forth. Sometimes all she wants is for you to hold her.

Instead of trying to create closeness by getting sexual, establish (or reestablish) closeness first, and then—if it's mutually natural—move into the sexual. Let sex be a deeply embodied expression of already-present loving connection. Let your connection with her be the aphrodisiac.

Stop saying, "Accept me as I am" when you actually mean, "Accept my sloppy or unkind behavior." Accepting *you* is not the same as excusing you or letting you off the hook when you've been disrespectful, rude, or neglectful.

Initiate the conversation when it comes to addressing relationship difficulties. Don't wait for her to bring these up; share the responsibility for doing so. If you're feeling cut off from her, don't blame her for this, but instead share your feelings regarding being thus disconnected, and do so vulnerably.

If you need to go for counseling, do so without her having to push you to it. Face the shame that may accompany such a venture, reminding yourself that it takes courage to go for therapy. And don't go just for her; go for yourself. Remember that just about everyone benefits from engaging in high-quality therapy, including those who think they don't need it.

Don't leave your unresolved wounds and conditioning unattended. Work on yourself, and keep working on yourself. Dig deep, feel more, come more alive, doing whatever healing work is needed.

Stop trying to turn her on by quickly going for, or overfocusing, on her erogenous zones. Slow down. Attune to the whole woman. Don't split her into sexy and not-sexy parts, or view her as having buttons to be pushed. Give your full attention to her presence, and you may find that her entire being can be an erogenous zone.

Make more quality eye contact, and don't wait for her to initiate this. If you find yourself avoiding her eyes, talk about this, and explore its possible origins. Keep your gaze open and direct, without any straining. Let everything show, including your possible fear of rejection or being invalidated. Notice what you'd like to hide, and don't.

Be vulnerable without losing your spine. Be transparent, nondefensive, and tender—with enough grounding for your vulnerability to be a source of strength.

Don't neglect personal hygiene. Stale sweat is rarely a turn-on. The same goes for bad breath, food stuck between your teeth, and unwashed body parts. Some women may not bring this up, not wanting to hurt you; if they don't, their aversion stays in place, while you remain unaware of why she seems a bit reluctant to physically engage with you.

Don't leave your clothes and or other stuff lying around for her to pick up and take care of. She's not your maid, and treating her like one is not going to foster intimacy.

Don't compare her to your mother or your previous partners or lovers. Comparisons can set up unwanted and messy triangulations, impaling both her and you.

Stop overemphasizing the visual in sexual functioning. Getting too caught up in how she looks keeps you insufficiently focused on the rest of her. By all means appreciate her appearance, but also stay attuned to her energetically—which is much more about feeling than seeing.

If she's let herself go physically, compassionately consider with her what that might be a symptom of (depression, deep hurt, wanting to be less sexual with you, and so on).

If you and she have children, don't assume that helping out is enough. Avoid the attitude that the children are primarily her responsibility, and that you are simply babysitting them when you're with them. Truly co-parent. Be aware of what and how much she is doing to take care of them, and step in more, without her having to ask. Don't undervalue how much energy and attention she is putting into their upbringing. If the kids are toddlers or infants, does she have to ask you to look after them so that she can simply take a shower? You may not think about asking to take a nap or shower while she handles the kids; don't make her ask for such things.

Look deeply enough at her to see more than her surface presentation. See her vulnerability, her wounds, her uncertainty, her subtle signals. Notice when her facial expression and energy don't match her words. Sense what she may not be saying. Sense her feeling you seeing her.

If you're doing something for her in the hopes of having sex with her, while acting as if this isn't the case, admit this—not just to yourself but also to her. Explore what's motivating you to do this, and *stop!* For example, you're giving her a massage to increase the odds of having sex with her; she *can feel this* no matter how "clean" your massage strokes are, and will be much less at ease than if you were giving her massage for no other reason than that you love and care for her. Another example: a woman comes home to a beautiful dinner her husband just made her, followed by a special bath he drew, with everything placed carefully and esthetically. She feels a growing unhappiness, knowing that she'll be *expected* to be sexual with him afterward. Don't pressure her with your mounting expectations.

■ ■ ■

Treat each of these points not as a "should," but as an invitation. Persist in working with them, not to be a "good" partner, but a full partner, a warrior of intimacy.

16

Gay Men

Outsiders No Longer

EVERYTHING I'VE BEEN DISCUSSING in this book—shame, power, challenge, relational intimacy—applies to straight and gay men alike. However, there are concerns unique to gay men. It's crucial that these concerns not be ignored or marginalized, so that gay men might be more fully included in the consideration of what it means to be a man in contemporary culture.

Much of what plagues straight males tends to plague gay males even more.

Take, for example, the admonition to "be a man," which more often than not degrades males—of whatever age—for not making the grade, shaming them for not measuring up, driving them into behaviors that estrange them from much of their humanity. They inevitably fall short of iconic or cultural notions of manliness, "betrayed" by their vulnerability, insecurities, and other qualities that don't meet manly stereotypes and easily become things to be ashamed of and to disown or reject, forming a hefty part of their shadow. But straight men at least are on a relatively well-trod continuum of masculinity—including having had significant support, since the 1980s, to shift into a healthier maleness, as most recently modeled (however uncommonly) by straight men who approach intimate relationship with women as a path to healing and awakening.

Things are not so straightforward for gay males. The very exhortation to "be a man" not only is also degrading to them, and hugely shaming, but is far more confusing than for straight males. "Manning up" on the playing field in athletic and moneymaking contexts is at least something potentially achievable—but in the context of sexually succeeding with females, an arena of considerable status for most straight males, a gay male is in no position to "man up." And even if he apparently does, being with females in ways that seemingly fit heterosexual norms, he knows that he is lying to himself, which only further divides and debilitates him. Straight males may have a hell of a time fitting in, but gay males—especially those who have not yet reached their adult years—are in an even more difficult position, their outsider or "other" status unrelentingly gnawing at their self-presentation and self-esteem.

Is there even a continuum of masculine evolution for a gay man? What do *maleness* and *manliness* and being *man enough* mean for gay men? And what might be the qualities of their warrior of intimacy? How might such a one approach homosexual relationship? What might characterize his sexuality? Much of what follows addresses these questions, with the caveat that I'm not gay and am in part basing what I'm saying on the work I've done with gay men over the past three decades, work that was in most ways the same as the work I did with straight men, but with at least one big difference: that sexual closeness with women was not a relevant topic, except insofar as it existed before they openly accepted and embraced their homosexuality. (Also, for the purposes of this chapter, I speak of being gay and being straight as discrete categories, but they do appear to exist, to whatever degree, on a complex continuum. With regard to sexual orientation, there are varying shades of bisexuality between homosexuality and heterosexuality; and with regard to how one communicates one's gender, there are varying shades of androgyny between masculine and feminine.)

Gay men have clearly been—and in many ways still are—outsiders culturally, their masculinity often viewed as something other than, or less than, true masculinity, something often seen through heterosexual eyes as having more in common with femaleness than maleness. After all, masculinity does not, in any conventional context, mean having one's sexual desire directed at other males. Even if we fully accept gay men's sexual focus, we may still not view this as anything that constitutes manliness or even masculinity—equating masculine sexual expression as something that is only directed toward women. I remember feeling like less of an outsider and more like a man, once I'd had sex, but were I gay, I imagine that I might have felt even more like an outsider—and less of a man in a strictly conventional sense—once I'd had sex with another man.

If we equate being sexually attracted to men as something that women do, we might also view gay men's maleness as belonging more to the feminine than masculine realm—while still perhaps being quite tolerant of gay men and their rights. Such tolerance is certainly better than its opposite, but stops short of any significant understanding of what it means to be gay in a mostly non-gay world. Homosexuality will remain too "other" to us until we humanize and empathize with it, seeing it not as something unfortunate or aberrant, but as something that, like heterosexuality, has both unhealthy and healthy forms. The stages of intimate relationship—ranging from me-centered to we-centered to being-centered—transcend sexual orientation.

Shame is probably the biggest obstacle that faces straight men, especially the shame of not being able to measure up to what culturally constitutes manhood; the shame that, as boys, they learned to get away from as quickly as possible—whether through aggressiveness (toward others and/or themselves), emotionally withdrawing, overachieving, cultivating a compensatory pride, or establishing themselves in positions where they seemingly couldn't be shamed.

The same is true for gay men, with the added shame of not just falling short of what supposedly makes one a man, but also of not even being in a position in which showing up as a man is possible in any conventional sense other than that of succeeding athletically, academically, or materially. And even in such success, they still remain outsiders culturally and sexually. They may still feel shame over not being an unambiguous and clearly accepted part of one's culture, simply because so many in that very culture categorically shun or marginalize them for not being heterosexual. And, once they've publicly affirmed their homosexuality, there still might be shame over feeling relief at not having to meet some standard of conventional manliness.

I have seen straight men in despair, often covering it with toughness and emotional hardness, determined not to crack, even though they were screaming from the inside to be let out. When they at last stopped keeping their vulnerability gagged and bound, and ceased letting their shame and fear paralyze them, what release, what deep tears, what rich opening and realization, what a reclamation of wonder and effortless presence, what a healing sense of belonging!

And I have also seen gay men in despair, sometimes toughing it out, and sometimes covering it with an armored softness, determined not to let their emotional pain fully surface, even though they were aching to be felt and seen and known beyond their sexuality. Their deeper vulnerability was usually not hard to access. When they ceased letting their shame and fear paralyze them, what release, what healing rage and tears, what rich opening and realization, what a reclamation of wonder and effortless presence, what deep tenderness and compassion—and fierce protectiveness—for the boys they were before they were ever called "fag" or "homo." And what about their sense of belonging? It's not that they necessarily joined heterosexual men in an awakened brotherhood—though this often happened—but that they came to rest in (and *as*) their bare essence, no longer outsiders at the level of pure being, no longer separated from others because of their sexual orientation.

Straight men vary hugely in their emotional and psychological makeup, and so do gay men, regardless of the commonly paraded stereotypes of the debonair, style-obsessed, conspicuously effeminate gay man. Some of my gay male clients have been very tender and transparent, softly constructed and expressed—and so too have been some of my straight male clients. What we often take to be feminine qualities—vulnerability, softness, tenderness, empathy, emotional literacy, conversational effusiveness and fluidity—are found in many men, especially gay men. But the more that gay men display such qualities, the more that all too many straight men tend to relegate them to the feminine (or lesser) side of the tracks, rather than seeing these qualities as legitimate expressions of maleness, whether gay or not.

And this is where gay men arguably have a cultural advantage over straight men: they have more permission—and a higher degree of acceptance—to openly possess and show qualities commonly associated with being female. This can have unpleasant consequences, as when homophobes speak of gay men as though they're less than men, embodying as they do qualities that supposedly belong to women. But aside from such ugly intolerance, having more cultural association between one's sexual orientation and emotional expressiveness and openness can be a big plus, if only because stepping out of emotionally repressed states—however partially or narrowly—is a far healthier practice than staying emotionally disconnected or contracted. The gay men I've worked with have been more readily and transparently expressive, quicker to reveal their inner workings, than many of the straight men I've worked with—however much they were troubled by such hard-to-hide openness.

Both straight and gay men are well acquainted with the pressure of keeping up appearances; neither are pleased about losing face, as usually happens when shame emphatically kicks in. Much of what straight men do is a strategy to avoid or minimize shame, a strategy to not let the sag and collapse and discombobulating presence of shame be visible to others. The same may be even more true for gay men. And why? Because, in general, not only do they carry the shame of falling short of what's expected of men in our culture but often also the shame of being apparently defective at the most basic level, possessing all the equipment of maleness, externally and internally, but generally having an innate leaning that disqualifies them, by many standards, from being healthily male (despite the long history of homosexual inclusion in societies worldwide).

Most gay men, like most straight men, likely grew up in families in which heterosexual parents—father and mother—were the role models for intimate relationship, for better or for worse. Even if it was far from functional, it was still the relational go-to form, usually with the potential to improve, at least to some degree. Whatever the quality of the parents' relationship, there nonetheless was probably at least some sense that a healthier form was possible.

But was there any model for a lasting man-to-man intimacy beyond the pleasantries of friendly brotherhood? Probably not. There was perhaps some sense of homosexual possibility, as conveyed through various media outlets, but the very shame implicit in seriously considering this would tend to keep it far in the background, setting up young gay men for secretive trysts, anonymous enough to be emotionally shed quite quickly, almost as if they had not occurred. In most cases, having no in-the-flesh models for man-to-man intimate relationship—and not just a sexual one—more often than not made the nonsexual part of gay relationship little more than a no-man's-land haunted by a closeness just out of reach, no matter how passionate or central the sex.

More than a few gay men are promiscuous—some secretly and some openly—and are commonly judged for this as being more screwed up than straight men. But *many* straight men are just as promiscuously *inclined,* even if they *might* act it out less often. A man can be with his wife, not have affairs, but use pornography, often behind her back, internally interacting erotically with many women, with as much promiscuous proclivity as any gay man. In both cases, men are avoiding real intimacy, whether in a nameless sexual exchange in a bathroom stall, or in front of a computer screen alight with pornographic visuals.

In a cultural context, the straight man arguably has it easier sexually, for he is into women only (with the exception of those who sexually engage with other men for non-gay reasons, ranging from acting out childhood sexual abuse to finding sexual outlets in prison)—and being lovers with a woman is still more accepted culturally than being lovers with a man, regardless of how liberally our society might okay gay relationship and marriage. The gay man, by contrast, has it harder, for he is viewed by many as engaging in something unnatural or even ungodly; a man who treats his wife horribly is still seen by such people as preferable to a man who treats his male lover with great care. Homophobia covered by layers of politically correct acceptance and tolerance is still homophobia.

Many men are terrified of their own potential for homosexuality, keeping it in the shadows, perhaps camouflaging it by emphatically denouncing homosexuality, even pronouncing it an abomination. But a certain percentage of men (and women) are, from before birth, wired for homosexuality. What are they to do about this, especially in cultures that still widely condemn it? They can try denial, they can make a show of being with women, they can model themselves after masculine icons, they can avoid behaviors commonly associated with being gay, they can live where few gay men live. But none of this works, any more than does acting a certain role in a play, and then trying to maintain that role for the rest of our lives. We talk of coming out of the closet, rather than out of the house, because closets are generally dark, cramped spaces, suitable for hanging clothes but not for housing us. Some gay men I've worked with had wives, kids, great careers, were seen by all their acquaintances as highly successful—but they were living a lie, and eventually that lie blew the closet doors off, to both their shame and their relief.

In premodern times, homosexuality was often culturally contained as a practice not between peers, but between a male (usually older and of significantly higher social status), and a less dominant male (usually younger and lacking in such status). Penetration and being in charge were the prerogative of the more dominant male; his sexual partner usually had but one option—submission, whatever its social perks. (This dynamic is also present in male chimpanzee and gorilla homosexual encounters; for females, the dynamic is very different, being all about bonding, so as to enhance security.) Back then, homosexuality was primarily rooted in the context of establishing and maintaining rank, thereby supporting the social order, however barbaric that might have been. Being penetrative was strongly associated with being masculine (just as it is in the rougher realms of current masculinity, as epitomized by prison and gang hierarchies). "Taking it up the ass" is still largely viewed, both literally and metaphorically, as the act of a weaker or submissive man, carrying a sense of diminishment and shame.

But contemporary homosexuality is not about rank, and there is no social order for it to play a supportive role in. More and more, it is about the meeting of peers, at whatever level. There's no conventional container for such relationships. And in fact, contemporary gayness feels like a social threat to many, the intrusion of a distinct "other" into everyday life. To really welcome the gay man into our non-gay midst is in the spirit of welcoming what we've disowned in ourselves back into the circle of our being. No outcasts.

Everyone begins life with a primal connection to a woman—their mother—and registers that shared beingness very deeply, for better or for worse. We may not recall our birth and early infancy through narrative (or everyday) memory, but we do recall it *emotionally*, since the parts of the brain that handle emotional memory are sufficiently developed at birth. Straight men may, however unknowingly, be automatically returning to deeply familiar, primordial territory when they intimately partner with women. But gay men, arguably, are not *automatically* brought back to this place of primordial resting and attachment in their intimate partnering. There's no amniotic or foundational femaleness to be enfolded in, no maternal harbor to rest in. However, such femaleness can be brought into a gay couple's relationship, not only through the cultivation of openheartedness and compassion, but also through becoming intimate with the feminine side that exists in every man, allowing it to be more in the foreground. Real intimacy transcends gender and sexual orientation.

Those of us who are not gay cannot fully embody our manhood without including gay men in our circle of being. Keeping them in the shadows, ostracizing or marginalizing them, forcing ourselves to be tolerant of them, viewing them as constituting a lesser form of maleness, avoiding them, reducing them to caricatures of manliness, ignoring their presence and the common ground we share—all this must shift into a true acceptance of homosexuality, but with no more excusing of its unhealthy manifestations than we would the unhealthy manifestations of heterosexuality. The gay man need not be part of our shadow; his humanity and ours are to be embraced and allowed to evolve into forms that benefit one and all, leaving us not as straight or gay men, but simply as *men*.

17

Deep Connection

Foundational Practices
for Intimate Relationship

INTIMATE RELATIONSHIP is arguably the twenty-first cen-
tury's ashram. It's not, however, a retreat or refuge from everyday life,
but a transformational growth center located in the very midst of it,
offering experiential courses in whatever generates and deepens intimacy, courses uniquely fitting for those entering its domain. Its goal
is not transcendence, but *full-spectrum intimacy*, not only with your
partner, but also with all that you are—dark and light, high and low,
petty and noble, deep and shallow.

If you are seeking transformation, you need look no further than
doing what it takes to fully be in such relationship. This is a great undertaking that asks much of us, and gives back more than we can imagine.

The path isn't neatly laid out, because we, with our partner, are
cocreating it as we deepen our intimacy, stepping into and embracing
a trailblazing mutuality, without having to know where we're going.

Implicit in this is a rare trust, an ongoing, shared willingness to
bring not only our very best to the relationship, but also to expose
our worst—not to be acted out or otherwise indulged in, but to be
faced and integrated and related to in ways that serve our relationship.
Nothing in us gets left out—it's all part of our relationship. This is
more than possible when—through our work on ourselves—our relationship becomes both sanctuary and crucible, a place of deep healing,
care, life-enhancing challenge, and a love that pervades all that we are.

What an adventure! And what an opportunity—not to romanticize, but to soberly face and embrace, beginning right where you are, embodying as much as possible a full-blooded "yes" to all the foundational practices that can make this a reality. And it's an adventure that doesn't plateau. I'm sixty-seven, and see no end to the deepening of my intimacy with my beloved Diane (who is sixty-three), and I am absolutely fine with that. Every day, I am grateful that she and I get to be together. There may not be much time left, but what's left is enough. The deepest growth, healing, and awakening I've ever experienced has been in my relationship with Diane. Hence my wholehearted recommendation that you do whatever it takes to move into or to deepen your intimate relationship. The foundational practices that follow are offered in the spirit of such intimacy.

When you realize you're being reactive, immediately say out loud, or under your breath to yourself, "I'm being reactive." How simple this sounds, and yet how challenging it can be to put into practice—mostly because of the shame we're on the edge of fully feeling as we become aware of our reactivity. Once you've stated that you're being reactive, *stop.* Say nothing more, no matter how tempted you might be to continue your reactivity. Soften your belly, breathe more deeply, and wait until you're ready to say what you're feeling *and nothing more,* until the grip of your reactivity has clearly waned.

Learn to express your remorse from your heart. Don't settle for shallow or emotionally flat expression. If you're not sorry, don't say you are. But if you've done something that's hurt the other, and the words "I'm sorry" get stuck in your throat, admit that you're having a hard time saying it. Such a confession, openly stated, will often soften you enough to allow your remorse a fitting voice. Try simply telling your partner that you feel shame about what you've done.

If you're being defensive and know it, don't hesitate to say so. Be your own whistleblower. Don't wait for the other to pressure you into owning up to your defensiveness. And don't slip into being defensive about being defensive!

Don't allow emotional disconnection to last any longer than necessary. When you lose touch with your partner, reestablish it as soon as possible. If you're staying emotionally disconnected to punish her or him, confess this without delay, regardless of how uncomfortable that may be.

Deepen your curiosity about what you least know about yourself. The better you know yourself—and such knowing is not just intellectual—the more available you'll be for truly intimate relationship.

Don't allow what's working in your relationship to obscure what isn't. When there's a relational conflict, resist trotting out your good points or using them to extricate yourself from the hot seat. Don't let your strengths camouflage your weaknesses.

Never threaten to leave the relationship in order to get your own way or to make your partner beg you to stay. If you feel like being manipulative, say so, rather than acting it out. Turn your desire to leave into something to explore rather than acting out. Threats are negative promises, and are usually dependent on moods—if you really want to leave a relationship, such wanting will remain present no matter how good, bad, or indifferent you feel.

Don't confuse accepting the other with accepting whatever the other does. If your partner has behaved disturbingly or hurtfully, and says, "This is just the way I am; accept me as I am" (perhaps along with alibis like "I'm just human" or "I never said I was perfect"), don't let yourself be seduced by this. And avoid the temptation to use this excuse yourself!

Learn how to give yourself without giving yourself away. As you open up and reveal more of yourself, don't abandon your boundaries. Instead, *expand* them to include the other, while maintaining your autonomy.

When your inner critic shows up in an interaction with your partner, immediately name it. Then report what it's saying. So instead of stating "I'm pathetic," say, "My inner critic says I'm pathetic." Don't allow your inner critic to masquerade as you nor disempower you.

Learn to recognize when the child in you takes over, clearly communicating that to your partner. Embrace and protect that aspect of yourself without adopting its viewpoint. When the child in you shows up strongly—especially during a relational conflict—ask yourself how old you feel, and share that with your partner. You might say something like: "Wow, my five-year-old boy just showed up!" or "The way I'm feeling is the way I felt when I was a kid being put down by my father."

Don't let the "nice guy"—the one who's confrontation-phobic—in you prevent you from taking strong stands. Recognize the wounding that animates the "nice guy" in you and keeps him a harmony junkie, and bring that wounding into the open.

If you find yourself on eggshells with the other, get off them completely, without getting pushy, aggressive, or disrespectful. Find a deeper sensitivity than that of being overly careful with the other. Explore the roots of your emotional and psychological tiptoeing, including your fears of what might happen if you stop being so careful, and openly share this with the other.

Learn to listen with your whole being, not letting your thoughts distract you. This means being mindful of what's arising in you as you listen, and not allowing it to get in the way of your listening.

When you're emotionally overloaded, make space for having a conscious rant. See the appendix for a detailed description. Read through it carefully before you attempt a conscious rant.

Instead of using sex to build connection, let sex be a fully embodied expression of already-present connection. When you want to have sex, but aren't feeling very connected to your partner, turn your attention to your emotional state, and do what it takes to bring *that* into your heart, including talking about it with your partner in a manner that deepens connection, however vulnerable this might make you feel.

Learn to look with compassion upon all that remains unhealed in you and your partner. Doing so helps creates a conducive space—simultaneously nourishing and challenging—for whatever healing is needed.

Remember that the deeper you dive, the less you'll mind any upsetting waves. View your relationship as an ever-evolving adventure, potentially deepened by all that happens, however unpleasant. You may hurt more as you mature—because you're more open to feeling—but you'll mind less.

Continue making your connection with your partner a top priority. Keep it central. Keep it alive and thriving, and don't begrudge the time it takes to do so.

Don't take any of the preceding practices as "shoulds," but rather as guidelines, invitations, and reminders. Invest enough time and energy in them, and they will become second nature—and well worth the effort!

■ ■ ■

Intimate relationship promises so, so much, but only delivers what we put into it. This does not mean that it's all work—far from it! Much of what we need to put into it is what we need to extend to the world anyway: our love, our compassion, our integrity, our courage, our yearning for a deeper life. And what a lucid joy it is to enter so fully in consciously shared living—shared heart, shared being, shared evolution—that everything that arises, no matter how painful, is permitted to further our intimacy.

And what a gift it is to be so close, so deeply attached and bonded, that we cannot get away, for very long, from facing things that we ordinarily would not face at all. Intimate relationship, fully entered into, keeps us on track.

Transformation through intimacy.

PART IV

Sex

The passion of the deepest sex primarily arises not from erotic excitation and stimulation, but from the presence of an intimacy rooted in deep trust, transparency, love, and emotional rawness and resonance, an intimacy that's the most potent of aphrodisiacs.

18

Eros Illuminated

An Introductory Look at Sexuality

SEX CAN BE a remarkably beautiful thing: an ecstatic communion in the flesh, overflowing with love and trust and full-blooded wonder. Sex as such succulently blends love, passion, gratitude, and emotional rawness, needing no fantasies for its arousal. It doesn't promise a loving closeness but *begins* with a loving closeness, being *an expression of already-present connection rather than a means to connection.* And its aphrodisiac? Our intimate, fully felt connection with the other.

And what's needed to access this? For starters, being committed to turning toward and working through whatever in us remains unhealed or is being kept in the dark, whatever we have tended to try to get away from through sexual activity. Much of what follows in this section is about releasing sex from the obligation of making us feel better or more secure or more manly. Doing so does not cut us off from our sexuality, or "unman" us, but frees us to settle into and express a sexuality that's profoundly satisfying and rejuvenating—a joyously embodied dance of passion, grace, and communion through which our essential manhood cannot help but be celebrated.

How central is sex for most men? Very.

Its apparent fulfillment—through whatever means—is the proverbial dangling carrot or go-to lure for all too many men, and tends to take up an exaggeratedly central position in their consciousness, regardless of how sexually active or inactive they may be.

This, however, is much more than just a matter of lust.

The biological imperative to be sexual—and to be prepared to be sexual—is far from a lightweight drive, and takes a dominant position in male mammals' to-do list when the time seems right (which may be most of the time). But to have this drive overamplified and on call for more than just sexual matters—like shoring up our self-image or decreasing our anxiety—keeps a man hooked to his sexual appetite, run by "the must in lust," rather than just periodically being caught up in it, increasing the odds that he'll be snared by pornography or the pull to cheat on his partner.

Sex tends to be the favored off-duty interest of many men, promising a pleasurable break from the rest of their lives. But the liberating power we often ascribe to sex can easily bind us to it. It's crucial not to underestimate the powerful narcotic pull that sex can have: consider all the men plugged into pornographic outlets, building enough erotic charge to seemingly necessitate masturbatory release, regardless of what kind of things they're viewing. It's easy to label those who are hooked on pornography as sex addicts, overlooking the fact that they're not so much addicted to sex as to getting away from the very emotional and/or psychological pain that continues to catalyze their pull toward pornography and what it promises.

In considering these men (including yourself, if you're in a similar bind), you may feel some aversion, some shame, but instead of stopping here, open yourself to their desperation, their underlying pain, their flight from relational intimacy. Let this awaken not only your compassion, but also your desire to help support their healing. Having compassion for the addict in them (and in yourself) does not mean that you let their behavior go unaddressed (nor that you tolerate their obsession with pornography), but that you do not lose touch with their basic humanity and suffering.

As much as men may long for freedom, often valuing it more than relationship—unless they've learned to find freedom *through* relational intimacy—they will not find it to any significant degree *until they've unchained their sexuality from the nonsexual tasks to which they've assigned it,* however unknowingly.

When JOHN was a young boy, his parents frequently fought in front of him, sometimes violently, and almost always contemptuously. They were not close, and made it clear that they didn't want to stay together. Their distance from and cruelty to each other frightened him; his way of comforting himself was to go to his room and lose himself in fantasy. As a teen, he found solace by keeping away from home as much as possible, and through masturbating, arousing himself by imagining girls in his school giving him their full interest while undressing before him.

As a man, he got heavily into pornography, feeling especially aroused when watching scenarios that featured a man and a woman being both very tender and very passionate in their sexual meeting. He had eroticized his desire to witness his parents meeting in loving connection, finding further excitement in being in control of this (even as he remained on the sidelines). At the same time, he'd chained himself to this ritual (so that it had become his go-to arousal strategy), using his sexuality to both act out and distract him from his unresolved childhood wounding. ■

Using sex for this purpose is very common. It may help us ease the difficulties of adolescence, but if we continue this into our adulthood, we're severely limiting our capacity to be in authentic relationship—because instead of taking responsibility for our old wounding and taking care of it, we'll just be continuing to act it out. How can we really be in intimate relationship with another when we have such a habit—the eroticizing of our unresolved wounds and unmet needs—being our sexual default (or what *really* turns us on)?

We need to stop isolating our sexuality from the rest of our being, and bring it—and whatever nonsexual factors are contributing to it—out of the shadows.

What we do sexually reflects what we're doing in the rest of our lives. The same conditioning is there, operating us to the degree that we're unaware of it, regardless of how sexually liberated or "sex-positive" we may think we are.

If you want to get closer to what makes you tick, take a lights-on look at your sexuality and all the factors that are part of it. Eros undressed, stripped down to what is animating it—this is an essential part of the work we are called to do, if we are to step into our full manhood and humanity, and is therefore a major section of this book. However much we may differ in our conditioning, we all have in common the capacity to cease letting it run us, including sexually. In the following chapters, we'll consider:

- the ways in which sex is still in the closet

- the nonsexual tasks to which we've assigned our sexuality

- eroticitis—obsessive interest in sexual activity, possibility, and opportunity

- the eroticizing of our unresolved wounds and insufficiently met needs

- pornography—its anatomy, pull, and impact, and how to outgrow it

- taking charge of our charge—no longer playing victim to our sexual arousal

- our relationship to our penis

- our fascination with breasts

- rape—its formative factors, why it's so prevalent, and what to do about it

- whether all men have an inner rapist

- releasing sex from the obligation to make us feel better or more secure

- sex as an expression of connection rather than a means of creating connection

19

Sex Uncovered

Freeing Your Sexuality from the Obligation to Make You Feel Better

SEX IS, IN MANY WAYS, still in the dark.

Yes, it's wearing much less and showing a lot more than it was fifty years ago, but it's still not truly out in the open, except in mostly superficial ways. Its ubiquitous exposure, graphic highlighting, and relentless pornification simply camouflage its deeper workings. However brazenly explicit or conversationally undressed sex now is, it still remains largely hidden, its depths mostly untouched, its heartland still largely unknown, obscured by the tasks to which we commonly assign it, especially those of making us feel better or more manly.

Just as being openly angry doesn't necessarily bring us any closer to truly *knowing* our anger, being openly sexual doesn't necessarily bring us any closer to truly *knowing* our sexuality.

An essential step to bringing sex fully out of the closet is realizing—and not just intellectually—that *the greater our investment is in distracting ourselves from our suffering, the greater our craving for sexual arousal and release may tend to be.*

The greater that craving is, the more likely it is that we'll become hyperfocused on sex. Consider how even the slightest hint of sex effortlessly seizes many a man by the mind and eyes, riveting his gaze to certain body parts of passing females, as though he were a swivel-headed puppet on a string, effortlessly held captive by perceived feminine allure (even if that allure is highlighted by false breasts).

Sex has that much power to distract, that much narcotic appeal, that much liberation-suffused promise. Sex functions in other ways, but its capacity to make us feel better quickly is arguably its primary lure, its hook par excellence. After all, doesn't just the possible promise of erotic engagement tend to push our pain more into the background?

THE SELLING OF SEX

Sex sells. And we're buying. Get enough people to think that someone or something is sexy, and you're in business. Get enough people convinced that a certain "amazing" approach to their sex life will arouse their partner into lusting for them again, and you're in business. There is so, so much that we expect sex to do for us—and how could we think otherwise, given the consistent megamarketing it gets, both collectively and in our fantasies?

It's so easy to assign an inordinate liberating power to sex, especially when we crave a potent, drugless, close-at-hand distraction from our suffering. Sex makes us feel better—or at least relieved—in a hurry, and our culture keeps bombarding with this promise. We see this, and perhaps cast a cynical eye, but don't often see the various labors to which we may have assigned our sexuality: make me feel better, make me feel more secure, de-stress me, prove that I'm wanted, make me feel whole, console me, resurrect my sense of self, make me feel more powerful or manly, help me feel less lonely. Sex has a lot on its back—we've saddled it with so much hope and expectation, whether in mundane or spiritual contexts.

And we might even find fault with sex, blaming it for our misuse of it, as exemplified by proclamations of our helplessness before our amplified sexual charge: "The flesh is weak" or "She brought out the beast in me, so I . . ." We can also put sex on a pedestal, equating doing whatever we want to do sexually with having sexual freedom, perhaps ennobling such indulgence by framing it as some sort of revolutionary or postconventional or tantric or sex-positive act.

In so doing, however, we just get fucked—mostly in nonsexual contexts—bringing little or no awareness to what we're actually up to while being sexual. Thus do we tend to keep sex in the basement.

Sometimes we may spiritualize it, burdening it with tantric or metaphysical expectations, as if it were the gateway to super-consciousness or "higher" realities. But in all this, sex is just doing time, enslaved to our nonsexual ambitions.

Sex sells. And we continue to buy. Cost is not an issue, given how valuable the potential payoff may be. The more stress we're under, the more dysfunctional our relationship is, the more insecure we are, the more unresolved wounding we carry, the more appealing sex may become to us. As long as we're having sex—or letting sex have us—we have a bit of distance from the mess or distress we're in.

This makes us ever more attached—perhaps to the point of addiction—to whatever most easily and powerfully amplifies our sexual charge, magnetizing our attention to whatever we deem sexy, with a special focus reserved for what is most sexually arousing of all for us.

THE LANGUAGE OF SEX

The word *fuck* says a fuck of a lot about what we may be up to during our sexual encounters. Its multiple meanings—including indifference, aggression, disappointment, and exploitation—are testimony to many of the nonsexual dynamics that may be at play while we are being sexual. More than we might like to admit, we may be "getting fucked"—getting screwed or getting the short end of the stick—while we're busy being sexual, and not just during intercourse, perhaps losing more than our integrity along the way.

There may be times when we are far from getting thus fucked during sex, but these, unfortunately, don't constitute the majority of sexual activity for many of us, and may in fact sometimes keep us hanging on in a relationship that is otherwise harmful for us, providing a little of what is so sorely missing in the rest of our relationship. The trouble is, we are then *overrelying* on sex to deliver the goods, which just increases the pressure to keep having it, a pressure that sooner or later backfires, leaving us immersed in the midst of what our sex was an antidote to, facing the far-from-sexy consequences of what we've marginalized or left unattended in our relationship.

Why is *sexy* such an incredibly popular adjective? Because in its very voicing or visual placement (like in ads) there's an instant implication of being attractive or appealing, of being wanted, of magnetically drawing others to us, of being special, of standing out so much that we cannot be overlooked. Being sexy may mean being "hot" (an extremely common, status-increasing term). *Sexy* and *hot* are labels that reflect and reinforce our culture's obsession not only with sex itself but also with employing pleasurably heightened sensation to distract us from our hurt, our depression, our anxiety, our apathy, our grief over what we've done with our lives.

Thankfully, there's an inherent dissatisfaction in trying to free ourselves from our underlying pain through maximizing pleasurable sensations—no matter how high or erotically charged we get, we come down, more often than not energetically drained, perhaps returning to our sexual habits with a touch more disillusionment.

BRINGING SEX OUT OF THE CLOSET

For all the overexposure that sex gets in contemporary culture, its *nonsexual underpinnings* still remain largely hidden. And not because we're blind, but because we may not really want to see them. And why? Because plenty of times, if we were to actually see what we were up to—besides being sexual—while in the throes of sexual arousal and activity, we might have to do something other than merely continue our sexual encounter. And who wants to interrupt or derail such a feel-good (or potentially feel-good) process? Our clothes may be off, and our appetites turned on high, but we might still be covering up, to at least some degree. There is a *deeper disrobing* needed, a deeper self-disclosure, along with a working through of whatever has driven us to use our sexuality to distance or distract ourselves from what is unhealed in us.

If enough of us were fully engaged in healing our wounds and awakening from our entrapping dreams, there wouldn't be a pornography epidemic. Pornography is so ubiquitous that it's been normalized (except in its darkest extremes), and those who question it are—whatever their maturity—often categorized as prudes, old-fashioned, sex-negative, repressed, conservative, or just plain uptight. But the pervasiveness of pornography *and* the commonplace tolerance of it indicate that something is terribly amiss in contemporary culture. The point is neither to repress nor indulge in pornography, but to *outgrow* it. And this begins with seeing through it and its dehumanizing impact, until its nonsexual roots (including our unresolved hurt and compensatory behaviors from our early years) are clearly exposed and worked with.

We can look back at the sexuality of the Victorian era, and think that we have come a long way since then, but in many of the really important ways we haven't, regardless of sex-positive advocacy (the uncritical acceptance of the sexually nonconventional), so-called open relationships, omnipresent sexiness, and so on. We're still keeping sex in the shadows to a significant degree, no matter how bright the lights seem. In both the Victorian era and our own, the underlying non-sexual and presexual dynamics of sex are mostly kept out of sight. Yes, we are far more open when it comes to the nuts and bolts and close-ups of sex, and have an easy surplus of every type of pornography at our fingertips, but to interpret this as somehow meaning that we have more sexual freedom is just misguided thinking: having more choices doesn't necessarily mean having more freedom.

The Victorian era was of course extremely screwed up about sex. To take but one example, consider its absurd, yet deadly serious, take on the dangerous results of masturbating (insanity, hair sprouting on the palms, and so on). But our era is arguably just as screwed up about sex. To take but one example, consider its general sanction of sexualizing prepubescent girls (as if ten-year-old girls should have the "freedom" to dress and act like prostitutes). It seems that our era and the Victorian one are two sides of the same erotic coin. The Victorians went to one extreme, and we to the other.

Consider their claim that masturbation is a terrible thing, and our common claim that it is a beneficial thing. Sure, it's not terrible, but is it a truly *beneficial* practice? If masturbation, hand in hand with its attendant fantasies, follows us into our adult relationships and remains an enticingly *central* operational possibility during sex with our partner, just how life-giving is that? Masturbation can provide some release, but it is usually far from intimacy, if only because at such times we may be so focused on ourselves and our urge for erotic discharge that our partner is little more than a prop in our masturbatory drama. And if we don't have a partner, our probable overreliance on sexual fantasy for masturbatory release will likely make any direct connection with future partners problematic.

For a man to be with his own sexuality in a genuinely uncloseted way, he needs to:

- explore the ways in which his sexuality hooks or obsesses him, recognizing its nonsexual dynamics and how he might be acting these out sexually;

- do enough work with his conditioning (his old wounding and reactivity) so that it doesn't get channeled into and expressed through his sexuality;

- be honest about whatever nonsexual payoffs he's seeking through sex;

- expose any shame he has about sex and his sexual functioning;

- not leave his heart, emotions, and vulnerability out of his sexuality;

- cease relying on sexual fantasy to get turned on or to stay turned on;

- release his sexuality from any pressure to make him feel better;

- stop isolating his sexuality from the rest of his being; and

- not let the supposed goal of sexual "completion" (orgasm) overshadow his connection with his partner, allowing such connection—fully and nakedly felt—to be his aphrodisiac.

■ ■ ■

Going to the heart of sex is not necessarily a sexy or hot journey, but it can be an exciting passage, a far-from-cozy adventuring. Discovering what we may actually be up to during sex can be a bit of a shock, but it is a potentially *liberating* shock, a kind of rude awakening that alerts us to our own need for healing, awakening, and integration.

As we bring sex *authentically* out of the dark, in both personal and collective contexts, we are furthered in our humanity, more deeply established in living in ways that serve more than just our own well-being. We don't lose our sexuality in this process, but are deepened and expanded in it, becoming capable of genuine intimacy, no longer burdening our sexuality with the obligation to make us feel better or more secure or whole, letting it be a wonderfully alive expression and celebration of *already-present* joy and wholeness.

20

Eroticitis

Obsessive or Compulsive Interest in Sexual Activity and Possibility

EROTICITIS, by which I mean an excessive or obsessive interest in sexual activity, opportunity, or possibility, is very common in contemporary culture, having become all but normalized. Frequently mistaken for healthy, robust sexual interest or a strong libido, eroticitis is commonly taken to be a sign of manliness, except in its uglier or clearly abusive extremes.

Eroticitis's disproportionate focus on things sexual both marks it and keeps it in business—and also provides a potent distraction from whatever wounding underlies and catalyzes the "need" for it.

Our task isn't to repress whatever eroticitis we may have, but to stop giving ourselves to it, to stand back far enough from it to see it clearly, to relate *to* it rather than *from* it. This task, this labor of love, does not desexualize or suppress us, but helps liberate our sexuality from the expectations with which we've saddled it (like "Make me feel like more of a man" or "Make me feel special").

If we are to truly free ourselves sexually, we have to understand, deglamorize, and outgrow eroticitis.

EROTICITIS AND SEXUAL EXCITATION

Eroticitis makes sexual excitation and its amplification far too important, overly attaching us to what most successfully fuels such excitation.

This intensifies not only our sense of internal pressure (getting seriously heated up), but also our urge for energetic discharge, with a special emphasis on the release provided by orgasm.

However, such release, whatever its cultural hype, is neither ecstasy nor liberation, but at best only brief relief, akin to the sensation felt when you at last remove an extremely tight pair of shoes. Repeatedly putting such shoes back on, in order to later have—no, *necessitate*—as pleasurable as possible an energetic discharge, is fundamental to the practice of eroticitis. The longer we leave the shoes on, the more satisfying the release when we take them off.

Thus do we become addicted not only to the release, but *also* to the buildup of tension that makes the release such a highly anticipated goal. This dynamic has many men by the balls and mind, binding them to the repetitive energetic circle of craving-tension-release-craving-tension-release.

Eroticitis keeps us in heat, ultra-available for sexualized activity. There's an engrossing edginess to eroticitis that has enough thrill—amped-up excitation—embedded in it to distract us from the discomfort of its swollen appetite. Excitation itself is not inherently problematic, but in the context of eroticitis, it is, driving us in unhealthy or destructive directions (for example, isolating ourselves in pornographic chambers).

Eroticitis is kept on the burner by our urge for release—through sexual means—from its contractedness and underlying pain (the wounding that first drove us into compensatory activities, erotic and otherwise). Compounding this is the additional friction—sometimes far from pleasant—generated by the pressure to ramp up, and keep ramping up, sexual excitation. Eroticitis can be one hell of an itch.

In eroticitis, we crave getting rid of the intensity of sexual desire itself—through orgasm—even as we fuel it again and again, putting ourselves in a position where we seemingly must have some sort of release, some sort of orgasmic payoff, some kind of pleasurable discharge and sedation—which only deprives us of much of the very energy that we need to truly investigate the source of our distress. Eroticitis is far from a happy thing.

SEX WITHOUT EROTICITIS

Eroticitis promises happiness, but real sex *begins* with happiness.

Such sex is intimate play, spontaneous and fully alive, needing no distress for its intensity, no preconceived or mechanical stimulation for its passion, no tight shoes, no fantasy for its ecstasy, no strategies (tantric and otherwise) for its depth.

Although sex in truly intimate relationship can include intensely heightened stimulation, this is not generated through strategic or merely frictional means. Instead, it spontaneously arises as a *natural by-product* of the partners' *already-present* connection and love-play. They already feel good; they already feel loose and easy; they're not expecting or pressuring sex to make them feel good. They are not suppressing their being and making a goal or grail out of sexual release, for they are already at ease, already present in loving erotic mutuality, already consciously and willingly surrendered to their passion's heat and light.

By overfocusing on the must in lust, eroticitis cheapens sexual desire, stripping it of much of its natural spontaneity and expansiveness, injecting it with compensatory fantasy. As such, eroticitis is no more than a misuse of imagination.

If we need to fantasize to have "good" sex, then we are not so much interested in sex as we are in mind games that primarily aim to maximize pleasurable sensation and release.

Sex does not require the thought- and image-generating activities of mind in order to function well, and in fact will not flow fully and freely and lovingly if thoughts and fantasies are allowed to intrude into and dominate its domain.

And what happens to eroticitis when sex is no longer allowed to go to mind (or be conceptually engineered)? What becomes of it when we put the effort into facing and healing the very wounding that first drove us into it? What becomes of it when love is already present, and both lovers are already open, relaxed, and in deep communion?

Eroticitis then loses its mind and operational imperatives, becoming the playful expression of sexual desire and passion, its face that of longing—not a tense or ambitious or desperate longing, but a heartfelt open-eyed longing—a yearning to share our depths with our partner through sexplay that's as loving as it is alive, as joyously embodied as it is intimate, as subtle as it is powerful. The point is not to shame ourselves for being caught up in eroticitis, but to put as much energy as possible into facing and working through whatever underlies it.

21

Eroticizing Our Wounds

Acting Out Old Hurt through Sexual Channels

THE MORE WE KEEP what's unhealed in us in the dark, the more likely it will show up in our sex lives.

Our unresolved wounds—and insufficiently met or badly handled needs—inevitably show up in our sexuality, however indirectly, often masquerading as a part of a healthy sexual life, the characteristics of which may be taken as nothing more than natural aspects of our sexuality. What's being *acted out sexually* then goes unseen, getting no more from us than an undiscerning green light. As such, sex does double duty, on the one hand dramatizing what's unhealed in us, and on the other briefly taking the edge off it.

As a boy, GEORGE was heavily rejected by his mother, which led him to (1) assume he was worthless, and (2) have a charge (a compelling excitation, whether negative or positive) both with not feeling wanted and with wanting to be wanted. He grew up expecting and attracting rejection—and found plenty of it—as well as craving full acceptance. As a teen, he eroticized this charge, absorbing himself in masturbatory fantasies in which he was unquestionably wanted sexually, without any trace of rejection.

This has continued into his adult years. His sexual fantasies are more elaborate, but are still basically all about him being surrounded by women who ache for him sexually, women who would never reject him. He's in charge; he decides who gets to have him. He hasn't at all worked through what his mother did to him—he simply has a place where she is excluded, even though his unresolved issues with her provide the fuel needed to keep this place afloat.

The negative excitation and contractedness he experienced as a boy when he was being rejected continues to be eroticized, so his strongest sexual excitement involves situations in which he is (or imagines himself to be) in clear control of the woman he's with, putting her in a position where it is extremely difficult to reject him. His core wound (being rejected) is not being faced and healed, but is being acted out through being eroticized. He continues to keep himself where he doesn't have to openly feel that wound, even as he pursues its unrequited longing (to be unconditionally wanted) in sexual contexts.

He may be getting what he wants, at least superficially, but he remains stuck, turned away from what he *needs* to turn toward: his core hurt, his original wounding. Only when he strips his fantasy of its erotic elements will he clearly see its underlying *nonsexual* dynamics and start to take care of the devastated boy he once was—and in many ways still is. ▪

It's very common to unquestioningly normalize sexual fantasies and practices that are not really expressions of our sexuality, but rather of our unresolved hurt and core wounding. Wanting to be smacked during sex is not some harmless bit of adult kinkiness, but an eroticizing of having been—especially as a child—thus struck or threatened with violence (or having had to repeatedly witness violence up close between family members), the excitation of which (regardless of its negativity) has remained with us, including in its translation into sexual contexts.

Watching and enjoying pornography in which women are being treated horribly is not just a matter of harmless adult arousal (better to watch it than do it, right?). Rather, it is a matter of unilluminated conditioning, likely resulting from (1) when we were boys, having watched females (mother, sisters, school acquaintances) getting treated badly; (2) *having felt a lot of charge, however negative, in seeing this* (perhaps also having felt immobilized as an observer back then, frozen to the spot, filled with adrenaline); and (3) sexualizing this charge, and seeking some release (however brief) from it through masturbating while watching pornographic depictions of women being abused.

The point is not to get morally righteous about this—for doing so only drives it further into the dark, and probably increases its appeal—but to look deeply enough into it to see its psychological, emotional, and social underpinnings. In my work with men, I've not yet heard a sexual fantasy or pornographic pull that was not directly and clearly related to childhood and/or adolescent dynamics. The hard part isn't connecting the dots, but taking action based on such insight, action that deepens our integrity.

WHY THE EROTICIZING OF OUR WOUNDS GETS LITTLE RECOGNITION

Although the eroticizing of our unresolved wounds and unmet needs is a major factor in sexual and psychological dysfunction, it is not often recognized as such. Part of the reason for this is that many of us don't want our sexual life interfered with, unless this involves amplifying its pleasurable possibilities; sex may be our only respite from an otherwise unpleasant or tedious life, and we're loath to tamper with it.

Another reason for why the eroticizing of our wounds gets skimpy press is that many of us are afraid to be openly critical of pornography and certain sexual practices, not wanting to be seen as puritanical, straitlaced, old-fashioned, sex-negative, conservative, or morally archaic. This fear keeps many of us overly tolerant, except when it's safe to be critical, as when everyone else seems to feel the same way (like in the condemnation of child pornography).

Cutting through *the myth of consenting adults* is crucial here—recognizing that the "yes" of many is not arising from their core of being, but from their wounding, their fear of saying "no" or of not being approved of or liked. If, as children, we associated saying "no" with danger or a withdrawal of love—and if we have not worked this through—we likely will not voice it (or voice it authentically) in situations where we don't really want to participate, but nonetheless think we *should* consent to (perhaps out of concern that we'll be met with disapproval or rejection, if we don't thus consent).

We may also say "yes" as an expression of defiance, as against controlling parents, eroticizing our acting out against their wishes. There is also a "yes" that is but the exhilaration of overriding our disgust, displeasure, or guilt. Another "yes" could be that of a woman who, ordinarily feeling powerless, uses her sexuality to overpower or control a man, thus feeling for a short while some degree of power. It's essential to know where our "yes"—and the "yes" of the other—is coming from, ideally before we act on it.

The point is not to analyze sex to death, to dissect it for emotionally removed study, but to go to its heart, learning to recognize all the ways we've misused it, all the ways we've chained it to the labor of making us feel better or more wanted or more secure. There is no better place to begin this exploration than by educating ourselves about what it means to eroticize our unresolved wounds. Call it Sexual Literacy 101, right down the hall from Emotional Literacy 101. It's a great class, far from tedious or flat, investigating as it does something that is remarkably interesting about us.

HOW THE EROTICIZING OF OUR UNRESOLVED HURT HAPPENS

1   We get significantly hurt in our early years—emotionally, physically, psychologically—without any resolution, which leaves us wounded.

2   Accompanying this wounding is a charge, an energetic imprint, an excitation (be it positive or negative) that infiltrates our lives, especially when circumstances arise that mimic the ones in which we first were wounded.

3   This charge becomes so familiar to us—however unpleasant it may be—that it seems to be none other than another natural part of us.

4 In our adolescent and/or adult years, *we plug this charge—our original wound-generated excitation—into sexual channels,* thereby both reliving it and finding some short-lived but strongly appealing release from it.

5 This continues, often addictively, until we awaken to what we're doing and turn toward our original wounding with compassion and fitting action.

WHAT OUR SEXUAL FANTASIES DRAMATIZE

The act of eroticizing our neglected needs and unresolved wounds not only means expressing them in sexual contexts, but also seeking—however unconsciously—their fulfillment through sexual fantasy and activity.

PAUL assumes that he's very sexual because he has sex or masturbates two or three times daily. He is chronically anxious and edgy, often feeling saturated or overloaded with fear and anger. Rather than working with this, he channels his surplus emotional excitation into his sexuality, finding considerable energetic release through doing so, using his ejaculatory capacity as a kind of discharge valve for his unwanted emotional energies. In this, he is reducing his sexual partner to little more than an outhouse for the energies of his anxiety and anger. He is, in short, eroticizing his need to rid himself of his emotional tension, while viewing himself, perhaps with pride, as having a very strong sex drive. ∎

When investigating our sexually harnessed "solutions" to our wounding and unmet needs, the explicit sexual details are usually not as important as the story line that precedes and underlies such solutions.

Imagine a lonely teenage boy finding intensely pleasurable sexual arousal when he views a certain part of a particular girl's anatomy. She's oblivious of him, even as he gives her a starring role in his masturbatory fantasies. When he's focused on her—or more precisely, on that part of her anatomy—he no longer feels lonely, no longer feels cut off from others, being consolingly absorbed in his heated picturing of her. As an adult, his central sexual fantasy continues to be viewing that part of a woman's anatomy in females who are approximately the same age as the girl who first stirred him erotically. His arousal is actually only *secondarily* sexual, with its primary catalyst being his longing to be distracted from his loneliness and sense of isolation. He likely doesn't question his pull to women much younger than himself, nor his obsession with that particular body part.

A quick way of uncovering much of a man's core wounding—and his "solution" to it—is to hear his most compellingly arousing sexual fantasy (whether it's current or not) in full detail, *and then strip it of its eroticism*. What remains is a concise portrayal of his wounding and his way of dealing with it, the detailing of which speaks volumes about the original context from which his fantasy arose.

In BRIAN's favorite sexual fantasy, he gets seduced by an older woman, following an intensely pleasurable meeting at her place; she never takes her eyes off him, and leads him in a slow but ever-deepening seduction, to which he happily surrenders. Take away the eroticism, and what's left? An older woman showing obvious interest in him, giving him her full attention, opening fully to him. As a boy, he was neglected by his father, and his mother only rarely gave him quality attention. So, he grew up with a charge around not being neglected—especially by an older woman. This charge became eroticized, manifesting as a fantasy in which he was far from neglected. That the seduction room in his fantasy resembles his childhood kitchen only reinforces the connection between now and then, as does the fact that the fantasy woman resembles his mother as she was in his childhood. ▪

MARTIN has a fantasy of being sexually very dominating, stopping just short of being violent. His partner in this fantasy is extremely passive. The theme is simple: overpowering another. The fact that such dominance has been eroticized is secondary. He was heavily shamed as a boy, criticized for his very existence; he fought back, even though that made things worse. So he grew up with a charge around being overpowered—which he was—and also with fantasies of turning the tables. Later in life, he sexualized this charge, seeking satisfying outlets for it. His most highly arousing sexual fantasy—and increasingly common practice—was, and still is, that of aggressively dominating another. He has not yet connected the dots, and continues to act as if his domination-centered erotic doings are just healthy, if somewhat kinky, expressions of his sexuality. ∎

Just like our dreams, our sexual fantasies are dramas worth exploring, tales that house much of who we are, both dressing up and revealing some of our core dynamics. However embarrassing the exposure of such fantasies might be to us, they are potential doorways deep into our being and conditioning. Our sexual fantasies dramatize what we've spent much of our lives arranging ourselves around. Undress them, stripping them of their eroticism, and you'll see their operational roots and bare script—and also the *you* who first sought release or escape from a life-altering core wounding.

Sexual fantasies can be extremely compelling, effortlessly seizing our attention, to the point where we're not relating to our fantasy, but are unquestioningly immersed in it. When we are thus absorbed, hermetically sealed into the arousing dramatics of our fantasy, we've no awareness of it, no clarifying perspective, being in the position of a dreamer who doesn't know he's dreaming, and who could be said to be dreaming that he is not dreaming. Awakening to what we're really up to in our sexual fantasies doesn't necessarily bring them to an end, any more than recognizing that we're dreaming brings our dream to an end—but it *illuminates* them, giving us options other than our usual or automatic responses.

The degree of drive or compulsiveness that characterizes our sexual fantasies reflects the degree of intensity of pain that we're attempting to bypass through our very immersion in such fantasies. This may be camouflaged by the complexity of some fantasies, but such complexity often just speaks of the desire to have many things in order and under control so that the outcome we long for can occur—an outcome that's nothing more than a solution for an early life in which many things were highly disordered or unpleasantly out of control.

■ ■ ■

The eroticizing of our unresolved wounds and insufficiently met needs is both an escape from our suffering *and* a sign of it. Once we recognize this, we are on our way to truly freeing our sexuality. Ceasing to eroticize the charge we still have with early life pain allows us to be present with that charge—and also with those aspects of ourselves that first endured such pain.

So instead of redirecting that charge, that contracted or compacted excitation, into the pleasuring possibilities of sex, choose to move closer to it, closer to the pain and wounding that underlie it. This isn't about no longer being affected by this charge—for it very likely will always be with us—but about not letting it run us.

Learning to bring our old wounding into our heart (ideally with some skilled help) is a challenging and deeply healing undertaking, leaving us more whole, more vital, more internally connected—and more able to come to sex already present, already connected, already feeling good, no longer employing it to distract us from our suffering.

Sex can simultaneously express our conditioning and keep it in the dark. And sex can, to whatever degree, also express our unconditioned essence and unadulterated individuality through a deeply loving, ecstatically transparent mutuality. It's up to us.

22

Pornography Unplugged

Understanding and Outgrowing Porn

FEW WOULD SAY that pornography has not reached epidemic proportions. More would claim that there's nothing necessarily problematic about pornography, countered by those who view it as wrong or evil. But in any case, pornography has become an increasingly central part of contemporary culture, and needs more than just condemnation or an overly tolerant eye cast upon it if it is to be seen through and outgrown. The very fact that so many men are addicted to it—and therefore not really available for healthy relationship—makes it something that we all need to face, and face deeply enough to recognize its roots and work through the wounding for which it's a "solution."

PORNOGRAPHY ILLUMINATED

Pornography—sexually explicit material designed to catalyze, intensify, and exploit sexual excitation in loveless, frequently degrading contexts—basically manifests as *dehumanization in erotic drag.*

Pornography is the business end of eroticitis (again, meaning obsessive or compulsive interest in sexual activity and possibility), exploiting the craving of those driven to distract themselves from their suffering through erotic excitation and discharge.

Pornography is erotic imagination gone slumming—losing contact with love, intimacy, and ecstasy—binding us to arousal rituals that obstruct our stepping into and embodying our full humanness.

Never has pornography been so ubiquitous and available. It hasn't become just a hugely pervasive Internet phenomenon, but also a major player in advertising. Sex sells, and the more sexually arousing an ad can be, the better for business, even if what is being portrayed degrades those in it, reducing them to erotic button-pushers. If more attention can be garnered through ads that highlight drugged-looking young teens and rape-suggesting scenes, then this is what gets photogenically pushed, mainlining us with more of what we may already be addicted to: sex as a potent go-to solution to much of what troubles us. The pornification of modern culture is so deeply established as to be largely normalized, except in its uglier extremes, and advertising reflects this. Pornography peddlers don't give a damn about the people they screw with, so long as they have their business.

Because pornography infects far too many relationships—often becoming the sexual baseline, the central heating system of erotic arousal—we need to deeply consider it, its roots, and the importance of outgrowing it. Pornography is especially common in me-centered relationships, being indulged in so much that it is often viewed as part of a healthy sex life. In we-centered stages of relationship, overt pornography may be uncommon and strongly suppressed; or it may be common and given an excessively tolerant nod. And in truly mature relationships, pornography is absent, the pull to it simply having been outgrown.

THE PRICE OF BEING POSSESSED
BY A PORNOGRAPHIC MINDSET

It's a vicious circle: pornography generates and is generated by a pornographic mindset, which can easily remain a man's default whenever he doesn't feel good about himself or is under stress, including in his intimate relationship. This mindset sucks the intimacy out of relationship, replacing or layering a man's flesh-and-blood lover with fantasy scenarios that reinforce his private lust rituals, thereby shutting out or reducing his lover to a bit player in his erotic drama. Pornography doesn't care who it messes with, and doesn't care that it doesn't care.

Pornography's pictures tell stories with usually the most scantily dressed of plots, stories that bring together viewed and viewer in quickly undressed hotbeds of sexual hunger. Whether or not there's actual sex, everyone gets fucked.

Whatever helps to amplify sexual excitation is brought into the picture or plot, if only in imagination. Sometimes this is relatively innocuous, and other times, it is darker, uglier, nastier, blurring the line between sexuality and outright violence. Pornography gives lust a bad name.

And pornography is not just limited to Internet videos, skin magazines, "adult" movies, lurid romance novels, or "hot" advertising—it is the primary operational strategy, the go-to methodology, of those who "have to" employ fantasy in their sexual encounters, especially as a means of getting turned on or staying aroused. (The alternative to this is learning to stay fully present, getting out of our heads and into our bodies and raw emotions, remaining more consciously connected to feeling than to thought, doing nothing to distract ourselves from our partners.)

Some might ask what's wrong with employing such fantasy during sex. The answer is not that it's wrong per se, but that it strands us in the shallows, distracting us from facing what's really going on in such encounters, including whatever tasks we may have assigned to our sexuality—the most common of which is to make us feel better. *If we're absorbed in fantasy, we're out of intimate connection, too caught up in our mind to truly see and be with the other.*

Pornography is perhaps *the* sexual booby prize. In binding our sexuality to our thinking mind, overvaluing erotic stimulation and fantasy, and reducing our partner to little more than a prop in our erotic dramas, we don't see that we are only screwing ourselves. To truly enjoy sex is then out of reach for us, for we do not enter its domain nakedly present and lovingly; instead we come in *already* overly attached to erotic expectations and rituals that originally arose as solutions to our suffering.

Teenage boys who have discovered the quick pleasure and relief that ejaculation can provide, likely will also find and use various visuals that help amplify their arousal. If, as they leave their teens, fantasy-centered erotic arousal and discharge remains their go-to practice for reducing distress and tension, and if they do not question or dismantle such conditioning, they may retain it through their adult years, even in an otherwise loving relationship. They might keep it in some poorly lit corner of their psyche, but when it comes to crunch time—as when they crave feeling *really* turned on—they'll animate it, perhaps through sexually fantasizing while engaging in sex, or through viewing porn, or both.

Like any other business, pornography exists to meet consumer desires, doing whatever it can to stimulate and feed those desires. Call it horny capitalism, there to profit no matter what the cost. The advertising industry milks pornographic angles as much as it can, because it is good for business. And the ads are getting more edgy, incorporating younger models (seemingly not so far past puberty) and "cool" suggestions of sexual predation and even about-to-happen rape.

Hypermasculine ads that glamorize callousness toward women, and associate violence with being manly, only add to this. If the darker extremes of porn could boost car sales, we might glimpse some hint of it, however subtly incorporated, loitering around the shadier outskirts of automobile ads. Naturally, this stirs up questions of morality: the claim for the moral high ground a standoff between religious zealots and stay-out-of-my-sex-life apologists.

However, neither condemnation ("it's sin") nor over-tolerance ("whatever consenting adults do is fine by me") of pornography—and neither repression nor indulgence of it—bring us any closer to facing and outgrowing it. Our fascination with and attachment to pornography will continue, flaming strongly, until we fully recognize how we've sexualized our distress, unresolved wounds, and emotional pain, looking to sex to distract us from our suffering and the roots of our suffering.

The energetic discharge provided by immersion in pornography doesn't truly ease us, but just sedates and dulls us, weakening our motivation to get to the heart of what's driving us to so desperately seek the excitement and payoffs of our pornographic leanings.

FACING THE PAIN THAT DRIVES
US TOWARD PORNOGRAPHY

If pornography is to cease being our erotic default, we need to acknowledge, reenter, heal, and integrate the psychological and emotional wounding that originally drove—and still drives—us into pornography's territory. By doing so, we liberate our sexuality from its desperation, mechanicalness, and heartless ruts.

This is far from an easy process, just as is facing and working through any addiction. I've seen many men with the best of intentions face the wounding for which their porn addiction was a solution, and then fall back into the familiar grip of such addiction, letting their shame over such slippage further fuel their immersion in porn. It's not so difficult for such men to seduce themselves with erotic tension and its pleasurably mounting expectations, thereby building up enough erotic excitation to convincingly necessitate—and perhaps even legitimize—some kind of sexual release in pornographic contexts.

In this, there is such untouched grief, such muted isolation, such endarkened loneliness, all calling from deep inside to be turned toward, to be faced and embraced, rather than continuing to be obscured by the addictive pull to porn and the arousal that it feeds.

Whatever its form, pornography is worth outgrowing. This begins with recognizing—more than just intellectually—how we create and reinforce our distress, taking our compassion-centered attention into whatever we are feeling and experiencing, especially emotionally, right before we give ourselves over to pornography. This does not mean a suppression of pornography and our pull to it, but rather relating *to* that pull while at the same time attuning ourselves to where we are emotionally (and also to where we were emotionally when we first got into porn).

Instead of repressing or indulging in our pornographic leanings, we'd do better by exploring them and journeying to the heart of the pain and wounding that underlies them. Instead of staying stuck in guilt for having a pull toward pornography, we need to gaze at it and our attraction to it with resolute compassion en route to contacting and openly feeling the hurt at the source of such attraction, finding the courage to ask for skilled guidance in this if necessary.

When relatively awakened sexual partners meet in deeply embodied mutuality and compassion, there is no diminishment of passion and raw vitality—theirs is a relationship in which destructive habits, pornographic and otherwise, can be fully faced, worked with, related to like souvenirs from our adolescence, and outgrown.

Enter sexuality's domain (whether you're with a partner or not) when you are unstressed and already loving, and you won't need to invite in your mind and its pornographic offerings, nor turn the lights out.

OUTGROWING PORNOGRAPHY

Men who are hooked on pornography have an *enormous* opportunity.

The work they need to do to outgrow—not repress but outgrow—pornography is the very work that brings them into their full manhood and humanity, unhooking them not just from pornography, but also from much of their conditioning (as I pointed to in chapter 20).

The degree to which a man is involved in pornography—including having a pornographic mindset—is the degree to which he's not available for relational intimacy.

There are plenty of objections to not having pornography, generally centered on the notion that those who oppose it are sex-negative, uptight, puritanical, deluded, narrowly moralistic, afraid to experiment sexually, and against sexual freedom. Pro-pornography advocates are out to make the case that pornography is not harmful, with arguments ranging from "different strokes for different folks" to studies indicating that the rate of sexual assault is lower in countries that have liberal pornography laws. They commonly argue that the right to choose includes the right to make bad choices, and that the objectification and degradation of women occurs in plenty of places besides pornography.

But pornography will not be outgrown through a debate between those who are for it and those against it; even if it were outlawed, it would continue. Pornography can only be outgrown when its roots are clearly seen—both personally and culturally—and worked through more than just intellectually. This means that our core wounding and our remedies for it need to be exposed and compassionately explored, until they no longer run us.

Outgrowing pornography begins with recognizing the grip and impact it has on us, and with ceasing to rationalize or justify its continued use. The following are some essential steps in doing so.

- **Work on awakening from your conditioning.** Bring what you've kept in the dark out into the open, so it can be healed and integrated with the rest of your being. Let go of the notion that you can do this all by yourself, and get whatever help you can, as soon as possible. Approach this not as a burden but as a sacred adventure.

- **Identify what you're feeling emotionally when you notice your desire to use pornography starting to stir.** Stay with and breathe into this feeling for at least ten minutes rather than distracting yourself from it through getting reabsorbed in pornography.

- **Attune yourself to the you who first felt this feeling.** Visualize and feel him, having the sense of bringing him closer, enfolding him in an embrace at once loving and protective. Stay with this no matter how strongly your porn habit pulls at you.

- **Turn toward your wounding with your full attention and care.** This allows you to see both its origins and your "solutions" to it.

- **Write out your full sexual history.** Include the nonsexual dynamics that occurred along the way (issues with your parents, and so on), giving special emphasis to your prevailing emotional state throughout. Include your erotic fantasies. If you're tempted to leave something out, write not only about it, but also about your desire not to mention it.

- **Make sure you understand what it means to eroticize your wounds.** (See the preceding chapter for a full description of this.)

- **Humanize those who star in your sexual fantasies and in whatever pornography catches your eye.** Let yourself see and feel beneath their surface presentation, refusing to view them as less than deserving of your compassion, no matter how compelling your lust may be.

- **Keep a picture of yourself as a little boy at hand.** Bring it out and look at it for at least a full minute when your urge to use pornography kicks in, breathing that little one into your heart as much as you can, giving him your full attention. This will help remind you of who you were before pornography gripped you, and also of the origins of some of the emotional pain that you let spur you toward using pornography.

- **Masturbate without using pornography or fantasy.** Focus not just on the sensations of sexual arousal, but also on your emotional reality. Keep your mind out of it. Stay connected to your heart as you proceed, slowing down when you start to rush. Make being present with yourself more central than coming.

- **Connect the dots between your early life conditioning and the nonsexual dynamics in your sexual fantasies.** Do this until it fully registers with you.

- **Don't be a mute bystander when it comes to pornography.** If others around you are talking approvingly of pornography or are talking about women in sexually degrading contexts, speak up, and not tentatively, remembering that your silence constitutes tacit approval of what they're saying.

■ **Do whatever it takes to reenter, heal, and integrate the emotional and psychological wounding that originally drove you toward pornography.** Take this on as a totally worthy challenge. Your doing so is a great gift to everyone.

■ ■ ■

To shift into a truly healthy sexuality includes doing whatever is necessary to outgrow pornography. This is far from a small challenge for men caught up in pornography, but it is a much-needed undertaking, asking the very best of a man, drawing him into the heartland of his conditioning, deepening his capacity to be in mutually empowering relationship. Any man who embarks on this journey deserves our deep respect, for he is on the way to making life a little better for all of us.

23

Taking Charge of Your Charge
Responsibility and Sexual Arousal

IS A MAN responsible for his sexual excitation or charge? And if so, at what point?

As soon as it has arisen.

He may not consciously bring it into being, for it can arise quicker than thought, more like a reflex than a response, but once it's there, he is responsible for what happens to it, including its amplification and transition into action.

It may seem that he can't help himself—mounting expectations, avalanching appetite, hugely compelling longing—but he can. The fleshing out of his charge, including through the quickest of fantasies or visual lingering, is his doing, his choice. His responsibility.

Once you've examined and started working with your eroticized wounds and your relationship to pornography and images of sexuality in the media, you can begin to own your charge as soon as it arises—and not just cognitively.

Take charge of your charge, right from its inception. Whatever you're doing with it needs to be recognized as your choice. If you're undressing a particular woman in your imagination, it's your doing, and cannot be blamed on her appearance or self-presentation or the intensity of your desire. The light may be green, but it's your highway and your signal box, and yours alone.

Unfortunately some men do blame women, saying in so many words that if she wasn't looking or dressing a certain way, they wouldn't be sexually fantasizing about her. Perhaps not, but she is not responsible for what they're doing with their charge.

It's easy to play victim to our sexual arousal and the intensification of that arousal, holding it accountable for any questionable behavior that happens, perhaps letting ourselves off the hook with statements like "What's a guy supposed to do?" or "I couldn't help myself" or "She turns me on" (in the sense that we don't turn ourselves on).

Being in charge of our charge doesn't mean that we won't get aroused, including times when we wish we didn't (like at a party when we're introduced to our boss's wife while he's standing beside her, looking at us). There's nothing to be disturbed about here, if we do not allow ourselves to fuel such excitation.

There are times when it is entirely fitting to let our arousal fully magnify, as when we're in loving connection with our lover.

What matters is what we *do* with such excitation. Hopefully we already have some options or practices on tap (see the following list), especially in circumstances where feeding our charge does everyone involved a disservice.

- Acknowledge your arousal to yourself as soon as you're aware of it.

- Identify what you're feeling emotionally, and keep some attention there.

- See and respond to whomever you feel aroused by as a complete being.

- Don't fixate on the other's body parts or isolate them from the rest of that person.

- Don't let your arousal strand you from caring about the other.

- Notice the ways in which you amplify or intensify your arousal, and don't let them hijack your attention. Learn to relate to them as options. If they're particularly compelling, shift your attention to your breathing as soon as you're aware that they've arisen, counting at least a dozen breaths (counting at exhale's end).

- Treat your arousal not as something bad, but as something worth exploring. Feel into the raw ache of it, the longing that's at its heart.

- When you feel a hit of arousal and have named it as such, take a few slow deep breaths, softening your belly, not allowing yourself to view the other as just a sexual beacon or possibility, seeing through any possible seductive energy coming from the other, so that you have your arousal rather than your arousal having you.

The amplification of your sexual arousal can be a wonderful part of your relationship with your lover, so long as it is not being used as a distraction from what's not working in your relationship. A couple that is emotionally disconnected may rely on sex to provide a sense of connection, but such reliance has a short shelf life, given that what it provides is little more than empty calories, a sugar rush of pseudo-closeness that quickly wears off, leaving the couple not only back in their unattended emotional disconnection, but largely drained of the very energy needed to face such disconnection.

Erotic charge can easily become too central to sex, existing as its hub, its most important feature. The heightened sensations of such heated excitation may be confused with emotional connection, when in fact this connection may not be happening to any significant degree. At these times, it may seem that we are feeling very deeply, but much of that is not so much emotional as just the sensations of sexual arousal compellingly pervading our system.

Sex that's centered or governed by charge cannot truly satisfy. Being possessed by charge when we are emotionally and empathetically disconnected reduces the other to a potential object for and fulfiller of our sexual appetite, blinding us to the nonsexual dynamics that are likely determining the direction we're going in with our sexuality.

Take charge of your charge. Sometimes it's entirely fitting to give it the green light. What a joy it is when arousal and emotional intimacy and love all are in passionate sync! Other times, it's entirely fitting to not permit your charge to grow. What a sobering joy there can be in breathing integrity into our interactions, embodying a "no" that makes possible a deeper "yes!" There is a soul-affirming satisfaction in holding our boundaries firmly in a potentially exploitive situation.

A man who won't take charge of his charge has not yet stepped into his true masculine power.

Taking charge of our charge is a discipline that may initially feel as though it's narrowing us, reining in our irresponsibly wandering attention and automated ogling. But it soon feels more liberating than entrapping, if only because it deepens our capacity for relational intimacy.

Charge has its place, and needs to be honored as such, rather than allowing it to run us sexually, reducing us to consumers in a culture obsessed by sexual opportunity and possibility. If enough men took charge of their charge, and made it their business to know its roots and psychological and emotional dimensions, pornography would have a hard time staying in business.

Don't overassociate sex with sensation (as does pornography). Doing so is severely limiting and relationally damaging, marooning us from intimacy, no matter how heatedly erotic we may get. Go for more than just "sensational" sex. And at the same time, don't bring excessive regulation to your erotic excitation. Charge itself is neither positive nor negative, and needs only to be consciously related to. Charge is inevitable; what matters is how we handle it.

The charge-centered fantasies we erect don't need moral dynamite or uncritical approval, but rather a compassion-centered exploration of whatever underlies them. Exploring our charge—exposing its roots—doesn't suppress its energies, but redirects them so that they might serve our deepest good.

Knowing that you're in charge of your charge makes it much more difficult to sexually exploit others. This isn't about men suppressing their sexuality or shaming themselves for it, but about bringing it into healthy alignment with the rest of their being. Taking charge of your charge deepens your integrity, making you more trustworthy, more capable of being in truly intimate relationship.

The passion of deep sex arises primarily not from erotic excitation and stimulation, but from the presence of genuine intimacy, an intimacy rooted in deep trust and transparency and emotional resonance, an intimacy that itself is the most potent of aphrodisiacs. In the presence of such closeness, charge is but sacred fuel.

24

The Penis
A Sensitive Topic

A MAN'S PENIS is usually so closely associated with his manliness that, in both physical and imaginal forms, it may occupy him to a degree that would astonish many women. It's always close at hand, on call to rise to the occasion, ready to spring to action.

Freud famously stated that women suffer from penis envy. He got the gender wrong. Many men have spent considerable time, at least for some stretches in their life, comparing their penis with those of others, with special status frequently given to the larger or lengthier ones.

Penis size—except in its extremes—is commonly said to not really matter to women, but it does to most men. For men, the notion of "bigger is better" applies in many areas—biceps, income, social status, height, shoulder width, penile length and girth—frequently commensurate with the inflation of their ego. In this context, a small penis may lead to overcompensation in other areas associated with a "large" manhood. This is perhaps most infamously illustrated by an anecdote about Napoleon, whose reportedly very small penis (apparently sold in desiccated form, in 1977, to a New Jersey urologist) shrank before his larger-than-life military exploits.

An erect penis—a hard-on, a boner, a woody, a one-eyed giant—is often not much more than an extension of a man's pride, rigid as a soldier at steely attention, helmeted head held high. Cocksure. Hardness has long been held to be a male virtue, and is still often associated with übermasculinity. Whereas softness in a man often has a negative

241

connotation, being sexually associated with flaccidity, not being able "to get it up," and with being insufficiently tough and too easily rendered emotional.

How painfully limiting it is to have one's manhood reduced to being little more than a walking erection, an emotionally impassive (except when it comes to anger) performer, hardened or stiffened against anything that might crack his armor, whether from within or from the outside! In such a context, a man will chronically be on guard against anything that might expose his softness or rob him of his erectility. After all, many view a man who can't "get it up" as less than a man. This is part of the reason why so many men try to make sure other men know that they're active sexually, perhaps even very active, as this is seen in more than a few circles as a sign of being manly, of being, so to speak, a cocksman, a conqueror of women, a success at getting laid.

An erect penis often has a sizable shadow, which tends to get overlooked or left unexplored. And what does this shadow usually house? A man's vulnerability and shame. An erection is blatantly out-front. A woman can hide her sexual arousal, but a man cannot, even if he wants to, given the hard-to-overlook presence of his hard-on. This may swell his pride, but it can also stir up his shame when he does not want there to be any overt display of his arousal. Think of a shy teenage boy in a position where the telltale bulge in his pants can be neither hidden nor made to obey any command to shrink.

And vulnerability? Aside from any visual concerns that a man might have about his erection, its sheer presence can be laced with concerns about what he can or needs to do with it, which can be anxiety-inducing if he has a history of losing (or sometimes losing) his erection when he most "needs" it, or if he has had a hard time using it skillfully. And to make things worse, he may be adamant about not discussing any of this with anyone, including his sexual partner (who might well be understanding and patient). So he may continue to harden himself against his vulnerability, shame, and sense of isolation, thereby doing little more than screwing himself, cutting himself off from real connection, forgetting that a loss of erection is entirely understandable under a variety of conditions, including times of distress.

The swelling penis can be the leading edge of a man's sexual excitement—you could say it has a mind of its own—plunging ahead so quickly that its movements dictate his, much like a large dog yanking on its leash so hard that the owner is jerked along behind it. This of course gives the impression that the penis, engorged with excitation, is in charge. And some of our sexual metaphors support this sense of not being in charge of the building up of our sexual arousal: "My lust overcame me" or "She makes me hard." Robin Williams encapsulates this: "God gave man a penis and a brain, but only enough blood to run one at a time." Nonetheless, we are in charge of our charge, usually unable to prevent the initial arising of sexual excitation, but nonetheless responsible for its amplification.

The penis can also provide a certain security, if only through its presence and familiar heft, however firmly cupped it may be by underwear. I remember watching my six-year-old brother stand motionless at one end of a soccer field while most of the rest of his team surged downfield; he was playing defense and had to stay back. He was clutching his penis through his shorts, seemingly comforted by doing so. My father saw this from the sidelines and roared at him to stop, which only made my brother cling to his penis more tightly, even as he looked around absent-mindedly. He might as well have been holding one of his stuffed animals.

Many men compartmentalize their penis (in much the same way that many women compartmentalize their breasts), isolating it from the rest of their body, giving it an autonomy that is far from natural for it. They may view their penis as representing *them* in a significant way, and treat it almost as though it were *independent* of them, being proud of it when it does well (staying erect during sex) and condemning it when it doesn't (loss of erection or reaching only partial erectile status). What they are overlooking is that no penis operates in a vacuum—it reflects whatever else is going on for its owner.

The penis doesn't lie.

If it retreats into flaccidity during sex (and there's no organic cause for this), this usually signals that whatever arousal level was originally there has seriously waned, no matter how much a man might think that he should still be erect.

And to even speak of him "being erect" indicates his identification with his penis—as it goes, so does he. Its rise is his, its fall his. When we say of a male that he's "playing with himself," we are usually referring to him making manual contact with his penis, conflating "himself" with his penis. Some of this is semantics, but it still speaks of how the male sense of self can be significantly fused with the penis. (Instead of saying, "My penis got hard," we may say, "I got hard.")

Again, the penis doesn't lie. A man may lose his erection during sex (the wind going out of his sails) when he sees what's really going on, besides all the erotic play: maybe he sees that his sexual partner is in emotional pain and trying to hide it; maybe he feels a flush of shame for how he pressured his partner into having sex; maybe he's just not very attracted to that one, especially as he starts to feel a bit more sober; maybe he was badly shamed for losing his erection with a former partner; maybe his conscience kicks in as he registers more fully than ever before that the person he's having sex with has a partner and children.

The penis may seem to be an independent operator (like the lone or hyperautonomous hero in many a male fantasy), unburdened by empathy or conscience or the pain underlying whatever sexual dynamics are at play. But in fact, it is not so separate, being intimately connected with the rest of us, however numbed such connection might be.

Some men give their penis a proper name, as if it were indeed an autonomous part of them, a kind of rogue peninsula. This reflects both the separation such men feel from their penis, and their sense that it's an independent force, an entity unto itself, something that has a mind of its own. Men can veer between identifying with their penis ("I got hard") and dissociating from it ("I don't know what's wrong with it"), but rarely do they cultivate intimacy with it, relating to it with conscious care until it's no longer an "it," but rather another aspect of their embodiment, no more and no less special than any other part of their body, to be honored regardless of its condition.

The penis is not just a cock, prick, schlong, dong, dink, tool, dick, pecker, knob, wiener, joystick, wanger, phallus, or—to take more literary license—groin ferret, flesh flute, longfellow, love muscle, quiver bone, or trouser snake. There are probably more English synonyms for the word *penis* than just about any other noun, synonyms that tend to isolate it—exaggeratedly singling it out—from the rest of what constitutes us, especially when they double as insults. Who wants to be around a prick? Who wants to be a dick, or be dicked around?

A man's relationship to his penis says much about his relationship to his egoity. If he identifies with his penis, rising and falling with it, letting its capacity to perform overoccupy him, he is likely to identify with his intellect in the same way, engaging in little or no self-reflection, commonly taking a fuck-or-get-fucked attitude toward life. And if a man dissociates from his penis, viewing it as an independent operator or something "down there" (that is, below his *head*quarters), he is likely cut off from the rest of his body, viewing it from the distance provided by his remaining stationed in his intellect.

The exaggerated importance commonly given to the penis—consider the focus given to any phallic symbol—tends to push the rest of a man's somatic reality into the background, unless it suggests sexual potency (think pumped up, prominently veined musculature). We might give our penis a proper name, but would we do the same for our elbows, heels, forehead, or hamstrings? The key is to relate to all that we are somatically with equal attention and care, not letting any one part hog the stage. This allows the entire body to become an erogenous zone.

If, for a few minutes, you pay close attention to any part of your body, it usually will come more alive, pulsing with sensation and presence, however subtly. When this focus is applied to the whole body (including the heart!) as a slow, thorough scan, the penis carries less charge (because any particular intensification of sensation is distributed through our entire physicality), and there is less of a need for it to be *the* energetic terminal for discharging heightened sensation. Even more important, it then becomes simply another part of our physicality, deserving of quality attention and care, but no more so than any other part of our body.

When a man embraces and honors his physicality, he no longer relates to his body as just an "it," but rather as an expression of who and what he truly is. It is in this context that the penis finds its most fitting place, no longer enslaved to reinforcing a man's egoity or self-importance, no longer burdened by obligations to perform for any sort of status, no longer reduced to a prick or anything else laden with negative connotations.

25

Breasts
Mammary Mania

BREASTS. Reading this word, what images arise for you? Can you sense to what degree these images are affected by our culture's fascination, visual and otherwise, with breasts and related matters, like cleavage and wardrobe malfunctions? Nothing catches most men's eyes like breasts, or the suggested presence of breasts, however they may be featured. Such easily magnetized focus is not, however, just a matter of lust, as we shall see—there is more to it than meets the eye, much of which is far from sexual.

Let's start by exploring what could be called the invasion of breast implants. *Invasion* is a strong term, but it is quite apt, given how pervasive such mammary enhancements are, colonizing more and more women. It is apparently important to increasing numbers of women to have bigger or perkier breasts—and probably even more important to many men—to the point where such physical alteration is becoming part of the new normal. (I am not speaking here, nor in the rest of this chapter, about breast implants or reconstruction chosen because of a mastectomy or huge weight loss.) Getting breast implants is now the most popular cosmetic surgical procedure in the United States, with liposuction coming in second (which women opt for ten times as often as men, with much the same rationale to look sexier that drives the bigger-is-better breast boom).

Plastic breasts are popping out everywhere, magnetizing attention and erotic interest despite their sometimes cartoonish artificiality, reinforcing our already well-implanted cultural obsession with mammary mass and shape. Women in the entertainment industry who don't have breast implants appear to be in the minority in their profession. More and more teenagers are getting implants, including as graduation presents. The fact that, collectively, we don't find this bizarre *is* bizarre, but understand-able, given our increasingly photoshopped cultural milieu and the central importance breasts—of whatever size—hold in the male imagination.

Consider this scenario: women taking their newly bought breasts out for a stroll, letting them lead the way, obscuring whatever pain or unresolved wounding fueled their purchase. If it makes you feel better, then just do it—such seems to be the prevailing, look-how-tolerant-I-am attitude toward breast implants (the same attitude is also often brought to pornography), with insufficient attention being devoted to the underlying motivations, both personal and cultural, for wanting to have them in the first place.

Yes, there's been some consideration given to the insecurity, not-enoughness, poor body image, and social pressures (read: many men prefer larger ones) that motivate most women who get implants—or who feel driven to use silicone bra inserts, push-up bras, or whatever else appears to increase their cup size—but this is more than offset by the increasingly popular notion that having larger or more prominent breasts is a good solution to such insecurity and related factors. After all, don't women feel better about themselves when they've got the breasts they want, or at least the breasts that most men apparently want them to have, breasts that'll enhance their sex appeal?

There may be some truth in this, but it is a very superficial and partial truth. The underlying insecurity and not-enoughness remain implanted, regardless of the new breasts' massy magnetism, compensa-tory cleavage and thrust, and power to reel in male gazes and fantasies. Boob jobs are mostly just time-delayed booby prizes, eye-catching overcompensations for unaddressed pain and insecurity (including being shamed for being flat-chested), exploiting the already-present obsession with breasts that pervades much of contemporary culture.

Getting breast implants can be an unhealthy undertaking for women. A 2007 study, for example, showed that the suicide rate was three times higher for women with breast implants than for women without them. This does not mean that having breast implants *causes* a higher rate of suicide, but rather that there's a positive correlation between suicide and having implants—*which implicates the factors generating the desire to have breast implants.* What's essential to consider here is what the women who have had breast implants were doing *before* getting them, especially with regard to their less-than-happy feelings.

If such a high percentage of men didn't make it so important that women have bigger breasts, would women still be going for breast enlargement (or otherwise trying to make their breasts appear larger)? In most cases, no. But the common male fascination, at least in contemporary Western culture, for bigger breasts shows no sign of abating, nor does our media's obsession with them (and with breasts in general). There is a natural attraction to breasts (for women as well as men), but we've gone far, far beyond that, into the airbrushed recesses of unnatural attraction—attraction that is little more than socially acceptable obsession and eroticized fetishism.

Boobs, tits, titties, knockers, jugs, bazongas, cupcakes, puppies, melons, fun bags, floaters, fog lights, hand warmers, hooters, warheads, bazookas, cans, rack—the list goes on, stretching far beyond the corseted decorum of *bosom.* The fact that there are so many synonyms for *breast* simply reflects how much our culture has been pervaded by the idea, sight, and promise of human mammary glands. *Here, size does matter*—how else to explain the inordinate attention and fame that some otherwise untalented women have received for having large, prominent breasts, even when such "attributes" are universally known to be implants?

The sight of big breasts, whether they're natural or not, is automatically arousing for many men; they may not particularly enjoy the feel of fake breasts, but the sight more than makes up for that. And just whose eyes are these men looking through at such times?

The rubbernecking lust and "I'd love to do her" fantasies that may be aroused by the sighting of a pair of out-front, gravity-defying breasts (with the rest of the woman's body, including her face, in the background) is arguably natural to some degree at a certain stage of a male's development—adolescence (which often extends into old age)—but not so natural once he is no longer a teenager.

He may still look, but if he has genuinely matured, he looks in the same way that he'd look at a lavishly blossomed tree or a shiny new car or a prominent pair of eyelashes or ears—whatever stands out in his visual field at the time. Curious, focused perhaps, but not titillated, for he no longer can isolate a woman's breasts from the rest of her. When he looks at her breasts, he sees her in her totality, and in seeing her thus, he is not drawn to any sort of fantasy regarding any part of her anatomy.

He has, in short, outgrown his capacity to *compartmentalize* her. Connecting with her is far, far more important than hooking up the horny adolescent in him (that is, if that aspect of him is still active) to her mammary display.

If he is in a deep relationship, his sexualized gaze is reserved for his beloved; he does not have to repress his urge to look with erotic interest at other women, for he's all but outgrown this desire. This does not, however, mean that his sexual passion is diminished! It simply no longer pulls at him to any significant degree. Unlike men who are trying to be "good," he does not avoid looking (looking, not ogling or staring) at other women's breasts (including those that are implants), nor does he eroticize what he's taking in.

HOW THE ORIGINAL APPEAL
OF BREASTS GETS EROTICIZED

Many men don't examine in much depth their interest in big breasts because they do not seriously question the appeal that such breasts hold for them. They typically take it as a given. But is it? Not necessarily! And is the appeal of big breasts—or breasts of any size (some men do prefer smaller breasts)—truly sexual? Not necessarily.

The eroticizing of our needs, our sexualized framing of them in conjunction with seeking their fulfillment through sexual activity, is a common occurrence (see chapter 21), and a fascination/obsession with breasts is no exception in this context. We may have developed a charge for breasts, and large breasts in particular, for all kinds of reasons, going back to infancy, a charge or excitation that we eventually eroticized (usually in our teen years), which only increased our pull toward breasts.

Picture an infant boy busy suckling, his mother's breast comfortingly and sensually—and perhaps also massively (a milk-engorged breast being no small object to an infant)—before him, literally in his face, there for his need. But did this create an obsession with breasts, and big breasts in particular? Not necessarily. Something else had to happen.

Perhaps his breastfeeding was done on a schedule that didn't work for him so that he was left too often with an unrequited craving for breast milk. Or perhaps his breastfeeding was done whenever he was hungry, but was cut off prematurely, as happened with many, many infants during the Dr. Spock era. (This would have left him with a craving made all the stronger by being in intimate proximity to his mother, but not having had access to her breasts.) Or perhaps he didn't get breastfed, but still had the urge to suck, like all newborns—no colostrum, no milk, no warm bare breast against his face, but only a familiar heartbeat when his mother held him close to her breasts.

So much nourishment, so very close by, such a rich warmth, such a soft sweet welcome, such exquisite gourds of motherly nectar, signaled by the sight of cleavage or by the breasts themselves—and he, growing up not seeing these wondrous sources of so much, but nonetheless still sensing them there, just behind the clothes and bras and don't-touch psycho-emotional walls. Such hunger here—and now imagine him *eroticizing* this completely understandable hunger (helped by his growing awareness of and exposure to our cultural obsession with breasts and breast size), and *staying stuck there*, growing up wanting women to display the same mammary largesse. Some men flee this (like Woody Allen in one of his early films being pursued by a gigantic, milk-squirting breast, before which he finally brandishes a crucifix), but many loiter in it, hooked by their eroticized yearning for breasts, especially large, spilling-forth breasts.

Many factors conspire to create our culture's breast fetish—and it is a fetish, in its unrelenting object-isolation and obsessiveness. Perhaps the key factor is a thwarted longing for deep maternal nourishment that has been eroticized and amplified to such an extent that we are immersed in and surrounded by it.

WHEN BREAST FANTASIES ARE STRIPPED OF THEIR EROTICISM

Where infants are faced with and enfolded by the breast, we are surrounded by and up to our eyeballs in it, bombarded by suggestions, sightings, and talk of breasts. One flash of a famous woman's bare breast at the Super Bowl a few years ago was an occasion of massive media coverage, before which all other news, including war horrors, paled. After all, a breast—a naked breast!—had been spotted for a second, spurring countless parents to cover their children's eyes. The breast is such a primal icon: picture McDonald's famous golden arches pointing skyward, and stick a nipple shape atop each, and you'll have a rough picture of what we're up against—a ubiquitous feeding frenzy both disguised and made palatable by our eroticizing of it.

The sexualizing of our craving for breasts or, more precisely, for what breasts represent to us, shows up dramatically in teenage males—and how could it not, given their common lack of access to breasts, coupled with their off-the-chart testosterone levels? Breasts, especially big, unsagging breasts, inviting and lusciously photogenic, hold a central place in many an adolescent male sexual fantasy—and let us not forget that adolescence, as a stage, extends far past the teen years for many men.

In fact, the budding pornographic mindset of many a teenage boy easily becomes the full-blown pornographic mindset of many a man, hyperfocusing in part on the titillating visuals of bare-breasted women in various stages of apparent arousal, women who—at least in fantasy!—*want him*. He doesn't have to buy such women dinner, or be nice to them, or do anything in particular to have them want him, because they *already* clearly do. And it is the longing for this unconditional acceptance that constitutes much of the charge, the source of the excitation felt *prior to its being sexualized*. Come to Mommy, and Mommy will give you what you want, no matter how you look and act, because she, as symbolized by prominent in-your-face breasts, is wide-open and totally available to *you*—this, once eroticized, is the naked essence of much of the breast fetish that occupies so many men.

And let's throw something else into the mix here: the imagery of big, unsagging breasts with deep cleavage is reminiscent of the round, rosy-hued, prominently jutting rear end of rutting female baboons—such blatantly presented double roundness and cleavage delivers a clear signal to any horny male baboons in the vicinity. Close in on those reddish mounds, get in between them, and make your penile entry: such are the operational dynamics of male baboons. Plenty of human males carry some of the same dynamics, closing in, if only in fantasy, on the round mounds of breasty heaven (a matter of buttocks having photogenically migrated to the chest?), made all the more appealing by clearly demarcated cleavage. (Consider how jaw-droppingly important cleavage is made by mainstream media, and of the efforts so many women make to increase it.) This is only a small aspect of sexual lust, but it is greatly magnified through our cultural fascination with breasts and breast size.

Many women have submitted to the adolescent male sexual fantasies that pervade our culture, as if their role were to somehow star in them (or at least play a supporting role) and present the kind of big-breasted or prominently breasted allure that can catalyze and spur male sexual excitement and release. But strip these fantasies of their eroticism, and what is left? The dramatics of being fed, or being wanted, of having wide-open access to satiation-oriented pleasuring. Much of the time, small or sagging breasts just don't get past the audition stage in such fantasies, and so, to the degree that women crave being desired by men—or crave the security or self-esteem or power that can arise from being so desired—they will try to make themselves more desirable, including by going under the knife for breast enlargement.

Men who are primarily me-centered typically tend to get off on breast implants, for they're usually overly focused on the visuals of sexuality, often employing such imagery in their arousal rituals, whether alone or with a partner. Prominent breasts, artificial or not, are commonly a rapid turn-on for them. Men who are more we-centered (focusing just as much on their partners' needs as their own) in relationship are not so sure about breast implants, but may still get off on them, without however, being particularly overt about it. Some may even be authentically critical of such artifice, scoring moral good-partner points by demonstrating an obvious sensitivity to the exploitation of women. But underneath such psychosexual properness, they still may lust for the very breasts that they publicly decry (sometimes to their own chagrin).

And for men who have stepped into their full manhood? Breast implants exert no erotic pull and, in fact, are a turn-off. (Nor do natural breasts usually pull at them strongly with any erotic significance, unless they belong to their partners.) When such men encounter a woman who has implants, they view her breasts in the context of all that she is, including the very forces that first drove her to seek breast enlargement (perhaps sensing the girl in her, the girl who first felt that she was not enough for males, be they boys or her father or men in general). Such men's erotic visuals are limited, without any repression, to their partners; they've simply outgrown the need to let their attention wander into and loiter in erotic possibilities, other than with their partners or lovers. (This is not to say that their sexual passion is in any way diminished—quite the opposite is true for those who are still sexually active.)

MOVING BEYOND BREAST FIXATION

Let us honor the whole woman: the little girl, the maiden, the mother, the sister, the virgin, the lover, the leader, the teen, the warrior, the queen, the elder, the daughter, the midwife, the spiritual adventuress, the deep partner, all of them together weaving the reality of the full woman, the woman unbound, the woman who is well on her way to becoming intimate with all that she is.

Such honoring makes room for a deeper compassion, including for men who are still visually Velcroed to breasts, and who do not yet recognize how they are eroticizing their wounds and unmet needs, especially the hurt over being insufficiently nourished. Such men have made themselves so very easy to erotically sway, so easily turned on by feminine allure (lit by the grail of the perfect breast), so easily over-powered by sightings of female fecundity (as symbolized largely by breasts), that a significant percentage of them may seek a balance of power through trying to overpower women.

May we as men cease casting the responsibility on women for our getting turned on, recognizing that *we* are in charge of our charge—and through doing so, cease viewing women in compartmentalized or dehumanizing contexts, cutting through our exaggerated fascination with their breasts (or other isolated body parts), until all that's left is deep appreciation of *woman* as a totality, a wondrous manifestation of that which both transcends and generates gender.

26

Fully Facing Rape

ONE OF THE BIGGEST problems with rape is that throughout human history it has been sanctioned and tolerated in a variety of contexts, with such an okaying influencing contemporary takes on rape, numbing many to the bare reality of it. The echo of this okaying, this legitimizing of or noninterference with sexual violence, may be faint but it persists.

Consider, for starters, the reputed practice of *jus primae noctis* (Latin for "right of the first night") by which a member of the nobility could take a woman on her wedding night and bed her, no matter how opposed she was to this, while the groom could do nothing to stop this. (The earliest mention of this practice is found in the epic of Gilgamesh.) Though there is some debate about whether this practice (also known as *droit du seigneur,* meaning "right of the lord") was actually exercised, kings and feudal nobles certainly had the power to enforce it, and not just on wedding nights, given that the men beneath them were little more than indentured servants, whose *property*—including their wives—could be taken from them at almost any time.

Also consider that, up until not so long ago, a married man had the right to have sex when he wanted it from his wife, no matter how opposed she was to this; marital rape was not called rape for a very long time, regardless of its severity. And consider wartime rape, which has a history as long as that of war itself, and still happens to this day, getting headlines but little countering action. In war, the raping of enemy women has been viewed—and often still is—as a male right.

And this is not just a matter of a few soldiers being out of control. Some armies, in the not-so-distant past, have set up "rape camps" for their soldiers, imprisoning thousands of enemy women, many very young, to serve the "needs" of such soldiers. (It is estimated that in the Bosnian conflict alone, more than sixty thousand women were thus "housed.") The number of rapes of German women by Russian soldiers during World War II has been reported to be over a million. The history of war is, in part, a history of rape, made all the more shameful by how much this has been marginalized.

Military rape is not just something that happens to enemy women; it is also a common in-house practice—targeting both women and men—in military contexts. The Pentagon recently released a report indicating a 35 percent increase in sexual assaults against women in the US military; there were about 26,000 cases (14,000 men and 12,000 women) of *reported* sexual assaults in 2012, compared with 19,300 in 2010. Of the 26,000 only 4 percent filed for an investigation, and only 9 percent of the cases processed actually went to court-martial. The Pentagon's estimated percentage of sexual assaults *not reported* is between eighty and ninety. Furthermore, some key US military officers, in charge of preventing sexual assault, being themselves recently (2013) under investigation for sexual assault only makes the military's commitment to seriously dealing with rape all the more questionable.

This is not some kind of anomaly, but simply reflects our culture's way of addressing rape: halfheartedly, as not much more than an unpleasant statistic, as if it were not all that serious a matter. It's estimated that almost one in five women (and just under 2 percent of men) in the US have been raped or otherwise sexually assaulted. Fewer than half the victims report this, and only 3 percent of the perpetrators are convicted. In more than half of the US states, rapists who have impregnated their victims can sue for custody and visitation rights. In the US, 15 percent of sexual assault and rape victims are under age twelve. These are appalling numbers, and need more than just a skimming over.

Rape as a man's right: this sentiment still finds some degree of legitimacy not only in the context of spoils of war, but also in those men for whom the sexualized overpowering of another is a turn-on, especially when they're able to dehumanize that other, reducing her—or him—to little more than a prop (or mere *property*) in their sexual fantasies and actions. The not uncommon hesitation of many men in positions of considerable power to take really strong stands regarding rape only contributes to the viewing of rape as something bad, but not *that* bad.

When a man feels overpowered by a woman (in the sense that her mere presence strongly arouses him), he may not feel good about this if she shows no sexual interest in him, perhaps not even noticing him. If he's (1) sufficiently bothered by her "ability" to so easily turn him on, *and* (2) makes her responsible for his arousal, "bringing out the beast in him" as she has done (however unknowingly), he may fantasize about "pouncing on her" (after all, what else is a beast to do?), thereby entering, however passively, into the retributive logic and eroticized violence that's central to rape. He may never act this out with a flesh-and-blood woman, perhaps limiting himself to using pornography in which women are "punished" or "put in their place"—hurt and debased—for their sexual allure. But in this he is, unwittingly or not, contextually aligned with rape, tending to relate to a woman's body as a site of conquest, a place to "prove" himself.

Most men are appalled by rape, but why are the remaining men—the majority of whom have probably never directly engaged in rape—not similarly disturbed? Perhaps because, at some level, it carries an appeal for them, a darkly engrossing charge, reinforced in part by history's cultural sanctioning of rape.

Cutting through this means not only weaning ourselves from alignment with *any* "rape is okay" mentality (including any "boys will be boys" rationale), but also facing and going to the very core of any sexual arousal we might feel through the actual or imaginary violent overpowering of another—and stripping that arousal of its eroticism so that we can clearly see its fundamental underpinnings. (See the description of eroticizing our wounds in chapter 21.)

This doesn't mean becoming asexual or shutting down our sexual passion, but freeing it from those old wounds and unmet needs of ours that we've compensated for—and acted out—through sexual means.

Rape takes the eroticizing of the desire to overpower, dominate, or hurt another, and acts it out sexually against the wishes of that person, violating her or him, using vaginal, anal, or oral penetration with the penis or an object. It may be the most underreported crime. The US Bureau of Justice Statistics states that 91 percent of rape victims are female, 9 percent male, and that 99 percent of offenders are male.

Some might think that all men are potential rapists, as if the desire to rape were somehow innate to males. But for many men, rape is not only abhorrent, but also something they know in their heart of hearts they could never engage in—there being no way they could find sexually violating another person to be at all arousing or appealing or doable.

DO ALL MEN HAVE AN INNER RAPIST?

Do all men (and women) have an inner child: a capacity or place within that is vulnerable, pre-rational, and far from adult or adolescent, a dimension of self that thinks, acts, feels, and sees like a child? Yes. However we may label or treat the child within, it is still there, still something we often regress into and identify with.

Do all men have an inner rapist? No. Let me explain, beginning with some background.

Perhaps our deepest challenge is to cultivate *intimacy* with all that we are, excluding nothing from our being. Such radical inclusion is not some sort of fusion (it doesn't settle for oneness) nor a mental practice or philosophical positioning, but rather an endeavor to take on wholeheartedly, if we are to fully heal and have a life in which passion, awareness, integrity, and love function in optimal tandem.

To be intimate with anything in particular, however, is *not* to be overrun or possessed or controlled by it—we get very close to it, knowing it extremely well, but not so close that we get lost in it or fuse with it. We can include it in the circle of our being without actually *possessing* its particular traits and qualities—we can relate, and perhaps relate quite intimately, *to* such traits and qualities, knowing them from the deep inside, even though we don't *have* them.

So it is crucial that we not confuse the *inclusion* of something in our being with actually *having* that particular something.

This may seem like splitting hairs, but it is a crucial differentiation that must be made clearly, if we are to avoid slipping into an embrace that makes such a grail of tolerance that we end up excusing what ought not to be excused (as when we say of another's abusive behavior that he or she's just being human or that he or she's doing their best).

However much room in ourselves we might make for a certain quality, we do not necessarily *have* that quality. As such, it is not innate to us. It is not a resident in us, but a visitor.

For example, we can include in our being—or expand our being to include—those who have an eating disorder, without ever having had one ourselves. To be intimate with those who suffer thus asks only that we allow them to occupy our heart. We may not have *had* an addiction to alcohol, but by including the alcoholic in our being, we humanize that one, becoming more intimately attuned not only to him or her but also to our own capacity for addiction.

I fully include my wife, Diane, and all her qualities in myself. So I am quite intimate with, for example, her great passion for gardening, but I do not *have* this passion; I like aspects of gardening, but I am definitely not passionate about it. *It's just not something I have.*

So expanding the circle of my being to include you—the deep practice of which is intimacy incarnate—does not mean that I then *possess* all the qualities and capacities that characterize you. That is, *including you in my being does not give me your traits.* I may develop considerable intimacy with your traits, but they still do not become mine.

So, again I ask, do all men *have* an inner rapist? Again, the answer is no.

But, when a man is ready to do so, he can include the rapist (or capacity for rape) in his being, without having that manifest or exist as an actual aspect of himself. Its presence in him then is not that of an endogenous piece of his psychological architecture, but rather that of a dark guest whose heart does not see.

Some might claim that all men have an inner rapist simply because they are men. But those who believe this claim are disregarding the fact that not all men actually *experience* having an inner rapist. Those who adopt the theoretical position that all men have a rapist within are overlooking something very basic: *our individuality.*

Some men who deny having an inner rapist (an attraction to rape, however passive or indirect) may in fact have one; but other men who deny having an inner rapist do so because they simply don't have one. A man who has significantly awakened from his conditioning and who has never fantasized about rape, never considered it, never felt aroused watching it in a film or in pornographic depiction or in imagination, very likely does not have an inner rapist. To state categorically that he must indeed have an inner rapist, just because he's male, demonstrates a misunderstanding of a man's true nature.

Yes, every man has the ingredients to commit rape (the capacities for violence, dehumanization, and sexual arousal), but not every man has the critical mix of these and related factors that together generate the desire or drive to rape.

It's important here not to get stuck in the excesses of relativism, and to remember that there *are* universals with regard to our interiority, such as the inner child. Everyone was once a child, so everyone carries a child-side in their psyche and emotional makeup, which, given the right conditions, shows up in, and may even dominate, our behavior, regardless of our age (this can be especially obvious when we're busy being reactive). Another universal is the capacity for force, along with the potential to misuse that force. We all also have a tendency to dehumanize others.

It may not be easy to admit that we have a capacity for violence, but under certain conditions it shows up; just about every parent knows this when imagining their child being violated, and without a thought severely injuring or even killing the violator, if necessary to save their child. But this violence, this entirely understandable, necessity-driven violence, is not itself depraved, sadistic, or otherwise aberrated.

But when a man's capacities for violence, dehumanization, and sexual arousal get sufficiently intertwined and are allowed to pornographically reinforce each other, he has entered the domain of rape, whether he acts it out or not. If the thought or depiction of rape turns him on, he needs to do more than just acknowledge that he has a rapist within, for the very energy and attention he put into it places him, however mildly or indirectly, on a continuum with actual rapists.

When the concept of "inner rapist" is used indiscriminately or under the banner of psychosexual correctness, there is a danger of trivializing rape, of bypassing the raw, ugly reality of it. It's crucial to use the term *inner rapist* only when considering those who actually *have* some sort of desire to rape, or who are at least aroused by the thought or depiction of it. As obvious as it may sound, we need to know what we actually are speaking of when we use the word *rape*. Using the word *rape* to describe activities other than actual rape lessens the impact that such violation should have on us, and strays dangerously close to normalizing it.

Again, *including* it, does not mean *having* it. To reiterate, we may choose to include the heroin addict in our being, but this does not mean that we must therefore have an inner heroin addict. Intimacy with the heroin addict does not mean fusion or union with that one, but rather a relational closeness that permits both clear focus and compassion. Turning *toward* the heroin addict does not mean we approve of or condone that one's behavior, but that we are refusing to exclude him or her from our heart. Such inclusion does not require an abandoning or collapsing of our personal boundaries, but rather a discerning expansion of them.

A mature man does not *have* an inner rapist (and this is also true of some less mature men). He has within himself the ingredients for committing rape, but no mixing bowl or catalytic agent for them. At the same time, he knowingly *includes* in himself every sort of male, holding them all with resolute and sometimes fierce compassion, allowing none to assume the throne of self, other than his essential uniqueness.

THE ISSUE OF CONSENT

The lack of consent central to rape doesn't have to be overtly expressed to be real. *The absence of any apparent opposition does not necessarily mean consent.* That is, being unable to say "no" doesn't necessarily mean saying "yes." And even saying "yes" doesn't always mean *yes;* many only say "yes" because they fear the consequences of saying "no," a fear that may date back to their early years, when any sign of noncompliance was met with aggression, censure, crippling shame, or a withdrawal of love.

Part of the problem here is that the whole notion of consent usually gets only a superficial look, featuring an unquestioning acceptance of another's yes, as if that yes were undoubtedly an adult yes uninfluenced by one's past, a yes that, of course, should be taken literally. The myth of consenting adults is prevalent in contemporary culture, all too often taken at face value, as if those engaged in such a "contract" were doing so as real adults. However, the very consent given may be coming not from a grown-up place in us, but from a place of unresolved woundedness so that we may be speaking more as *adult*erated children than as actual adults.

This means that we need to know not only where we're coming from when we agree to something but also where the other is coming from when he or she makes such an agreement. Implicit in this is some degree of self-knowledge in both parties, along with an obvious transparency. Furthermore, being clear about where we're coming from includes being out-front about our motivations, including that of *wanting* the other to say "yes"—and perhaps wanting to go ahead even if that yes feels partial, reluctant, or artificial to us. If we're being run by our sexual appetite, our caring about possibly disrespecting the other's actual boundaries will matter little to us; after all, they've said "yes," so why not proceed?

Rape is a crossing of another's sexual boundaries without their permission—or with their *coerced permission.* It is an eroticized trespassing and violation of their being. Its tools are various combinations of physical force, threat, coercion, abuse of authority, manipulation, and a capacity to shut off empathy and override conscience. Rape features aggression and lust in a darkly compelling embrace, being allowed to possess and run one, in contexts ranging from the mundane to the evil.

CUTTING THE TIES TO RAPE

If you are a man with rape-oriented (or otherwise coercive or violent) sexual fantasies and pornographic preferences, you need—as soon as possible—to take the following steps, not letting your shame or appetite obstruct you from doing so.

- Acknowledge to yourself that you indeed do have these fantasies, and that this puts you, however slightly, on a continuum with actual rapists. This may be far from a comfortable admission, but it is necessary, if you are to significantly explore any charge you might have with rape.

- Stay present with whatever shame this brings up, not letting it morph into any sort of aggression or other compensatory activity (including rape-oriented fantasy or pornography). This means getting to know your shame very, very well.

- Explore, ideally with a suitably skilled psychotherapist, the nonsexual dynamics of your rape-oriented fantasies and the origins of these dynamics. This is far more than just an intellectual undertaking; the dots it connects between your past and present clarify the psychological and emotional underpinnings of any appeal that rape may have for you. When this is fully felt and worked with, it decreases your *charge* with such fantasy, aligning it with what originally fueled it: the negative excitation of early dynamics that featured violence, being overpowered, being strongly suppressed, and so on.

- When such fantasies start to arise, immediately inquire into what is being felt (other than sexually), especially in emotional contexts. That is, what emotions or emotional states are present right before, and at the onset of, such fantasies? Loneliness, anger, sadness, depression, hurt, shame? Identify these, name them out loud, and then simply sit with them, being as present as possible, getting to know them more closely. Also, ask yourself how old you feel while this is occurring. (Odds are, it'll be a younger, probably much younger, you.) No matter how strong or compelling your lust may be, stay with your emotional state, not seeking flight from it, but *intimacy* with it—and also with the you who first suffered it.

■ Do whatever it takes to cease dehumanizing those who populate such fantasies. Feel them close to you, as if they were beloved to you, as if you felt a drive to protect the sanctity of their being. Do all you can to *empathize* with them (perhaps visualizing someone you truly care for, and then projecting this feeling of care onto those who occupy your fantasies).

■ Realize that such fantasies may continue to arise well after you've taken the preceding steps, but that as your relationship—and decreasing submission—to them grows firmer and clearer, your desire to act them out will decrease. This is not about repression, but about seeing through these fantasies (clearly recognizing their roots and nonsexual factors) and outgrowing them.

■ View pornography as something to outgrow. (See chapter 22.)

■ Honor the fact that you're cutting through a habit that's had you by the balls, and that in so doing, you are doing a lot of good. Among other things, you are, however indirectly, helping men reclaim their humanity and align their sexuality with their hearts, thereby making them far more capable of being in truly healthy relationships.

■ ■ ■

Essential to a man's work on himself is cutting any ties to rape and the sanctioning of it—and not just intellectually. This may be quite a challenge for many, since it requires that a man face and work through whatever draws him toward rape's continuum. It's not enough to be on good behavior, to repress any urges in which sex and violence operate together. Something deeper is needed, namely to work so sincerely and so deeply with his aggression and wounding that he becomes *incapable* of rape, for the sake of one and all.

27

Ecstatic Intimacy in the Raw

Awakened Sex

WORKING WITH YOUR SEXUALITY, making it more conscious and caring and connected, is a profoundly beneficial—and impactful—process, not just for you but for *everyone*.

Too many men have chained themselves to a sexuality that's significantly detrimental to them and others, turning away from what could free them. What a gift it can be to them when other men decisively break this pattern and take a no-bullshit stand for a sexuality that's rooted not in unresolved wounding, but in a potently embodied, open-eyed love. A love that makes it impossible to dehumanize or otherwise mistreat those we're being sexual with. A love that's as passionate as it's awakened. A love that makes it possible to sexually shift from maximizing pleasurable sensation to fully embodying an ecstatically open intimacy.

To work with your sexuality is to work with all that you are. Sexuality involves your physical, emotional, mental, psychological, energetic, social, and spiritual dimensions, all of which must be taken into account as you explore it. This is no small undertaking, but it is entirely doable, and rewarding not just sexually, but in every area of your life.

Liberating your sexuality from the task of making you feel better or more secure or more manly is a labor of love. So is taking charge of your charge, and so is outgrowing pornography. However much this asks of you, it gives back much, much more. It unchains your masculinity from eroticitis and from being defined through your sexual performance.

Sex that's no longer employed to distract you from your wounding and unmet needs is sex through which you can express your full joy, depth, exultation, and communion with both your lover and the deepest dimensions of being.

Such sex is a joyously expansive celebration of already-present ease, trust, emotional rawness, and love. It is not some exotic thing to manipulate yourself into, but rather a *natural* result of working through whatever wounding you've eroticized, and outgrowing our culture's erotic obsessiveness and pornification.

There's an innocence in such sex, an awakened innocence, through which you gain access to an enormous wonder that sometimes manifests as a dissolution of your everyday self into a far deeper sense of self, a joy-saturated knowingness that's extraordinarily healing and affirming. And when this happens, it won't necessarily be something before which the rest of your life almost always pales, but something that very likely will already be occurring (albeit in perhaps less stunning a fashion) in your life because of the work you've done on yourself, work that aligns you with your essential manhood and humanity.

Sex that goes beyond the maximizing of pleasurable sensation and orgasm is sex that truly satisfies, sex that is but love-ravished gratitude and passion in succulent entanglement, sex that blows open the gates of perception, sex that's free of desperation and erotic frenzy, sex that can weep with joy. Such sex can be slow, exquisitely tender, melting, as well as passionately alive. It may open veils that you never knew were there, depositing you in places of reality-unlocking significance.

Sex can be all this, and it also can be very ordinary—it doesn't matter, once we've freed our sexuality from the expectations we'd originally burdened it with. No desperation, no need to have sex be spectacular. No need to have sex deliver us someplace special. No need to have sex be fueled by our pain or the sticky shadows of yesterday. This is the ease that sooner or later comes from working with our sexuality, relieving us of any pressure in our sexual functioning.

Turn toward your sexuality, bringing it and everything that contributes to it out into the open, and step, as best you can, into the work described in these chapters on sex, knowing that you are doing so for more than just yourself.

A deep bow to all men who take this on and stay with it. You are warriors of the highest order, and I honor you as such.

PART V

Wrapping Up

28

Full-Spectrum Healing

Bringing Together All That You Are

TO HEAL is to make whole.

To begin to heal is to see what's fragmented in you, compartmentalized, pushed away, or kept in the shadows—and to approach it not with missionary zeal or quick-fix ambitions, but with patience and compassion.

Healing is about illuminating, opening to, and integrating all that you are, including the aspects of yourself that you've denied, neglected, ostracized, or disowned. This is far from a short-term process, asking that you move into and through it at a pace that doesn't overstretch or unduly tax you, a pace that allows for proper digestion and assimilation. If you move too quickly, you'll overwhelm yourself and lose perspective; if you move too slowly, you'll lose your momentum and passion for the process, increasing the odds that you'll quit.

But move we must, if we are to heal—taking rejuvenating rests and breaks along the way, and doing our best to make haste slowly, both challenging and nurturing ourselves, honoring the bedrock necessity and importance of our healing.

Healing doesn't necessarily mean curing. It's not a matter of getting rid of your endarkened or less-than-healthy qualities—as if excising a tumor—but of openly facing, exploring, and making as wise as possible use of them. This is the essence of self-acceptance. Nothing gets left out. Everything has its place. The deeper your healing, the more you become whole, and the more capable of relating skillfully to everything that you are.

Many of us are in pieces, with little or no communication between the fragments. Much of the time we go from piece to piece, identifying ourselves as whichever one is dominating the foreground, letting it masquerade and speak as us. Some pieces we keep out of sight, embarrassed or disturbed by their presence, perhaps acting as if we don't have them, projecting their qualities onto others. Think of men who loudly condemn being gay and who, at some point, are revealed to be gay; their shame over being thus oriented had been overcompensated for and camouflaged by their adamant attacks on homosexuality, until their façades were demolished.

As you shed your luggage, letting go of whatever no longer serves you, you travel lighter, and the more lightly you travel, the easier it is to enter the heart of your difficulties and skillfully work with them, finding in this the healing you most deeply need, the healing that brings you into the intrinsic wisdom, compassion, humor, and joy of being.

Healing can be seen as the full-blooded resurrection of a wholeness that honors the uniqueness of each of its parts, without letting any particular part dominate or govern the rest.

Such awakened wholeness is our birthright. Without it, we remain at war internally and externally, psychologically and emotionally in pieces, shredded by circumstances. And at the same time the invitation to heal remains, calling to us through even the most difficult of conditions. Heeding that call, breathing some attention and energy into it, marks a huge turning point for us, drawing forth the deep warrior in us.

WHEN YOUR PAST OCCUPIES YOUR PRESENT

Part of healing is time-traveling, going back psychologically and emotionally (and consciously!) to the central scenes of our original wounding, scenes where we became a divided nation in order to proceed with our lives. In this, we go back not just in narrative (or everyday) memory, but also in—and sometimes only in—emotional memory.

It's as if we've found a control panel in the dark, bringing in enough light and presence to do some rewiring, not to get rid of our painful memories—which is impossible—but to lessen their hold on us so that they cease being our default locale when we're suffering in circumstances that mimic those in which we originally suffered.

Past, present, future—such a neatly sequential trio, or so it seems. However, it's not just the study of quantum mechanics that deconstructs and calls in question the apparent orderliness of time, but also the developmental dynamics of our lives. Events and behavioral patterns from our early years can easily determine how we now operate, often colonizing our present with our past; this may be obvious externally, but not so obvious internally. If we, for example, were heavily shamed by a parent for not measuring up, such shaming may still be running us. We hear its voice more than we might want to admit, whether when we keep picking partners who similarly shame us, or when we work hard for the kind of success that seemingly will put us in a position where we cannot be shamed. Here, our shame itself may not be seen, being obscured by our solutions to it; but it squats in us, fueling our direction.

So our past is often very much present in us, manifesting in the form of behaviors that first arose in response to difficult circumstances, and still arise, almost as if frozen in time, when similar difficulties occur.

Such behaviors are mostly automatic, featuring very predictable reactions, regardless of their outer trappings. Our unresolved wounds may be out of sight, but the behaviors associated with them usually are not. We may, for example, get strongly reactive over something very small, like a malfunctioning pen or slightly-slower-than-usual computer, losing ourselves in our dramatics—to the consternation of those around us—while remaining unaware of what is underlying and animating our reactivity.

Once current circumstances have pushed us past a certain energetic threshold, old conditioned responses can easily kick in and take over. Not that we have to be victims of this, but we can do little to stop such conditioning from initially seizing us. But if we see it for what it is, we can alter our course, even though the characteristic sensations of such a takeover may persist quite strongly (changing course in the middle of a storm doesn't necessarily cause our agitation to immediately disappear!).

And it's not just our past that may take charge of or invade us (with our permission), but also the past of others with whom we're associated, and our collective past. Think of how challenging fear can be, and then factor in the reality of collective fear, not as a distant something on someone else's horizon, but as a living force pervading our living space, carrying the message that we are, in various ways, threatened or endangered, no matter how removed we may be from the darker stuff of life.

A man who doesn't know his personal history well (and more than just cognitively), to the point where he is not being dominated by it, cannot be fully trusted, for whatever lies unfaced and unillumined in him can take over, run the show, and operate in ways that do great damage, both to himself and to others.

For many of us, our past *is* a major part of our shadow, apparently gone but in reality still very much here and now, determining far more of our behavior than we might want to admit. Our past will remain present until we consciously and compassionately take our present/presence into our past, inhabiting what was once fled, mobilizing what was once immobilized, freeing what was once trapped, bringing into our heart what was once rejected, providing as optimal an environment as possible for a healing integration of all that we are. This leaves us not in pieces nor run by any particular part of ourselves, but *knowingly whole.*

INTEGRATING BODY, MIND, EMOTION, PSYCHE, AND SPIRITUALITY

A relationally rooted, integrative approach to healing takes into account *all* of our dimensions—physical, mental, emotional, psychological, sexual, social, and spiritual—cultivating intimacy (hence *relationally rooted*) and working with them in the context of our innate wholeness. In this approach, no part of us is left out or marginalized. *Everything* that we are is considered in the process of our healing.

What follows provides some framework for what it means to work in this way, with your body, mind, emotions, psyche, and spirituality.

Working with Your Body

- Your body is not "down there"—except from the viewpoint of your head. Take your undivided attention into the parts of your body that feel the farthest away or that you feel least in touch with, and keep it there until you sense these parts becoming more alive, more present, more clearly *you,* no longer "below" you.

- Your body is not just an "it," but rather an expression of you. What you truly are is not *in* a body, but is being expressed *as* a body. Remembering this will help you cease treating your body as an "it" or a container. (Having a well-grounded meditative practice can help immensely with knowing this directly.)

- Attune to the interior of your body as well as to its exterior. Become more sensitive to its rhythms, its emotional currents, its shifting sensations. Listen to it, and listen closely, especially when you are distressed or reactive.

- Remain aware of your body when emotions and thoughts arise. The more consciously embodied you are, the more skillful your actions are likely to be.

- Your body is not an obstruction to wisdom or spiritual deepening. Your body does not lie. Through its tensions, structuring, pains, and leanings, it reveals both your present and your past (as you can discover through skilled bodywork).

- When you feel disembodied or disconnected, bring more awareness to your body. Breathe deeply into and soften your belly, slowly scanning your entire body with undivided attentiveness. Become more aware of what you're feeling emotionally, directing as much attention as possible into that feeling—and also into what first drove you to dissociate or disconnect from your body. (Ideally, do this with a somatically attuned therapist.)

- Do a regular body-centered workout. Incorporate aerobic, weight-bearing, and stretching work. Do a sweat-inducing aerobic workout at least every two days; also ease into doing a weight workout every two days, alternating with your aerobic workout. And slowly and mindfully, stretch after your aerobic and weight workouts.

Working with Your Mind

- Thinking that you are aware is altogether different from being aware of thinking. Working with your mind means being consciously and undividedly attentive to whatever arises in it—thoughts, fantasies, images, judgments, comparisons. (A well-grounded meditative practice is very helpful with the practice of this.)

- Most of what arises in your mind arises unbidden. Becoming aware of this is the beginning of meditation. Observing what your mind is doing, and maintaining this awareness for more than a few minutes is not easy, but must be learned if you are to cease being automatically run or hooked by what passes through your mind.

- Observing, rather than identifying with or getting absorbed by, your mind requires both discipline (in the form of sustained focus) and relaxation. Concentration and spaciousness. A relaxed but relatively unwavering awareness. This is the essence of meditation, cultivated not just in retreat settings, but in daily life.

■ When your mind wanders or gets fuzzy, shift your awareness to your body, especially your breathing and emotional state. Stay as present as possible with this, keeping your attention more focused on sensation and feeling than on thought.

■ Become more aware of the spaces between your thoughts. Make a practice out of periodically letting your attention remain focused on these spaces, for just a few minutes at a time.

■ Keep these points in more than mind. When you get derailed by your train of thought (a common occurrence for all of us!), don't let this discourage you from deepening your awareness of your mental dimensions.

Working with Your Emotions

■ Become more emotionally literate. Get to know each of your emotions very well, and learn how to skillfully express and contain them. Value them, treating them not as problems, but as guests, allies, the lifeblood of communication.

■ Deepen your capacity for empathy. The more intimate you are with your own emotions, the more intimate you'll be with the emotions of others, and therefore more able to empathize with them. Without empathy there is no compassion.

- There are no negative emotions. But there are negative or unwholesome things we *do* with our emotions (as when we turn our anger into hostility).

- Remember that emotion and reason work best when they work together.

- Read my book *Emotional Intimacy,* treating it as a companion to this book. Knowing its contents (and practicing its exercises) will help you deepen your emotional literacy, both in personal and relational contexts.

Working with Your Psyche

- Get to know your personal history very well, connecting the dots between your past and present, both intellectually and emotionally. This will help you recognize when your conditioning is running you. It will also make you more understanding of and responsible for your behavior, and more capable of truly intimate relationship.

- Identify whatever traumas there may be from your past, and work with them. This means not just thinking about them, but unhooking yourself from them, both somatically and emotionally, *and* getting whatever help you need to do so (like from a therapist who works with trauma not only cognitively, but also physically and emotionally). Don't think you have to do this by yourself. Remind yourself that reaching out for help is an act of courage.

- Get familiar with your various parts—the inner critic, the child, the adolescent, the self-doubter, and so on. Develop the capacity to be able to name these parts (which actually are *more verb than noun,* being *activities* rather than indwelling entities) when they enter the foreground, while not letting any of them usurp the throne of self. The better you know these parts, the less likely it is that they'll run you.

■ Don't limit psychological work to cognitive study. Connect it with your body, your emotions, your spirituality. When you're facing some old wounding, illuminate its dynamics, yes, but also go into it emotionally and physically, allowing your whole being to participate, learn, and heal.

Working with the Spiritual

■ Spirituality is not synonymous with being religious. I define spirituality as the cultivation of intimacy with what you, in your heart of hearts, know to be sacred or ultimate. As such, it does not require belief. It is at once personal and transcendent.

■ Educate yourself about *spiritual bypassing,* doing your best not to slip into it. Spiritual bypassing means using spiritual practices and beliefs to avoid painful feelings, unresolved wounds, and relational challenges. It is very common. (For more, see my book *Spiritual Bypassing.*)

■ Distinguish soul from spirit. By soul, I mean your personalized essence, the heartland of your individuality. It is the face of spirituality. Spirit transcends individuality; in its healthy forms, such transcendence embraces what has been gone beyond, requiring no departure from our humanness.

■ Don't spiritually "should" yourself. Recognize and cut through spiritual cultism and correctness. Find what works for you spiritually, tailor it to your own unique needs, and consistently practice it, allowing it to evolve as you evolve.

■ Healthy spirituality is not an escape from life's difficulties, but an awakened embrace and illumination of them. It is love and nonconceptual awareness functioning as one.

EMBODYING WHOLENESS

In the most effective healing work, all of our dimensions are approached and worked with in ways that not only allow them to function together as optimally as possible, but that also reinforce and deepen our wholeness.

Whatever is occurring—physically, mentally, emotionally, spiritually—is encountered and worked with in the context of our innate wholeness. This means we don't lose touch with our wholeness as we work with particular aspects of ourselves. Doing so reinforces our natural integrity of being. It also keeps things in healthy perspective—the perspective not of a particular aspect of ourselves, but of our intrinsic unity of being.

As complex as this all might sound, it is actually quite simple, being very natural to us. Being fragmented, alienated, disconnected, is what's unnatural, leading to unnecessary complexity and complications, stranding us from much of our humanity. Wholeness is not a fantasy; it is our natural state.

The healing of our fragmented self, the reunion of our far-flung, scattered selves, the integration of all that we are, the journey toward awakened wholeness—this is essential work, truly honorable work, work that heals and liberates, both personally and collectively. Let us do whatever we can to support and embrace it.

29

The Passage
to Authentic Manhood

Your Flaws No Longer in the Way

WHAT A DEEPLY transformational journey the passage to full manhood is—rising and falling, soaring and bleeding, ever deepening—abundantly supplied with soul-enlivening challenge and firsthand teachings, catalyzing needed healing and breakthrough, uprooting us again and again so that we might stand our truest ground. Call it a full-blooded odyssey to the heartland of true masculine power and what it means to be a man.

Eventually just about everything feels like a stepping-stone for your passage, as the conventional definitions of manhood fall around you in ruins, with only what truly serves your evolution rising from the rubble.

You are on a quality quest, making your way to what really matters, breathing courage and integrity into your stride, no longer shaming yourself for—inevitably—stumbling as you proceed. Instead of trying to get rid of your flaws, you are learning to compassionately relate to them, sooner or later finding that they're no longer in the way.

However difficult it was to begin your journey, you now have momentum. And you're recognizing that your softness and vulnerability are not problems, but sources of strength, coexisting with your resolve, guts, drive, and ability to get things done, whatever the challenge.

Undertaking this passage of deep healing, awakening, and integration brings forth the very best in you, including the warrior of intimacy and life-affirming action, the one who is so deeply needed to help us get on track in this quickly shifting century, this perilous turning point time.

Though this book ends here, it doesn't stop. My hope is that those who read it deeply will carry forward its essential teachings, making them their own. I wrote it for men, but it is for women, too. We all are midwives for the awakening man, birthing him through the work we do on ourselves, work that is at the heart of all that I've written here.

Having a Conscious Rant

THE POINT of a conscious rant is to defuse overloaded or potentially harmful reactivity in a way that hurts no one, including ourselves.

In a conscious rant, you totally cut loose emotionally, exaggerating your sounds and movements without any editing, all within the confines of a context that is well boundaried—the ground rules for which you've thought out and clarified beforehand. This is very different from everyday reactivity. The context has been set; into the ring you step, knowing the boundaries and knowing that you don't have to hold anything back. You have permission to be outrageous.

Your task is to do this full-out. If you get self-conscious or only express yourself partially, deliberately exaggerate what you're feeling. Be as melodramatic as possible, going for sheer vitality, not humor—though conscious rants can sometimes end up being hilarious once they're fully rolling.

If you're with another person (your partner or a good friend), your parameters for having a conscious rant will have been preset clearly so that it does no harm. It's as if you were in an acting class, and your task was to give volcanic vent to your emotional state, *without doing any harm and with a clear beginning and end.* (Note: If you're upset with a particular person, don't face them during your rant; and if your upset with them is big, conduct your rant on your own or with someone else. In other words, your partner or a close friend can be witness or coach to your ranting about anything or anyone—except for them.)

Conscious rants can be done for any difficult, overwhelming, or otherwise upsetting state you're in. Here are instructions for having a conscious rant when you're feeling really frustrated, angry, despairing, or aggressive:

Stand in the middle of a room where you have enough privacy to be loud. And if such a room isn't available, stand in the middle of whatever room you have, with a firm pillow in one hand. Your partner or a close friend can be in the same room, having already cocreated with you an agreement for the ground rules for the conscious rant you're about to have. And if you have no one (or cannot have anyone there) to witness what is about to happen, it still works well if you do it alone.

Fully focus on what's disturbing. Breathe deeply, bending your knees slightly. Now let your anger or outrage speak, and speak uninhibitedly—don't be polite, don't be careful, don't try to be a model of clean anger. Bust loose! (If you have to keep the noise down, hold the pillow to your face so that it completely covers your mouth. Squeeze the pillow as hard as you can, and let loose!) If you feel self-conscious, be more outrageous. No rehearsing! Stomp your feet, make fists, spontaneously speak with your whole body. If you have a gripe, blow it up to major proportions; if you think you were treated unfairly, lay into whoever dared treat you that way; and so on.

Keep your rant full-blooded, keep it dramatic, keep it spontaneous, and really exaggerate it whenever you feel yourself fading energetically. Give yourself at least three or four minutes of full-out expression. After that, you may continue for a bit, but stop when you are running out of steam; then lie flat on your back, spread-eagled, and breath slowly for a couple of minutes. Then let your breathing return to normal, and get up when you feel ready.

In summary, the steps for a conscious rant are:

1 Name your prevailing emotion(s).

2 In an already established context (for suitable containment), cut loose, expressing what you're feeling. Exaggerate your speech, your tone, your body movements enough so to lose any self-consciousness.

3 Do this all-out until you naturally start to tire (usually in fewer than five minutes), then lie down or sit comfortably for as long as you like.

Acknowledgments

A RESOUNDING THANKS to the dynamic duo of Tami Simon (founder of Sounds True) and Haven Iverson (my gifted editor at Sounds True) for coming up with the idea of publishing a book for and about men, and for asking me if I'd be interested in writing it. I immediately said yes. I'd been writing about shadow, assuming my next book would be about that, but the men's book-to-be pulled at me much more strongly. So I dove in, getting a first draft done quite quickly. The words had poured forth easily, and I assumed that after completing the usual round of edits a few months later, I'd basically be done—and ready to move on to my next book.

Half a year later, I still hadn't begun another book. The men's book had a resolute grip on me, going through two rounds of editing, the first being a developmental edit—through which I rewrote much of the book as I reorganized it—and the second a "regular" edit, with a bunch more rewriting and pruning. For the second round, my wife, Diane, read every chapter very carefully while keeping a keen eye on the overall feel of the book and its central themes, suggesting changes rooted in her uncommonly deep knowing of me—and in her sense of what best served the book's core needs. Resisting mightily at times, I embraced her guidance, and the book is much better for it, leaner, cleaner, more alive. She and I do all our psychospiritual work together, literally side by side, and so completing the book in such intimate conjunction was very fitting.

A deep bow to the men who have come to me for work, whether through individual sessions, couples work, trainings, or group work. My time with you helped forge the heart of this book.

And gratitude to all those, male and female, who are committed to fully embodied healing, awakening, and integration. Your contribution to my bringing forth this book is immeasurable.

About the Author

ROBERT AUGUSTUS MASTERS, PhD, is a relationship expert and psychospiritual teacher and guide, with a doctorate in psychology. He's the cofounder, with his wife, Diane, of the Masters Center for Transformation, a school featuring relationally rooted psychospiritual work devoted to deep healing and fully embodied awakening. He's the author of fourteen books, including *Transformation Through Intimacy*, *Spiritual Bypassing*, and *Emotional Intimacy*.

His uniquely integral work, developed over the past thirty-seven years, intuitively blends the psychological and physical with the spiritual, emphasizing full-blooded embodiment, authenticity, emotional openness and literacy, deep shadow work, and the development of relational maturity.

At essence his work is about cultivating intimacy with all that we are—high and low, dark and light, broken and whole—in the service of the deepest possible healing, awakening, and integration. He works side by side and in very close conjunction with Diane. His website is robertmasters.com.

Further reading from Robert Augustus Masters

EMOTIONAL INTIMACY
A Comprehensive Guide for Connecting
with the Power of Your Emotions

Emotions link our bodies, thoughts, and conditioning at multiple levels. And the capacity to be intimate with our emotions—to know them deeply—is essential for creating truly fulfilling relationships, relationships in which awareness, love, passion, and integrity can function as one. In this comprehensive book we learn to:

- Deepen our emotional literacy

- Cultivate intimacy with all of our emotions

- Identify how we numb our unwanted feelings, and learn ways to revive them and welcome them back

- Identify our emotions, fully experience them, and skillfully express them

- Resolve and heal from old emotional wounds

- Recognize gender differences in emotional literacy and expression

- Bring greater intimacy and depth into our relationships

- Face depression, anxiety, and crippling shame

- Understand how "blowing off steam" can often make us feel worse, and what constitutes healthy catharsis

- Fully engage with fear, anger, joy, jealousy, shame, grief, guilt, awe, and the full spectrum of our emotions

There are no negative or unwholesome emotions—only negative or harmful things we do with them. Through real-life examples, exercises, and an abundance of useful insights, this book provides a lucid guide for reclaiming our emotions, relating to them skillfully, and allowing them to resonate in ourselves and with others more fully and richly, immeasurably deepening our lives.

To purchase a copy, visit SoundsTrue.com

About Sounds True

SOUNDS TRUE is a multimedia publisher whose mission is to inspire and support personal transformation and spiritual awakening. Founded in 1985 and located in Boulder, Colorado, we work with many of the leading spiritual teachers, thinkers, healers, and visionary artists of our time. We strive with every title to preserve the essential "living wisdom" of the author or artist. It is our goal to create products that not only provide information to a reader or listener, but that also embody the quality of a wisdom transmission.

For those seeking genuine transformation, Sounds True is your trusted partner. At SoundsTrue.com you will find a wealth of free resources to support your journey, including exclusive weekly audio interviews, free downloads, interactive learning tools, and other special savings on all our titles.

To learn more, please visit SoundsTrue.com/freegifts or call us toll-free at 800-333-9185.